Management of Software Engineering
Innovation in Japan

Yasuo Kadono

Management of Software Engineering Innovation in Japan

 Springer

Yasuo Kadono
Ritsumeikan University Graduate School
of Technology Management
Ibaraki
Osaka
Japan

ISBN 978-4-431-55611-4   ISBN 978-4-431-55612-1 (eBook)
DOI 10.1007/978-4-431-55612-1

Library of Congress Control Number: 2015946773

Springer Tokyo Heidelberg New York Dordrecht London

Springer Japan KK is part of Science+Business Media (www.springer.com)

Preface

Managing information technology (IT) is one of the most important and challenging aspects of contemporary business. As IT is a fundamental driver of competitiveness for companies in a wide variety of business sectors, it is essential that the strategies and practices of IT management are well understood. However, from the viewpoint of the demand side of IT, many companies in Japan that use enterprise IT systems have not been fully satisfied with the speed of delivery, quality, cost, or productivity of software delivered by IT vendors, although the ultimate goal of Japanese IT vendors is to serve as catalysts for their customers' IT management of enterprise systems. Conversely, from the supply side viewpoint of IT, total sales of the Japanese information service industry have grown at a sluggish pace since reaching 10 trillion yen in 2005. It still, however, has a considerable presence in the world.

In fact, IT vendors in Japan face a wide range of old and new issues in their business environment. These include the need to respond to rapid technological innovations, an orientation toward custom-made applications for the domestic market, global competition with new entrants from emerging countries, man-month-based multilayer subcontractors, leadership of senior managers at IT vendors, software engineers' skill building, and IT management in user companies. In particular, because sustaining shop-floor usability is given priority over introducing technological innovation when IT is deployed in user companies in Japan, the dynamics of user–vendor interactions enable the development of finely tuned custom-made applications. This tends to establish long-lasting relationships between user companies and IT vendors. Thus, the development of custom-made applications can cause a high entry barrier for newcomers from home and abroad. As a result, the Japanese software industry has not established transparent relationships with the international market. This fact, coupled with the Japanese-language barrier, has resulted in the Japanese software industry having for some time been described as a maze, or as having "Galapagos syndrome."

In this book, we address these issues relating to the Japanese software industry as part of the management of software engineering innovation. We simultaneously look at the whole picture from both the supply and demand sides of software. The first step for the Japanese software industry to achieve sustained success in solving issues relating to managing innovation in software engineering is to grasp an appropriate perception of the present situation in the Japanese software industry in areas such as software engineering capabilities, business performance, and the business environment. Therefore, the objectives of the research are to assess the achievements of software engineering capabilities, as represented by IT vendors in Japan, and to understand better the mechanisms of how software engineering capabilities relate to IT vendors' business performance and business environment.

To achieve these objectives, an original measurement tool called Software Engineering Excellence (SEE) was developed. An aim of the research is to encourage innovation; therefore, in developing the SEE measurement model, state-of-the-art cases were surveyed by more than 50 experts in academic, business, and governmental circles in Japan and the United States, and literature reviews relating to software engineering disciplines were conducted in the broadest sense, focusing on the management of innovation. The scope of the survey also includes Barney's resource-based view of vendors, informed by paying attention to factors such as degree of rarity and inimitability of management resources.

In this study, SEE can be used to evaluate overall software engineering capabilities of IT vendors on the basis of the following seven factors: deliverables, project management, quality assurance, process improvement, research and development, human resource development, and customer contact. In addition, "business environment" expresses the company profile and structure of an IT vendor including, e.g., origin of vendor, number of software engineers, average employee age, business model, customer base, and corporate culture. Thus, business environment factors complement the relationship between SEE and business performance of software vendors, such as profitability, growth, productivity, and efficiency of the management.

This book is structured in two major parts. The first part, Chaps. 1–3, introduces the Japanese software industry and examines Japanese vendors' software engineering capabilities through social surveys and statistical analyses. In Chap. 1, the above-mentioned old and new issues of the Japanese software industry are introduced and the research objectives are articulated based on a literature review of the information service industry in Japan, innovation in software industry, and the research approach. Then, we clarify the relationships among Japanese IT vendors' software engineering capabilities, business performance, and business environment through the remaining chapters of the book. In Chap. 2, the research model and survey results of SEE are introduced. Because the SEE survey results are valuable pieces of information in the study of Japan's software industry, the figures relating to the survey results are included in Appendix. In Chap. 3, statistical analysis results based on the SEE surveys, such as order effect and series correlation, are demonstrated using cross-section analysis, path analysis, stratified analysis, panel analysis, and longitudinal analysis. Additionally, the issues of managing innovation in software engineering in Japan are discussed.

The second part of the book, Chaps. 4 through 8, includes research relevant to managing innovation in software engineering in Japan in the broadest sense. In Chap. 4, the competitive environment in the Japanese software industry and the differences of characteristics among manufacturer spin-off, user spin-off, and independent vendors are discussed based on Porter's five forces and Barney's resource-based view. In Chap. 5, IT management of individual IT user companies is discussed through large-scale social surveys, called IT management effectiveness (IME) surveys. Additionally, the causal relationships among the following six factors are empirically verified: awareness and actions of top management, linkage between management and IT, IT development capability, IT investment and deployment, IT readiness, and business value creation from IT. In Chap. 6, beyond SEE and IME, a new social research scheme, which includes both the demand side (IT user companies) and the supply side (IT vendors) is designed to accelerate innovation in IT management. In Chap. 7, future scenarios of Japanese software industry structures, giving priority to the effects of offshoring in China, are preliminarily assessed through agent-based simulation. In Chap. 8, an epilogue pursues a research methodology for assembling large-scale social surveys to collect data, statistical analyses, simulations, and other complementary considerations based on the content of the preceding Chaps. 1 through 7.

Although the chapters are intended to cover issues relating to IT management and software engineering innovation in the broadest sense, the research approach—using social surveys, statistical analyses, and simulations based on the resource-based view—has limitations. For example, if the rules of the game in the Japanese software industry change in a rapid and unpredictable manner, e.g., Schumpeterian revolutions, or a paradigm shift caused by a breakthrough in technology, then it will be difficult to adapt the findings discovered by the approach in this book to a new business environment. However, the current business environment is entrenched in the Japanese software industry and is likely to be unchangeable for good or bad, just as in other industries in Japan and other cultures. Thus, through the eight chapters of the book, our hope is that readers, including all the stakeholders in IT management, i.e., the supply and demand sides of IT, researchers, and policymakers at home and abroad, will find enlightenment in the Japanese software industry referred to as the maze or Galapagos syndrome.

The author gratefully acknowledges the valuable suggestions and kind support for statistical analyses received from Professor Hiroe Tsubaki at the Institute of Statistical Mathematics, and the warm support and constant encouragement received from Professors Takao Terano and Hiroshi Deguchi at the Tokyo Institute of Technology. In truth, however, this book would never have been completed without the help of the thoughtful experts in academic, business, and governmental circles in Japan and the United States who have shared their concerns and problems with me, and of a number of supportive respondents to the five-times large-scale surveys of SEE and IME. The author is particularly grateful to the Ministry of Economy, Trade and Industry (METI); the Software Engineering Center, Information-Technology Promotion Agency, Japan (SEC, IPA); Dr. Seishiro Tsuruho (former head of SEC); the Japan Information Technology Services Industry Association (JISA); Kozo Keikaku Engineering Inc.; and the Management Science Institute Inc. (MSI). Additionally, this research was partially supported by grants-in-aid for scientific research from the Japan Society for the Promotion of Science (JSPS; B:20310090; C:24530497). I am also grateful to Professor Alan Stoke for his skillful editorial work. I also want to thank Springer Japan. And, last but not least, I thank my family—my wife, Yoshimi, and my son, Yuki—for all of their help and support.

Tokyo   Yasuo Kadono
August 2014

Contents

About the Author

Yasuo Kadono is a professor at Graduate School of Technology Management of Ritsumeikan University, and a visiting professor at Tokyo University of Foreign Studies, Japan. He received his PhD in business administration at Tsukuba University. He also received his master's and bachelor's degrees in applied mathematics and physics at Kyoto University. He has extensive practical experience with McKinsey & Company, Accenture, Sumitomo Metal Industries, and Management Science Institute. He has also produced important research projects in academic, business, and government circles. Consistent with his academic and business career to date, his teaching and research interests include management of technology, competitive strategy, and information technology.

Chapter 1
Introduction to Software Engineering Innovation in Japan

Abstract The Japanese information service industry continues to have a considerable presence in the world, although its total sales have grown at a sluggish pace since it passed 10 trillion yen in 2005. However, IT vendors in Japan are facing a wide range of old and new issues in their business environment, such as responses to rapid technological innovations, an orientation of custom-made applications for the domestic market, global competition with new entrants from emerging countries, man-month-based multilayer subcontractors, origin of vendor (e.g., manufacturer spin-offs, user spin-offs, and independents), leadership of senior managers at IT vendors, skill building of software engineers, and IT management in user companies. In this book, we address these issues relating to the Japanese software industry as part of management of software engineering innovation, and we simultaneously look at the whole picture from both supply and demand sides of software. In this chapter, we articulate the research objectives based on a literature review of the information service industry in Japan (e.g., market size and history, government policy, and industry structure), innovation in the software industry (e.g., issues of the Japanese software industry, nature of Japanese software innovation, and types of innovation), the approach to research (e.g., the resource-based view and relevant software engineering disciplines), and measurement models. Next, we seek to clarify the relationships between the software engineering capabilities of Japanese IT vendors, their business performance, and their business environment through the eight chapters of the book.

Keywords Resource-based view · Information service industry in Japan · Software engineering · Innovation · History · Policy · Industry structure

1.1 Motivation

The Japanese information service industry has stagnated recently. However, this industry is still large. In fact, in fiscal year 2013 the Japanese information service industry was a 10,427,909 million yen market, of which 7,502,070 million yen was for software development and programming as shown in Fig. 1.1 (Ministry

© Springer Japan 2015
Y. Kadono, *Management of Software Engineering Innovation in Japan,*
DOI 10.1007/978-4-431-55612-1_1

1

Total Sales
(Million Yen)

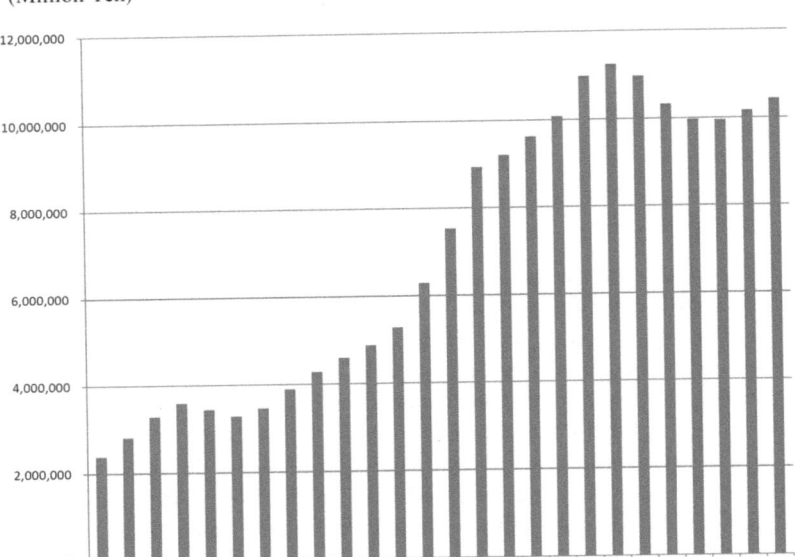

Fig. 1.1 Total sales in information service industry in Japan

of Economy, Trade, and Industry (METI) 2014). On the other hand, according to
the Ministry of Internal Affairs and Communications (MIC), it is projected that the
worldwide information service industry market, including IT services and software,
reached US$ 1 trillion 221 billion in 2013 (MIC 2014). Japan's share is estimated to
be 8.5 %, assuming that US$ 1 is 100 Japanese yen. Thus the Japanese information
service industry still has a considerable presence in the world.

However, many companies in Japan that use enterprise software have not been
fully satisfied with the quality, cost, and productivity of software that IT vendors
deliver, or the speed of delivery. At the same time, IT vendors in Japan are facing
drastic changes in their business environment, such as technological innovations
and new entrants from emerging countries, e.g., China and India. Additionally, there
are particular issues that are present in the Japanese information service industry,
such as vendors relying on man-month-based multilayer subcontractors and on
legacy business models that depend on supplying custom-made applications for the
domestic market (Cusmano 2004; Kadono 2007; Kimura 2014).

These are both old and new issues for the Japanese software industry. An existing
paper on the Japanese software industry noted that when information technologies
are introduced, Japan's most salient characteristic is sustaining shop-floor usability,
rather than stressing technological innovation (Baba et al.1995). As a result, the
Japanese software industry has not established transparent relationships with the international market; this is compounded by the Japanese language barrier. Therefore,
it has been called a maze, or Galapagos, for a long time (Kadono 2009).

Simultaneously, from a financial perspective, the Japanese software industry has not been necessarily profitable over the years. For example, the operating profit ratios of most Japanese IT firms have been around 5% for many years, compared with foreign firms' over 20% (MIC 2014). Therefore, as the previous paper noted, the Japanese software industry is a paradox, at once highly productive and yet unsuccessful.

Today however, although the Japanese software industry is unfortunately still unsuccessful, we are skeptical about the argument that it is highly productive. And we think that the longer the information service sector in Japan neglects the above issues, the less competitive it will continue to become in the global market. In addition, the problem will cause other Japanese sectors to be less competitive in the world because IT is a fundamental driver of competitiveness in a wide variety of business and public sectors.

In this book therefore, we address these Japanese software industry issues as part of the management of software engineering innovation. To this end, we need to look at the whole picture of the Japanese software industry from both the supply side and the demand side, such as human resource development in software vendors (e.g., senior management leadership and unhappy software engineers), IT management in user companies, and Japanese culture and society (e.g., multilayer subcontractors).

1.2 Literature Review

Regarding the issues above, we gather several insightful findings from relevant research and government reports. We then conduct a literature review from the viewpoints of the information service industry in Japan, innovation in the software industry, and the approach to research, including the perspective of international comparison.

1.2.1 Information Service Industry in Japan

1.2.1.1 Market Size and History

In 2013 fiscal year, the information service industry was a 10,427,909 million yen market in Japan, of which 7,502,070 million yen was for software development and programming; orders for software totaled 6,365,857 million yen, accounting for 61.0% of the entire information service industry, while the software products market was 1,136,213 million yen. Total Sales by type of operation in the Japanese information service industry from 1988 to 2013 are shown in Table 1.1. Additionally, the numbers of regular employees in the Japanese information service industry from 1988 to 2013 are shown in Table 1.2. The total number of persons reached 327,813, and the number of persons dispatched from other enterprises (aggregate person-days) was 9,355,804 in fiscal year 2013 in the Japanese information service industry (METI 2014).

Table 1.1 Total sales by type of operation in information service industry in Japan (million yen)

Fiscal year	Total sales	Software development, programming	Orders for software	System Integration (SI)	Software products	Game software	Others[a]
1988	2,386,276	1,377,232	...	...	...	...	1,499,372
1989	2,817,459	1,631,911	...	...	...	...	1,753,229
1990	3,290,630	1,931,785	...	...	...	...	2,528,606
1991	3,597,797	2,142,731	...	...	...	...	2,701,877
1992	3,439,329	2,018,989	...	...	...	...	2,639,817
1993	3,284,918	1,966,111	...	...	...	...	2,438,668
1994	3,464,486	2,130,355	1,857,751	...	272,604	...	2,450,640
1995	3,890,898	2,493,421	2,103,373	...	390,048	...	2,563,699
1996	4,282,278	2,814,638	2,381,159	...	433,479	...	2,687,721
1997	4,592,785	3,107,137	2,672,693	...	434,444	...	2,156,467
1998	4,872,831	3,403,542	2,958,317	...	445,226	...	2,147,181
1999	5,278,383	3,687,072	3,196,507	...	490,565	...	1,591,312
2000	6,288,604	4,407,373	3,696,387	1,667,220	710,987	201,367	1,881,230
2001	7,529,044	5,479,205	4,621,724	2,267,292	857,481	235,052	2,049,839
2002	8,934,344	6,603,896	5,457,331	2,984,927	1,146,565	459,456	2,330,448
2003	9,207,575	6,712,520	5,502,245	3,092,534	1,210,275	501,141	2,495,055
2004	9,623,327	6,861,728	5,661,229	3,255,215	1,200,499	480,455	2,761,600
2005	10,073,854	7,225,501	6,038,604	3,477,661	1,186,897	486,906	2,848,353
2006	10,976,154	7,979,348	6,581,999	3,982,086	1,397,349	691,069	2,996,806
2007	11,238,011	8,128,131	6,666,219	4,099,594	1,461,912	694,115	3,109,880
2008	10,961,285	7,900,991	6,622,624	4,139,551	1,278,367	599,922	3,060,295
2009	10,322,556	7,387,893	6,152,374	3,856,252	1,235,519	573,215	2,934,662
2010	9,966,737	7,035,572	5,978,029	3,787,123	1,057,543	432,802	2,931,165
2011	9,954,579	7,089,448	6,107,381	3,920,838	982,067	368,440	2,865,131
2012	10,168,266	7,304,470	6,243,654	3,940,285	1,060,816	400,777	2,863,796
2013	10,427,909	7,502,070	6,365,857	4,061,383	1,136,213	442,438	2,925,839

a Includes Information Processing (such as Calculation Service), Data-Input, System Management on Commission, Information Selling Service, Database Services, Various Surveys, and Others

Table 1.2 Number of regular employees in information service industry in Japan

Fiscal year	Number of establishments	Total number of regular employees (Persons)	Technical	Other	Number of the employees dispatched to other enterprises (Aggregate person-days)	Number of the persons dispatched from other enterprises (Aggregate person-days)
1988	1345	144,222	112,762	31,460	...	...
1989	1510	155,690	121,675	34,015	...	...
1990	1531	165,649	129,249	36,400	2,362,779	4,179,140
1991	1561	180,979	141,917	39,062	2,361,770	4,343,109
1992	1559	186,757	146,012	40,745	2,268,706	3,982,017
1993	1578	188,930	146,429	42,501	2,145,338	3,390,608
1994	1614	187,224	143,194	44,030	1,835,847	3,192,753
1995	1600	183,242	139,559	43,683	1,870,482	3,383,386
1996	1620	184,435	140,083	44,352	1,892,673	3,688,620
1997	1650	189,716	144,694	45,022	1,845,468	4,248,154
1998	1655	196,128	151,770	44,358	1,765,874	4,750,163
1999	1957	224,897	174,316	50,581	1,679,058	4,961,675
2000	1865	234,588	180,331	54,257	1,765,661	5,290,261
2001	2293	275,431	209,480	65,951	2,022,072	6,017,406
2002	2318	273,827	210,494	63,333	3,021,457	6,255,732
2003	2830	288,363	224,925	63,438	2,859,939	6,610,312
2004	2813	289,103	225,372	63,731	2,766,423	7,271,452
2005	2793	304,593	230,994	73,599	2,764,040	8,655,907
2006	2737	308,730	232,370	76,360	3,030,716	10,342,669
2007	2716	316,770	238,208	78,562	3,137,283	12,146,368
2008	2703	321,217	243,823	77,394	3,228,622	12,080,668
2009	2650	328,772	249,496	79,276	3,098,653	10,521,759
2010	2579	327,255	249,327	77,928	3,055,707	9,638,444
2011	2662	329,407	250,294	79,113	3,019,747	9,351,409
2012	2670	328,953	251,919	77,034	3,034,461	9,297,110
2013	2643	327,813	251,213	76,600	2,911,263	9,355,804

Retracing the history of the Japanese information service industry, the first computerization of Japanese enterprises emerged in 1955, just after the introduction of the first commercial computer by Univac in 1951 (Japan Information Technology Service Industry Association (JISA) 2014). The first software firms were established in the second half of the 1960s. Until then, most computer programs were either developed internally by users or supplied free of charge by computer makers. As larger numbers of computers were introduced, the demand for software increased. Thus the emergence and evolution of the software market was driven by the rapidly increasing demand for new user programs. The leading computer users created software firms when close relationships were desired with specific customers. Between 1973 and 1988, the average costs for computerization per firm almost doubled. The steel industry, particularly, made a significant contribution during the early stage. Banks and other financial companies then did the same, overtaking the steel industry approximately 1980 as leading users in the domestic software business. In 1980s, 3000 billion yen were spent in the banking sector as a whole. It is estimated that each major bank spent approximately 150 billion yen, and large local banks approximately 30 billion yen (Baba et al. 1995; Financial Information System Center 1992).

In 1990, the total size of the Japanese information service industry reached 3 trillion yen under the title of strategic information systems and system integration. It exceeded 5 trillion yen in 1999 when distributed computing using personal computers and communication networks was deployed universally in enterprise IT systems. Although the total sales of the information service industry in Japan exceeded 10 trillion yen in 2005, it has grown at a sluggish pace for 10 years, including the period of the Lehman Shock in 2008, as shown in Fig. 1.1 and Table 1.1, despite the emergence and evolution of the Internet era.

The number of employees engaged in the software service industry has been closely linked to the industry's total sales, as shown in Table 1.2. The companies listed in the information service industry have been emerging since the 1980s. As of May 2014, 337 companies in the information service industry were listed on the First and Second Sections of the Tokyo Stock Exchange, the Market of the High-Growth and Emerging Stocks (Mothers), and the Japan Association of Securities Dealers Automated Quotations (JASDAQ); this is the second largest category in the Japanese industrial classification (METI 2014; JISA 2014).

1.2.1.2 Government Policy

Regarding government policy and the Japanese information service industry, the Machinery and Information Industries Bureau in the Ministry of International Trade and Industry (MITI) was established in 1973. At roughly that time, a major policy objective was to help the Japanese leading IT players, such as Nippon Telegraph and Telephone Public Corporation (Dendenkosha), Fujitsu, Hitachi, NEC, Toshiba, Mitsubishi Electric, and Oki Electric, develop generation 3.5 computers to compete against the IBM370 series in the liberalization initiative of the computer market. In the first half of the 1980s, the shift to an information-oriented society was actively discussed, especially in the areas of software cost, security, and network connections. However, the Japanese software industry did not necessarily evolve in parallel with a series of innovations in computer hardware. In fact, Japanese semiconductor companies became the world leaders in very-large-scale integrated circuits, e.g., 64 K DRAM and 1 M DRAM, in the late 1970s and 1980s, unlike the Japanese software industry.

In the second half of the 1980s, the basic policy shifted towards international cooperation; the government was focused on arrangements to promote private initiatives in information services. In 1987, the Vision of Information Industry in 2000 was published. The Japanese government then promoted several large information service projects until 2000: the Information-Technology Promotion Agency, Japan (IPA) and private IT vendors, such as the fifth-generation computer, the sigma project, Electronic Commerce (EC), Computer Aided Logistics Support (CALS), and local software centers (Hasegawa 2013).

It has been seen as urgent to adapt Japan to the world's rapid and drastic changes in the socio-economic structure caused by the utilization of information and telecommunications technology. To this end, to promote measures for forming an advanced information and telecommunications network society expeditiously and intensively, in January 2001 the Strategic Headquarters for the Promotion of an Advanced Information and Telecommunications Network Society (IT Strategic Headquarters) was established within the Cabinet. At this writing, Japanese IT policy is formulated mainly by the IT Strategic Headquarters within the Cabinet, METI, and MIC. (IT Strategic Headquarters 2012; METI 2014; MIC 2014).

1.2.1.3 Industry Structure

It is instructive to consider the Japanese software industry structure from the perspective of path dependence, i.e., the origins of the industry (Arthur 1989). Japanese software vendors can be classified into three categories according to the type of company from which they originated: hardware manufacturers, users, and independent vendors.

First, manufacturer spin-off vendors are defined as hardware suppliers; they include firms such as computer makers, e.g., Fujitsu, NEC, Hitachi, and IBM; or subsidiary companies under the control of hardware suppliers. In the early days of the Japanese information service industry, manufacturer spin-off vendors, as well as Nippon Telegraph and Telephone Public Corporation (Dendenkosha), i.e., the precursor of Nippon Telegraph and Telephone Corporation (NTT), established distinctive competencies (Selznick 1957) due to time compression dis-economies (Dierickx and Cool 1989) based on governmental policies and support, as previously noted.

Second, user spin-off vendors are defined as subsidiary companies of buyers, i.e., IT user companies. Particularly in 1960s and 1970s, leading computer users such as steel companies and financial institutions increasingly began to establish subsidiary software vendors because close relationships were desired for their business purposes. Some are thought to have gained inimitable capabilities, including expertise in specific functions and unique products/services. Therefore, the parent companies of user spin-off vendors might not be concerned about their business performance attributable to their management policy.

Third, independent vendors are defined as neither manufacturer spin-off vendors nor user spin-off vendors; they include firms such as system integrators, e.g., NTT DATA and Nomura Research Institute. On occasion, manufacturer and user spin-off vendors became independent in the long term, not under the control of the parent companies. Additionally, some software engineers formerly in charge of software development in computer makers or user companies founded their own independent vendors in 1970s and 1980s.

The structure of the software industry in Japan is shown in Fig. 1.2, analyzed using the five forces model (Porter 1980). The central box shows three types of origin of software vendors in Japan, namely, manufacturer spin-offs, user spin-offs, and independent vendors. The buyers in the right-hand box include IT user companies, while the suppliers in the left-hand box include hardware vendors and temporary staffing as variable costs. One of the most remarkable characteristics of the Japanese software industry is that all types of IT vendors rely on man-month-based multilayer subcontractors. For example, three-to-four-layer subcontracting, including subsidiary IT firms, temporary staffing from other vendors, and individuals is common in a large project in Japan.

The upper box shows new entrants: offshore IT vendors from China and India are emerging in the Japanese market. Recently, Japanese local IT vendors began

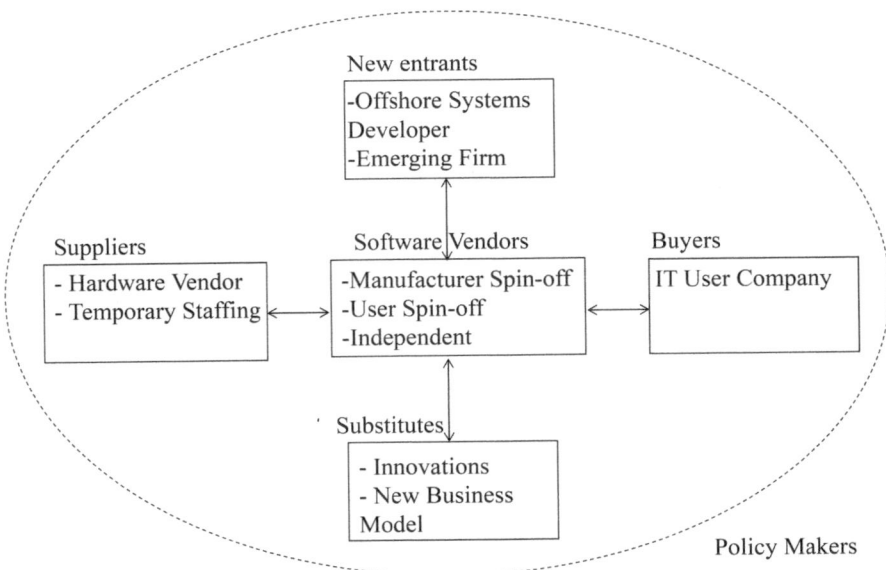

Fig. 1.2 The five forces model of the software industry in Japan

facing competition in pricing as well as services from these offshore vendors. The lower box shows the recent trend in which Japanese purchasers expect to substitute packaged software and cloud computing for custom-made software. Policymakers, such as the Japanese government, e.g., the IT Strategic Headquarters within the Cabinet, the Ministry of Economy, Trade and Industry (METI), and the Ministry of Internal Affairs and Communications (MIC), are considered to be a sixth force, as demonstrated above.

Informed by the five forces model, we interviewed experts in the IT industry and searched the literature, and assembled the following as environmental threats and opportunities to the industry: new entrants, e.g., China and India, US/EU vendors, difficulty in recruiting bright people, low-profitability, low-growth, mature oligopoly, packaged software, e.g., Enterprise Resource Planning (ERP), decline in IT demand, development-time pressure (quick delivery requests) from clients, price pressure from clients, quality requirements from clients, return on investment (ROI) requirements by clients, low IT literacy of clients, self-development by clients, shortage of subcontractors, new technology adoption, product differentiations, competition (clients switching vendors), erosion of software engineering capability, decreasing numbers of bright IT students, staff turnover, Merger and Acquisition (M&A), retirement of senior software engineers, and stagnation in IT innovation (Porter 1980, 1985; Barney 1986, 2007; Besanko et al. 2007; Cusumano 1991; Lippman and Rumelt 1982; Dodgson et al. 2008; Mongomery and Wernerfelt 1991; Prahalad and Hamel 1990; Arthur 1989; Dierickx and Cool 1989; Selznick 1957; Penrose 1959; JISA 2014; SAP 2014; McKinsey & Company et al. 2013; Kadono 2007).

In Chap. 4, based on these environmental threats and opportunities, we pursue the characteristics of Japanese IT vendors from the viewpoint of vendor types, i.e., manufacturer spin-offs, user spin-offs, and independents, in more detail (Kadono et al. 2009).

1.2.2 Innovation in the Software Industry

1.2.2.1 Issues of Software Innovation in Japan

As mentioned in the previous subsection, in the beginning of the Japanese information service industry, the limited number of manufacturer spin-off vendors and the NTT established distinctive competencies due to time-compression dis-economies based on governmental policies and support.

Additionally, because sustaining shop-floor usability is given priority over introducing technological innovation when IT is deployed in user companies in Japan, the dynamics of user-supplier interactions enables the development of finely tuned custom-made applications, and tends to establish long-lasting relationships between the user companies and IT vendors. The development of custom-made applications can cause a high entry barrier for domestic and international newcomers.

Simultaneously, most custom-made applications are developed jointly by the internal staff of the user company and software engineers from IT vendors, as a team or individually. Thus, if necessary, software engineers may be dispatched from man-month-based multilayer subcontractors. As a result, software engineers within the prime contractors tend to focus on dispatching engineers, and sometimes irresponsibly cede effective project management roles to the subcontractors.

This man-month-based multilayer-subcontractor structure in the Japanese software industry tends to inhibit the evolution of original Japanese innovations and innovators, such as new business models, e.g., packaged software, cloud computing, and entrepreneurs.

In fact, most Japanese software engineers acquire practical skills through on-the-job training in projects but tend to have limited opportunities to formally acquire professional skills based on computer science or software engineering disciplines. As shown in Chap. 2 in detail, most IT vendors hire new recruits from universities and graduate schools every year, but many of them have not majored in computer science or software engineering and seem under-qualified. Therefore, for new recruits the median is over 400 training hours for professional skills per year. On the other hand, for experienced software engineers, the median is almost 40 h per year; they are dispatched to develop custom-made applications for IT user companies.

In contrast, in the U.S., software engineering and computer science are scientific disciplines that develop the knowledge required for creating software professionally in the horizontally integrated software industry. Therefore, the U.S. provides sources of information on software engineering and computer science disciplines, e.g., the Software Engineering Body of Knowledge (SWEBOK), Carnegie Mellon University's (CMU) Capability Maturity Model/Capability Maturity Model Integration (CMM/CMMI) and the Project Management Body of Knowledge (PMBOK), that we review in the subsequent section. Furthermore, in the emerging countries, the numbers of IT engineers in the information service industry exceeded 1.4 million persons in China and India in 2009, most having majored in computer science or software engineering. These countries have therefore successfully become the world's offshore centers of software development, reflecting national policies of innovation (JISA 2014; Special Economic Zones in India (SEZ) 2009).

Consequently, the Japanese software industry experiences a vicious cycle in the factors such as sustaining shop-floor usability in IT user companies, university education in software disciplines, man-month-based multilayer subcontractors, senior management leadership of IT vendors, and introducing technological innovation.

1.2.2.2 Innovation Differences between Japan and the U.S.

In general, the software industry includes businesses involved in the development, maintenance and publication of computer software to solve business problems. The industry also includes software services, such as training, documentation, and consulting. In the U.S., the following sectors comprise the software industry (Rubin et al. 2008). First, the infrastructure software sector includes development of infrastructure software such as operating systems, middleware, and databases, e.g., Microsoft, IBM, Oracle, and HP. Second, the IT consulting and services sector includes services and custom solutions, e.g., IBM Global Services, Accenture, and other IT consulting organizations. Third, the packaged software development sector includes Enterprise Resource Planning (ERP) systems, e.g., SAP, Oracle. In addition, the cloud computing players have recently grown rapidly, e.g., Google, Amazon, and Salesforce. The market of orders for software in Japan is mainly comparable to the U.S. markets for IT consulting and services and packaged software development in the U.S.

Due to the historical differences in the liberalization of the ICT industries between Japan and the U.S., Japan's software industry is much more vertically integrated, whereas the U.S. software industry is much more horizontally integrated. Therefore, we can observe several different characteristics in analyzing innovation in the two countries.

First, regarding the supply side in the U.S., private programmers and individual organizations tend to create break-through innovations, creating software patents and intellectual property (Chiang 2010). The U.S., e.g., Silicon Valley, has been one of the most enthusiastic centers of IT innovations in the world; it created several technology trends and new paradigms, e.g., big data, digital enterprise, social media, clouds, IT staff, IT means business, mobile, bring your own device (BYOD), cyber security, and analytics (Greengard 2012, 2013; McKinsey & Company et al.2013). In Japan it is more common for large manufacturer spin-offs to work with university laboratories to develop innovations and patents in software products and services.

Second, in terms of the demand side, IT user companies in Japan seem to recuse themselves from adopting new technology at an early stage. In comparison, the U.S. software industry is highly packaged in that many large software development organizations, particularly in the area of ERP software, provide a specific set of software solutions, e.g., accounting, production management, sales management, logistics, etc. (SAP 2014). Organizations can then customize the pre-packaged software solutions rather than creating a large set of custom-made software solutions (Farhoomand 2007). The average of new packaged software development went from 22% in 1998 to 48.1% in 2008 (Rubin et al. 2008), while in Japan, even in fiscal year 2013, the software development and programming market was 7,502,070 million yen, of which orders for software totaled 6,365,857 million yen (METI 2014). Further, a comparison of the use rates of cloud network technology among Japanese and U.S. enterprises in March 2013 shows that the rate in the United States reached 70.6% against 42.4% in Japan. There is a wide disparity between Japanese and U.S. enterprises in the use of cloud computing as a key ICT component (MIC 2013).

Still, there are several common characteristics in the innovations and industry structures between Japan and the U.S., although the path dependencies (Arthur 1989) have been considerably different from each other. In terms of innovation processes, IT innovation and patents are growing, particularly given the growth of open systems and mobile application development. The software industry is going through a consolidation in both Japan and the U.S., where numerous mergers and acquisitions are taking place. We expect to see partnerships between different industries both in Japan and the U.S. In particular, telecommunication companies, software vendors, media companies, and mobile application developers are looking into partnering with each other to deliver entertainment content as well as business content in addition to traditional voice and data services.

1.2.2.3 Innovation Types

One of the controversial areas in managing innovation is the variation in what we understand by that term. First, shared by the following authorities, we assume that innovation is a process of making something new, i.e., innovare in Latin, in its broadest sense:

- New combinations: The introduction of new goods, new methods of production, the opening of new markets, the opening of new sources of supply, and the introduction of a new organization of any industry (Schumpeter 1926)
- Innovation is the specific tool of entrepreneurs, the means by which they exploit change as an opportunity for a different business or service. It is capable of being presented as a discipline, capable of being learned, capable of being practiced (Drucker 1985).
- Companies achieve competitive advantage through acts of innovation. They approach innovation in its broadest sense, including both new technologies and new ways of doing things (Porter 1990).

Second, the manufacturing capability model (Fujimoto 2003) for the automobile industry suggests that organizational routines ultimately influence business performance both through deep competitiveness, e.g., quality, productivity, product, and development lead-time, and through superficial competitiveness, e.g., cost, delivery time, and product appeal. Therefore, we consider the order effect on innovation paths in developing our research model. In terms of a broad sense of software engineering, an IT vendor's routines and deep competitiveness might include such factors as human resource development, project management, customer contact, quality assurance, and process improvement; an IT vendor's superficial competitiveness might include deliverables; and an IT vendor's business performance might include profitability, growth, and efficiency, in general.

Third, as shown in developing the research model in Chap. 3, based on interviews with IT vendors and experts in Japan and the U.S., we have identified three key factors for successful innovation: salesforce management, operational improvement, and R&D. Some vendors who manage their sales forces effectively succeed in efficiently dispatching their software engineers to upcoming customer projects. As a result, one such vendor operates at an average of 90 % capacity. Other profitable vendors have accumulated data on quality, cost, delivery, and productivity for more than 30 years to improve their operations continuously, i.e., kaizen (Ohno 1988; Osono et al. 2008). Most large-scale system integrators in Japan work earnestly on R&D activities in addition to doing effective salesforce management and efficiently improving their operations.

These three key factors are considered to be innovations in service, process, and product, respectively (Dodgson et al. 2008; Tidd and Bessant 2013). We have mentioned the user-driven shop-floor nature of the Japanese software industry and the viewpoint of service science (Stauss et al. 2008); when we investigate managing software engineering innovation in Japan, it is reasonable to consider service innovation, which includes the interface between the software user and vendor, e.g., project management and customer contact, in addition to product and process innovations.

Finally, in Chap. 3 we assume the structural model hypothesis, proceeding from development of human resources as the common original source, through refinement of deliverables, toward improvement in business performance, with leverage from the following three types of innovation in the management of software engineering: (1) product innovation: proceeding from human resource development to research and development, (2) process innovation: proceeding from human resource development to quality assurance and process improvement; and (3) service innovation: proceeding from human resource development to project management and customer contact.

In Chaps. 2 and 3 we analyze the causal relationships among the factors, proceeding from human resources development, via product, process, and service innovations, through refinement of deliverables toward improvement in business performance. We perform a structural equation model analysis, a path analysis, and a cross-section analysis, using data collected from the social surveys on software engineering (Bollen 1989). Furthermore, we go beyond the cross-section analysis results to understand the full range of relationships among the factors relating to software engineering capabilities, business environment, and business performance in the long term. We perform a panel analysis and a longitudinal analysis by making best use of the data obtained from the surveys (Meredith and Tisak 1990).

Similarly, we can learn several insightful findings from previous relevant studies. For example, according to the empirical study of critical success factors in the competitive advantage of an organization (Pastuszak et al. 2012), organizational learning directly influences performance through innovation, and organizational learning is essential for continuous performance improvement and long-term competitiveness. Additionally, we can find useful information for businesses for building critical capabilities to create and maintain competitive positions in the marketplace by examining key determinants of firm competitiveness; the determinants derive from three capability-based constructs, i.e., quality, marketing, and knowledge management systems (Yee et al. 2012). Furthermore, the exploratory study on the relationships between innovation and organizational performance suggests that an innovation orientation is related to overall organizational performance and that the highly innovating firms had a positive relationship with top line growth, customer satisfaction, bottom line growth, and profitability.

1.2.3 Research Approach

1.2.3.1 The Resource-Based View

Because a goal of this research is to encourage innovation, a key portion of the literature review includes the resource-based view, informed by which we give attention to factors such as an IT vendor's resources and capabilities. Understanding the value of an IT vendor's resources and capabilities is an important first consideration in understanding the IT vendor's internal strengths and weaknesses.

In studying the internal strengths and weaknesses of a firm's resources and capabilities, a resource-based view rests on two fundamental assumptions. The first assumption, resource heterogeneity, is that firms can be viewed as bundles of productive resources and that different firms possess different bundles of resources. This assumption is based on Penrose's work, which tries to understand the process through which firms grow and the limits of growth (Penrose 1959). The second assumption, resource immobility, is that some of the resources, derived from institutional leadership and distinctive competence, are very costly to copy (Selznick 1957). If the resources a firm possesses enable it to exploit opportunities or neutralize threats, are possessed by only a small number of competing firms, and if they are costly to copy, then they may be firm strengths and thus potential sources of competitive advantage (Barney 2007).

The definition of a firm's resources and capabilities and the assumptions of resource heterogeneity and resource immobility are quite abstract and not directly amenable to the analysis of a firm's strengths and weaknesses. However, Barney has developed an analysis framework called the VRIO framework. The VRIO framework is structured in a series of four questions to be asked about the business activities in which a firm engages:

- The Question of **Value**: Do a firm's resources and capabilities enable the firm to respond to environmental threats or opportunities?
- The Question of **Rarity**: Is a resource currently controlled by only a small number of competing firms?
- The Question of **Imitability**: Do firms without a resource face a cost disadvantage in obtaining or developing it?
- The Question of **Organization**: Are a firm's other policies and procedures organized to support the exploitation of its valuable, rare, and costly-to-imitate resources?

Particularly in our research, we pay considerable attention to Questions 2 and 3. Valuable but common resources and capabilities can be only a source of competitive parity, but valuable and rare resources and capabilities can be sources of at least temporary competitive advantage. Valuable and rare organizational resources can be sources of sustained competitive advantage only if firms that do not possess them face a cost disadvantage in obtaining them compared to firms that already possess them, i.e., if they are imperfectly imitable resources (Lippman and Rumelt 1982; Barney 1986a, b).

Software engineering capabilities are the essential management resources (core competencies) in the software service industry (Prahalad and Hamel 1990); therefore, in developing a measurement model in Chap. 2, we survey state-of-the-art cases in the software service field through a number of experts in academic, business, and governmental circles in Japan and the U.S., paying attention particularly to the degree of rarity and imitability of the software engineering capabilities in a broad sense.

1.2.3.2 Software Engineering Relevant Disciplines

Software engineering is defined as (1) the systematic application of scientific and technological knowledge, methods, and experience to the design, implementation, testing, and documentation of software (ISO/IEC 1993), and as (2) the application of a systematic, disciplined, quantifiable approach to the development, operation, and maintenance of software; that is, it is the application of engineering to software (ISO/IEC/IEEE 2010).

As we mentioned previously, in the U.S., software engineering as well as computer science are systemized scientific disciplines which develop the knowledge required for creating software professionally. Therefore, the U.S. provides sources of information on software engineering and computer science disciplines. Although the theory of measurement (Kyburg 1984), its application to computer software (Zuse 1997), a technique for identifying meaningful metrics for the software process (Basili and Weiss 1984), and a fundamental framework and a set of basic principles that guide the definition of product metrics for software (Pressman 2010) are topics that are beyond the scope of this book, it is worthwhile to establish a measurement model to assess the degree of execution of software engineering based on the disciplines of software engineering in a broad sense.

The measurement model we construct Chap. 2 is understood to be complementary to existing models, or disciplines, such as the Software Engineering Body of Knowledge (SWEBOK), Carnegie Mellon University's (CMU) Capability Maturity Model/Capability Maturity Model Integration (CMM/CMMI), the Project Management Body of Knowledge (PMBOK), and Fujimoto's manufacturing capability model.

First, regarding the SWEBOK 2004 (IEEE Computer Society 2004), we reviewed the SWEBOK knowledge areas and adopted the following areas into the measurement model to address IT vendors' innovative capabilities in software engineering: software requirements, software design, software construction, software testing, software maintenance, software configuration management, software engineering management, software engineering process, software engineering tools and methods, and software quality.

SWEBOK V3.0 (IEEE Computer Society 2013) is the most recent completely revised and updated version of the internationally respected "Guide to the Software Engineering Body of Knowledge." Newly imagined as a living, changing document, and thoroughly rewritten, SWEBOK V3.0 has been developed and created by leading authorities, reviewed by professionals, and made available for public review and comment, continuing its 20-year reputation as the most authoritative, fundamental, and trusted definition of the software engineering profession.

Second, regarding the CMM/CMMI (CMU 2014), we adopted the certification levels from 1 to 5 into the model to access the process improvement factor because we considered these levels to be a symbolic measure of process-improvement capability in software engineering.

Third, as already mentioned, because project management and customer contact are on the interface between the vendor and user of software, we also reviewed the Project Management Body of Knowledge (PMBOK) (PMI 2014) and enhanced the model and the question items on these factors, e.g., top management involvement and quality of the user requirement specification, consistent with insights obtained from service science (Stauss et al. 2008).

1.2.3.3   Measurement Models

Unlike the physical sciences using direct measures such as mass, velocity, or temperature, we tend to consider it to be difficult to measure attributes in the social sciences. Even in the social sciences, however, it is necessary to conceive a systematic method to assess the quality of activities; the method must be based on a set of clearly defined rules that will improve quality of the existing activities.

Such consensus is attained in several performance investigations of companies, including the self-measurement system for the Malcom Baldrige National Quality Award developed by the National Institute of Standards and Technology (NIST) in the U.S. in 1987; Malcolm Baldrige served as Secretary of Commerce, and his managerial excellence contributed to long-term improvement in efficiency and effectiveness of government (NIST 2014). The Award Program, responsive to the purposes of Public Law 100-107, i.e., quality improvement of product and process, led to the creation of a new public-private partnership.

In Japan, Nihon Keizai Shimbun's NICES is a private-sector multi-evaluation system to pursue the image of an excellent company from the viewpoint of an investor, consumer, business partner, employee, society, and of its potential; it includes responses to questionnaires and public financial data (Nihon Keizai Shimbun 2013). NICES conducts a large-scale survey of over 500 companies and performs a statistical analysis, such as using a structural equation model (Bollen 1989), to evaluate the priorities of the respondents.

Similarly, as shown in Chap. 2, we conceived the Software Engineering Excellence (SEE) rating to assess an overall degree of software engineering capabilities from the viewpoint of the supply side, i.e., the IT vendor. Additionally, in Chap. 5 we derive the IT management effectiveness (IME) as an overall performance indicator from the demand side, i.e., an IT user company (Kadono and Tsubaki 2002). The overall performance measurement is evaluated by an appropriate weighted average of detailed factors using statistical methods, such as principal component analysis and factor analysis.

1.3   Research Objectives

To add rigor to the previous argument about the productivity and success in the Japanese software industry, to assist the Japanese software industry to overcome the various issues mentioned previously, and to achieve medium- and long-term success, we pursue the following research objectives in the book (Fig. 1.3):

- How does the Japanese software industry develop its productivity?
- How does productivity relate to success for IT vendors?

To achieve these objectives, we first develop a measurement tool called SEE to evaluate the overall level of software engineering capabilities as an extended interpretation of productivity. Based on the literature review in the previous section, the SEE covers broad disciplines relating to software engineering capabilities, such as SWEBOK, CMM/CMMI, PMBOK, etc.; it therefore consists of Deliverables, Project Management, Quality Assurance, Process Improvement, Research and Development, Human Resource Development, and Customer Contact, as shown in Chap. 2.

Second, we verify the relationship between an IT vendor's productivity and its success; to do so we use the methodology that we reviewed in this chapter, such as the structural equation model and longitudinal analysis. The degree of a vendor's success can be evaluated by Business Performance such as profitability, growth, and stability.

Third, in addition to the research objectives regarding productivity and success, we need to address complementary issues, i.e., the Business Environment, including not only the supply side but also the demand side, for the Japanese software industry to pursue the ideal management of innovation in software engineering:

- What are the relevant environmental factors to consider in the relationship between productivity and success?

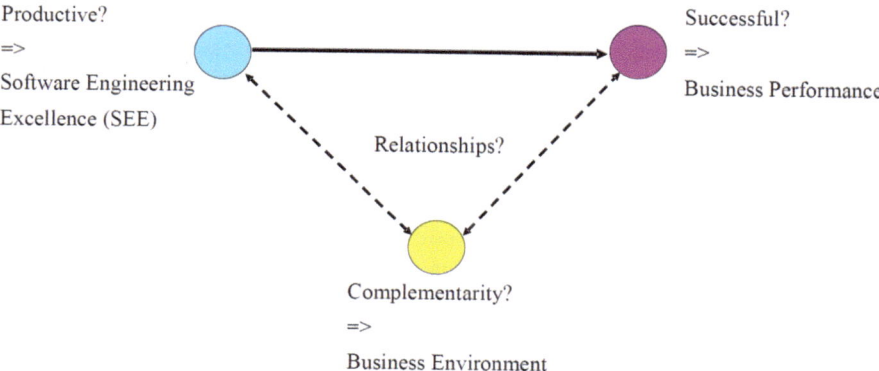

Fig. 1.3 Is the Japanese software industry productive and successful?

| | IT user companies | | |
	Business	IT	IT vendors
Management	CEO	CIO	
Operation	User divisions	IT divisions	

Fig. 1.4 Stakeholders in IT management

This is because sustaining shop-floor usability is given priority over introducing technological innovation when IT is deployed in user companies in Japan. That is, the ultimate goal for Japanese IT vendors is to serve as catalysts for their customers' IT management of enterprise systems; this is one of the most formidable management issues for senior managers in every sector in Japan.

The stakeholders in IT management of enterprise systems include both the supply side, i.e., IT vendors, and the demand side, i.e., IT user companies. Furthermore, the IT management organization in a user company consists of its Chief Executive Officer (CEO), Chief Information Officer (CIO), user divisions, and IT divisions, as shown in Fig. 1.4.

1.4 Overview of the Book

The book is composed of two major parts. The first part, Chaps. 1 to 3, introduces the Japanese software industry and examines various software engineering capabilities and the relationships among them, business performance, and the business environment of Japanese vendors through social surveys and statistical analyses.

In Chap. 2, to solve the issues relating to managing innovation in the Japanese software industry as mentioned in Chap. 1, we attempt to assess the achievements of the software engineering capabilities as represented by IT vendors in Japan; we additionally attempt to better understand the mechanisms of how software engineering capabilities relate to IT vendors' business performance and business environment. To this end we designed a research survey to investigate SEE; we administered it together with METI and IPA (METI and IPA 2007). SEE was originally developed based on interviews conducted with over 50 experts in academic, business, and governmental circles in Japan and the U.S. and on literature searches in the field of software engineering in a broad sense, as we reviewed in Chap. 1. Therefore, SEE can be used to evaluate the overall software engineering capabilities of IT vendors with regard to the following seven factors: Deliverables, Project Management, Quality Assurance, Process Improvement, Research and Development, Human Resource Development, and Customer Contact. We introduced two additional primary indicators as well: Business Performance, e.g., profitability, growth, productivity, and efficiency of management, and Business Environment, e.g., origin of vendor, number of software engineers, average age of employees, business model, customer base, and corporate culture. The SEE survey resulted in 233 valid responses. We found that vendors with a larger number of software engineers tended to obtain a higher SEE score, as did vendors whose employees were older, though they tended to be less profitable. Finally, there was no significant relationship between the SEE score and operating profit ratio of the IT vendors in Japan. Because the SEE survey results are precious pieces of information in the study of the Japan's software industry, the detailed findings are demonstrated in Chap. 2, and figures relating to the survey results are included in Appendix.

In Chap. 3, the objective of the research is to better understand the mechanisms of how software engineering capabilities relate to firms' business performance and business environment for the Japanese software industry. Based on the SEE survey results shown in Chap. 2, statistical analysis results are demonstrated using cross-section analysis, path analysis, stratified analysis, panel analysis, and longitudinal analysis. Focusing on management of software engineering innovation, we empirically verified the common order effects originating with human resource development and proceeded along the paths of service innovation, product innovation, and process innovation. Based on the panel analysis, we demonstrated several series correlations among the software engineering capabilities. The longitudinal analysis suggested positive relationships among software engineering capabilities and business performance in the long-term. However, the relationships between the software engineering capabilities and business performance vary significantly depending on the origin of a vendor: manufacturer or user spin-off or independent. Based on the analysis results, the several implications for managing innovation in software engineering in Japan, such as economies of scale and organizational inertia, are discussed in this Chapter.

The second part of the book, Chaps. 4 through 8, includes research relevant to managing innovation in software engineering in Japan in the broadest sense: characteristics of Japanese software vendors, IT management for user companies, a new social research scheme, modeling of the software industry structure, and a hybrid method to predict scenarios in the Japanese software industry.

In Chap. 4, the objectives of the research are to describe the competitive environment in the software industry in Japan and to understand the characteristic differences among manufacturer spin-offs, user spin-offs and independent vendors. Based on management frameworks such as Porter's five forces and Barney's resource-based view, we developed a model to measure environmental threats and competitive strengths/weaknesses. We then conducted factor analysis of the data collected from 100 major IT vendors in Japan. On this basis, we extracted eight threat factors, e.g., industry stagnation, difficulty in recruiting bright people, ROI/ quality demands from clients, price cutting/quick delivery demands from clients, and adoption of new technology. We also identified six strength/weakness factors, e.g., human capital, scale merit, expansive business, inimitability, and stability. Regression tree analysis suggested that manufacturer spin-off vendors tend to significantly expand their business with well-resourced R&D, while user spin-off vendors seem to depend heavily on demand from parent companies, as a result of which some are thought to gain inimitable capabilities. On the other hand, many independent vendors supply temporary staff to principal contractors and do not show specific strengths; even so, some independent vendors with inimitable assets are thought to be role models for software vendors in Japan.

In Chap. 5, the purpose of the study is to clarify the mechanism of how IT creates business value, particularly from the viewpoint of IT management in individual companies. To do this, we developed a hypothetical structural model that consists of six performance indicators, namely: awareness and actions of top management, linkage between management and IT, IT development capability, IT investment and deployment, IT readiness, and business value creation from IT. Based on analyses of data collected from 509 major companies comprising various types of business in Japan, we found that awareness and actions of top management lead to business value creation from IT via other intermediate factors, such as linkage between management and IT, etc. Based on the structural model, we propose a framework called "IT management effectiveness" with which the overall effectiveness of IT management is measurable.

In Chap. 6, we assume that the stakeholders in IT management of enterprise systems include not only the demand side, i.e., IT user companies, but also the supply side, i.e., IT vendors. We attempt to design a new social research scheme including both the demand side and the supply side to accelerate innovation in IT management. To do so, we first analyze the processes and results of the five surveys we have administered, researching into IT management effectiveness on the demand side and SEE on the supply side. Second, based on service dominant logic, we construct a new social research scheme for IT management innovation that is more dynamic and interactive between IT user companies and IT vendors than traditional social research schemes. One advantage of the new social research scheme is to be able to pursue management sophistication in the use of IT through three stages: Quality, Cost, and Delivery (QCD) assessment, potential growth factor analysis, and benchmarking with world-class cases. Another advantage is to be able to construct an information circulation platform to accumulate information and knowledge on cases of management sophistication in the use of IT.

Furthermore, through a case in the information service industry, we consider the role of science for society in a future-oriented manner that co-creates value beyond the border, i.e., aufheben, between the supply side and the demand side.

In Chap. 7, our goal is a preliminary assessment of the future software industry structure in Japan, giving priority to the effects of offshoring in China, based on surveys on software engineering capabilities of Japanese IT vendors conducted together with METI. An agent-based simulation model, focusing mainly on customers' price preferences and on the quality of vendors' communication with customers, concludes that Japanese vendors can possibly lose market share if Japanese customers prefer the lower prices offered by offshore vendors. The results suggest that Japanese vendors should improve their communication skills to satisfy their customers' requirements regarding the quality of enterprise software, while also taking into account their customers' price preferences to avoid direct price competition with Chinese vendors. Otherwise, some Japanese vendors within the current man-month-based multilayered software industry culture will not survive in the drastically changing Japanese market.

In Chap. 8, we investigate the potential to predict future scenarios in the Japanese software industry by making use of a hybrid method; that is, we attempt to develop a new research framework by integrating data obtained from large-scale fact-finding surveys, statistical analyses based on dynamic modeling, and simulations. On this basis, we suggest guidelines for a global technology strategy for Japan's software industry with a view to winning a sustainable competitive advantage. Additionally, it should be possible to develop evidence-based visualizations of industry growth scenarios by integrating intellectual instruments such as management theory, research surveys, statistics, and simulations.

References

Arthur, W. B. (1989). Competing technologies, increasing returns, and lock-in historical events. *Economic Journal, 99,* 116–131.

Baba, Y., Takai, S., & Mizuta, Y. (1995). The Japanese software industry the hub structure approach. *Reseach Policy, 24,* 473–486.

Barney, J. B. (1986a). Strategic factor markets: Expectations, luck and business startegy. *Management Science, 32,* 1512–1514.

Barney, J. B. (1986b). Organizational culture: Can it be a source of sustained competitive advantage? *Academy of Management Review, 11,* 656–665.

Barney, J. B. (2007). *Gaining and sustaining competitive advantage.* New Jersey: Pearson Prentice Hall.

Basili, V. R., & Weiss, D. M. (1984). A methodology for collecting valid software engineering data. *IEEE Transactions on Software Engineering, SE-10,* 728–738.

Besanko, D., Dranove, D., Shanley, M., & Schaefer, S. (2007). *Economics of starategy.* New York: Willey.

Bollen, K. (1989). *Structural equation with latent variables.* New York: Wiley-Interscience.

Carnegie Mellon University. (2014). Software Engineering Institute. http://www.sei.cmu.edu/cmmi/. Accessed 14 Aug 2014.

Chiang, C. (2010). Product diversification in competitive R & D-intensive firms: An empirical study of the computer software industry. *Journal of Applied Business Research, 26*(1), 99–108.

Cusmano, M. A. (1991). *Japan's software factories.* Oxford: Oxford University Press.

Cusmano, M. A. (2004). *The business of software.* New York: Free Press.

Dierickx, I., & Cool, K. (1989). Asset stock accumulation and sustainability of competitive advantage. *Management Science, 35,* 1504–1511.

Dodgson, M., Gann, D., & Salter, A. (2008). *The management of technological innovation.* Oxford: Oxford University Press.

Drucker, P. (1985). *Innovation and entrepreneurship.* New York: Harper & Row.

Farhoomand, A. F. (2007). The global software industry in 2006. Asia Case Research Centre.

Financial Information System Center. (Ed.). (1992). *White book on financial information system.* Tokyo: Zaikei Shouhou Sha.

Fujimoto, T. (2003). *Capability-building competition.* Tokyo: Chuohkouronshinsya.

Greengard, S. (2012). Ten tech trends will change IT in 2013. http://www.baselinemag.com/it-management/ten-tech-trends-that-will-change-it-in-2013. Accessed 14 Aug 2014.

Greengard, S. (2013). Six top tech trends to watch in 2014. http://www.baselinemag.com/innovation/six-top-tech-trends-to-watch-in-2014.html/. Accessed 14 Aug 2014.

Hasegawa, S. (Ed.). (2013). *History of Japan's trade and industry policy (7) machinery and information industries*. Tokyo: Keizai Sangyo Chosakai.

IEEE Computer Society. (2004). SWEBOK 2004.

IEEE Computer Society. (2013). SWEBOK V3.0. http://www.computer.org/portal/web/swebok/swebokv3.

ISO. (1993). ISO/IEC 2382-1:1993 Information technology–Vocabulary–Part 1: Fundamental terms, 01.04.07.

ISO. (2010). ISO/IEC/IEEE 24765:2010 Systems and software engineering–Vocabulary.

Kadono, Y. (2007). The Issues on IT Industry in Japan. Nikkei Net. http://it.nikkei.co.jp/business/news/index.aspx?n=MMITac000017122007. Accessed 14 Aug 2014.

Kadono, Y. (2009). *Business opportunities in Japan: Negotiating the Japanese Maze?* Bangalore: NASSCOM, Global Trade Development (Keynote speech).

Kadono, Y., & Tsubaki, H. (2002) *How IT create business value*. Proceedings of Pacific Asia Conference on Information Systems (PACIS).

Kadono, Y., Tsubaki, H., & Tsuruho, S. (2009). *A study on characteristics of software vendors in Japan: from environmental threats and resource-based view*. Proc., the 13th Pacific Asia Conference on Information Systems.

Kimura, T. (2014). The forty five evils brought by man-month-based business, and multilayer subcontractors in IT industry. *Nikkei Computer*.

Kyburg, H. E. (1984). *Theory and measurement*. Cambridge: Cambridge University Press.

Lippman, S., & Rumelt, R. (1982). Uncertain imitability: An analysis of interfirm differences in efficiency under competition. *Bell Journal of Economics, 13*, 418–438.

McKinsey & Company, Bughin, J., Chui, M., & Manyika, J. (2013). Ten IT-enabled business trends for the decade ahead. *McKinsey Quarterly*.

Meredith, W., & Tisak, J. (1990). Latent curve analysis. *Psychometrika, 55*, 107–122.

Ministry of Economy, Trade and Industry, & Information-Technology Promotion Agency, Japan (METI & IPA). (2007). *Fact-finding investigation on software engineering capabilities of enterprise systems in Japan*. (The responsibility for the investigation lies with Yasuo Kadono). sec.ipa.go.jp/reports/20071204/SE_level_research_2006_2.pdf. Accessed 14 Aug 2014.

Ministry of Economy, Trade, and Industry (METI). (2014). *Current survey on selected service industries: Information service industry.*

Ministry of Internal Affairs and Communications (MIC). (2013). *White Paper—Information and Communications in Japan.*

Ministry of Internal Affairs and Communications (MIC). (2014a). The policy of information and communications in Japan. http://www.soumu.go.jp/main_sosiki/joho_tsusin/joho_tsusin.html.

Ministry of Internal Affairs and Communications (MIC). (2014b). White paper: The information and communications in Japan. http://itpro.nikkeibp.co.jp/atcl/watcher/14/334361/072100007/?ST=ittrend&P=1.

Mongomery, C. A., & Wernerfelt, B. (1991). Source of superior performance: Market share versus industry effects in the U.S. brewing industry. *Management Science, 37*, 954–959.

National Institute of Standards and Technology (NIST). (2014). Malcom Baldrige National Quality Award. http://www.nist.gov/baldrige/about/improvement_act.cfm.

Nihon Keizai Shimbun. (2013). NICES. http://www.nikkei-r.co.jp/domestic/management/nices/.

Ohno, T. (1988). *Toyota production system: Beyond large-scale production*. New York: Productivity Press.

Osono, E., Shimizu, N., & Takeuchi, H. (2008). *Extreme Toyota: Radical contradictions that drive success at the world's best manufacturer*. Hoboken: Wiley.

Pastuszak, Z. S., Stacy H.-P., Lee, T.-R., Anussornnitisam, P., & Kaewchur, O. (2012). Establishing interrelationships among organisational learning, innovation and performance. *International Journal of Innovation and Learning 2012, 11*(2), 200–215.

Penrose, E. T. (1959). *The theory of the growth of the firm*. New York: Wiley.

Porter, M. (1980). *Competitive strategy*. New York: Free Press.

Porter, M. (1985). *Competitive advantage*. New York: Free Press.

Porter, M. (1990). *The competitive advantage of nations*. London: Macmillan.

Prahalad, C. K., & Hamel, G. (1990). *The core competence of the corporation*. Harvard Business Review.

Pressman, R. S. (2010). *Software Engineering: a practitioner's approach* (7th ed.). McGraw-Hill.

Project Management Institute. (2014). A guide to project management body of knowledge (PMBOK). http://www.pmi.org/PMBOK-Guide-and-Standards/Standards-Library-of-PMI-Global-Standards.aspx. Accessed 14 Aug 2014.

Rubin, H., Johnson, M., & Iventosch, S. (2008). The US Software Industry. *Country Report*.

SAP. (2014). Invester relations. http://www.sap.com/corporate-en/about/investors.html.

Schumpeter, J. A. (1926). *Theorie der Wirtschaftlichen Entwicklung* (The Theory of Economic Development).

Selznick, P. (1957). *Leadership in administration*. NewYork: Harper & Row.

Special Economic Zones (SEZ) in India, Ministry of Commerce & Industry. (2009). Formal approvals granted SEZs as on 15 January 2009, SEZ India website. www.sezindia.nic.in. Accessed 20 Sept 2009.

Stauss, B., Engelmann, K., Kremer, A., & Luhn, A. (2008). *Services science: Fundamentals, challenges and future developments*. Berlin: Springer-Verlag.

Japan Information Technology Service Industry Association (JISA). (2014). Research on IT human resources and training measures for globalization. http://itjobgate.jisa.or.jp/world/index.html.

The Strategic Headquarters for the Promotion of an Advanced Information and Telecommunications Network Society (IT Strategic Headquarters). (2012). The new strategy in information and communications technology (IT) roadmaps. http://www.kantei.go.jp/jp/singi/it2/pdf/120704_siryou1.pdf.

Tidd, J., & Bessant, J. (2013). *Managing innovation* (5th ed.). New York: Wiley.

Yee, K. P., & Eze, U. C. (2012). The influence of quality, marketing, and knowledge capabilities in business competitiveness. *International Journal of Innovation and Learning 2012, 11*(3), 288–307.

Zuse, H. (1997). *A framework of software measurement*. New York: DeGruyter.

Part I
Industry and Software Engineering Capabilities from Surveys and Statistical Analyses

Chapter 2
The Surveys on Software Engineering Excellence

Abstract In Chap. 2, to solve the issues relating to managing innovation in the Japanese software industry as mentioned in Chap. 1, we aim to assess the achievements of the software engineering capabilities as represented by IT vendors in Japan; we additionally aim to better understand the mechanisms of how software engineering capabilities relate to IT vendors' business performance and business environment. To this end we designed a research survey to investigate software engineering excellence (SEE); we administered it together with METI and IPA. SEE was originally developed based on interviews conducted with over 50 experts in academic, business, and governmental circles in Japan and the U.S. and on literature searches in the field of software engineering in a broad sense, as we reviewed in Chap. 1. Therefore, SEE can be used to evaluate the overall software engineering capabilities of IT vendors with regard to the following seven factors: Deliverables, Project Management, Quality Assurance, Process Improvement, Research and Development, Human Resource Development, and Customer Contact. We introduced two additional primary indicators as well: Business Performance, e.g., profitability, growth, productivity, and efficiency of management, and Business Environment, e.g., origin of vendor, number of software engineers, average age of employees, business model, customer base, and corporate culture. The SEE survey resulted in 233 valid responses. We found that vendors with a larger number of software engineers tended to obtain a higher SEE score, as did vendors whose employees were older, though they tended to be less profitable. Finally, there was no significant relationship between the SEE score and operating profit ratio of the IT vendors in Japan. Because the SEE survey results are precious pieces of information in the study of the Japan's software industry, the detailed findings are demonstrated in Chap. 2, and figures relating to the survey results are included in Appendix.

Keywords Software Engineering Excellence (SEE) · Business performance · Business environment · Social survey

© Springer Japan 2015
Y. Kadono, *Management of Software Engineering Innovation in Japan,*
DOI 10.1007/978-4-431-55612-1_2

2.1 Structural Model and Research Question

In order for the Japanese software industry to solve the issues relating to managing innovation in software engineering, and lead to sustained success, the first step in all achievement is to grasp an appropriate perception of the present situation in the Japanese software industry, such as software engineering capabilities, business performance, and business environment, we mentioned in Chap. 1. In other words, we need to understand how software engineering capability as a core competence (Prahalad and Hamel 1990) for the industry is significant for achieving medium- and long-term success.

Therefore, the objectives of the research in Chaps. 2 and 3 are to:

1. assess the achievements of the software engineering capabilities, as represented by IT vendors in Japan, and
2. better understand the mechanisms of how software engineering capabilities relate to IT vendors' business performance and business environment.

To achieve these objectives, we developed a measurement tool called Software Engineering Excellence (SEE). SEE was originally developed based on the interviews conducted with through over 50 experts in academic, business, and governmental circles in Japan and the U.S., and on literature reviews in the field of software engineering in a broad sense, and so on, as we surveyed in the previous Chapter (ISO/IEC/IEEE 2010; Pressman 2010; IEEE, Computer Society 2013; CMU 2014; PMI 2014; Barney 2007; Fujimoto 2003; Dodgson et al. 2008; Tidd and Bessant 2013). Therefore, SEE can be used to evaluate the overall software engineering capabilities of IT vendors from the viewpoint of the following seven factors: Deliverables, Project Management, Quality Assurance, Process Improvement, Research and Development, Human Resource Development, and Customer Contact.

We introduced two other primary indicators as well: Business Performance and Business Environment. Business Performance indicates the overall business performance of individual IT vendors, such as profitability, growth, productivity, and efficiency of the management. Business Environment expresses the company profile and structure of an IT vendor, including, e.g., origin of vendor, number of software engineers, average age of employees, business model, customer base, corporate culture. Business Environment complements the relationship between SEE and Business Performance of software vendors. The structural model of the research is shown in Fig. 2.1.

2.2 Measurement Model and Literature Review

Based on the structural model, we develop the measurement model and conducted surveys on SEE in 2005, 2006, and 2007, together with Japan's Ministry of Economy, Trade and Industry (METI), and Information-Technology Promotion Agency (IPA).

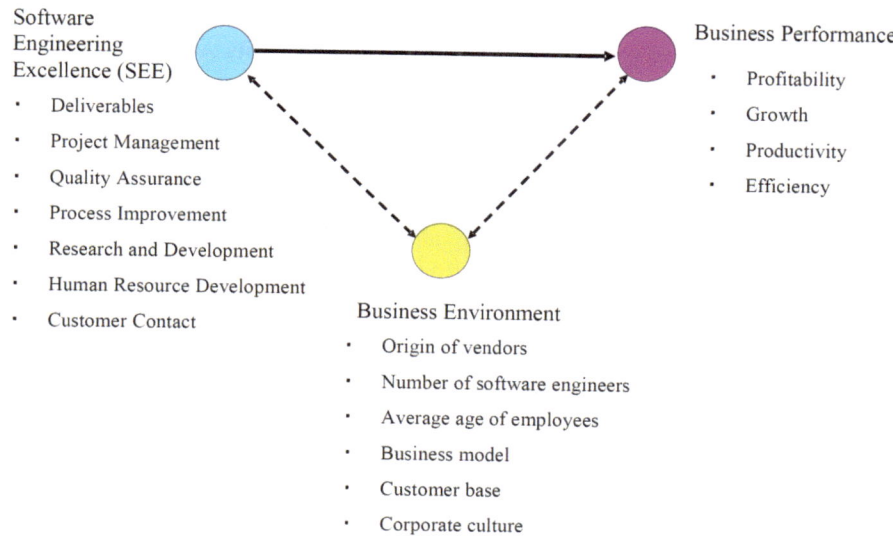

Fig. 2.1 Structural model of Software Engineering Excellence (SEE)

Software engineering capabilities are the essential management resources in the software service industry, so, in developing a measurement model in Chap. 2, we survey state-of-the-art cases in the in the software service field, through a number of experts in academic, business, and governmental circles in Japan and the U.S., paying attention particularly to the degree of rarity and imitability (Barney 2007) in the software engineering capabilities in a broad sense.

The SEE measurement model is also understood to be complementary to exist-ing models of software engineering in a broad sense, including computer science disciplines, maturity model, and capability models, which are reviewed in Chap. 1: Software Engineering Body of Knowledge (SWEBOK), Fujimoto's manufacturing capability model, Carnegie Mellon University's Capability Maturity Model/Capa-bility Maturity Model Integration (CMM/CMMI), and Service Science, and so on.

First of all, existing Process Improvement models in the field of software en-gineering are explicitly included inside the SEE model in the following way. Re-garding SWEBOK (IEEE, Computer Society 2013), we reviewed the SWEBOK knowledge areas and adopted the following areas into the SEE model to address IT vendors' innovative capabilities in process and product: software requirements, software design, software construction, software testing, software maintenance, software configuration management, software engineering management, software engineering process, software engineering tools and methods, and software quality.

The manufacturing capability model (Fujimoto 2003) for the automobile indus-try suggests that organizational routines finally influence business performance through both deep competitiveness, e.g., quality, productivity, product and devel-opment lead-time; and superficial competitiveness, e.g., cost, delivery time, and product appeal power. Therefore, we go into greater depth, with question items of the measurement model: IT vendors' routines and deep competitiveness, i.e., Human Resource Development, Project Management, Quality Assurance, Process Improvement, Research and Development, and Customer Contact; and IT vendors' superficial competitiveness, i.e., Deliverables; and Business Performance, i.e., operating profit ratio.

Regarding CMM/CMMI (Carnegie Mellon University), we adopt into the SEE model the certification levels from one to five, so as to assess the Process Improvement factor, since we considered these levels to be a symbolic assessment measure of Process Improvement capability in software engineering.

Moreover, informed by the viewpoint of service science (Stauss et al. 2008), we see that Project Management and Customer Contact are on the borderline between user and vendor of software, so we expanded the questionnaire to include user-side items, e.g., top management involvement, and quality of user requirement specification.

Based on the above literature review and the discussions with experts in academic, business, and government circles, we came up with the SEE measurement model. The SEE measurement model has a hierarchical structure with three layers: observed responses to question items, seven detailed factors, and SEE as a primary indicator.

Software Engineering Excellence (SEE) as we have defined it consists of the following seven factors:

1. Deliverables: achievement ratios on quality, cost, speed, and productivity; understanding of project information;
2. Project Management: project monitoring, assistance to project managers, project planning capability, PMP (Project Management Professional) ratio;
3. Quality Assurance: organization, methods, review, testing, guidelines, management of outsourcers;
4. Process Improvement: data collection, improvement of estimation, assessment methods, CMM/CMMI (Carnegie Mellon University's Capability Maturity Model/Capability Maturity Model Integration);
5. Research and Development: strategy, organization, sharing of technological skills, learning organization, development methodology, intellectual assets, commoditized software, readiness for state-of-the-art technology;
6. Human Resource Development: training hours, skill development systems, incentive schemes, measurement of human resource development, moral support;
7. Customer Contact: ratio of prime contracts, scope of services offered, direct communication with customers' top management, deficit prevention, and clarification of user specifications.

Business Performance considers general performance indicators such as:

- Profitability: operating profit ratio,
- Growth: sales growth ratio,
- Productivity: sales per person,
- Efficiency: capital ratio.

Business Environment includes the following items, which are relating to the controversial issues in the Japan's software industry shown in Chap. 1, and suggested by the interviews with experts in academic, business, and governmental circles:

- Origin of vendor: manufacturer spin-off, user spin-off, or independent,
- Number of software engineers, including programmers,
- Average age of employees,
- Business model: ratio of customized development, ratio of prime contractors,
- Customer base: manufacturers, financial institute, information communication technology, public services, wholesale/retailer, services, utility, construction,
- Corporate culture: aspirations of senior managers, spirit of challenge, information sharing, agility.

2.3 Software Engineering Excellence (SEE) Surveys

2.3.1 Conduct of the SEE Surveys

Based on the measurement model of SEE survey, we administered it in 2005, 2006, and 2007, together with Japan's Ministry of Economy, Trade and Industry (METI), and Information-Technology Promotion Agency (IPA) (METI and IPA 2007; Kadono et al. 2012).

The questionnaire of SEE on the practice of software engineering and the nature of the responding company was sent to the CEOs of major Japanese IT vendors with over 300 employees, as well as the member firms of the Japan Information Technology Services Industry Association (JISA), and was then distributed to the departments in charge of software engineering.

As shown in Table 2.1, in the 2005 SEE survey, there were 55 valid responses, a response rate of 24%; and in the 2006 SEE survey, there were 78 valid responses, a response rate of 15%. In the 2007 SEE survey, responses were received from 117 companies, with a total of 100 valid responses, a response rate of 10%. Although the responses are limited compared with the total IT vendors in Japan, the number of software engineers and programmers who belong to the responding companies accounts for over 30% of the total number of them in Japan according to the re-

Table 2.1 Software Engineering Excellence surveys

Fiscal year	2005	2006	2007	Total[a]
Questionnaires sent	230	537	1000	NA
Valid responses	55	78	100	151
Manufacturer spin-off	17	27	27	42
User spin-off	15	15	20	33
Independent	23	36	53	76
Response rate (%)	24	15	10	NA

[a] Total number of unique respondents over the three surveys

port published by JISA (JISA 2014). Therefore, the SEE survey results are precious pieces of information in the study of the Japanese software industry.

In the 2005 SEE survey, we preliminarily analyzed the relationships among SEE, Business Performance and Business Environment based on data collected from 55 major IT vendors in Japan. We conducted path analysis, by which we found that SEE factors exert a direct positive impact on Business Performance, and that the Business Environment directly and indirectly (i.e., via SEE) affects Business Performance (Kadono et al. 2006). In the 2006 SEE survey, we increased the number of surveyed Japanese IT vendors from 55 to 78, in order to more deeply investigate the impact of software engineering on Business Performance and the Business Environment, as we describe the analysis results in detail in Chap. 3.

Consecutively, in the 2007 SEE survey, we collected data from the 100 major IT vendors in Japan. Since the sample size of each type of vendor in the 2007 SEE survey, i.e., manufacturer spin-off, user spin-off and independent, is large enough to perform stratified analysis, we statistically investigate the differences in characteristics attributable to vendors broken down by origin in Chap. 3. For the further analysis, such as panel analysis and longitudinal analysis, we have integrated the 233 valid responses received over the 3 years into a single database including 151 unique companies, consisting of 42 manufacturer spin-off vendors, 33 user spin-off vendors, and 76 independent vendors.

2.3.2 Calculation Results of SEE

After collecting data from vendors in 2005, 2006, and 2007, we calculated the standardized factor loadings of the seven factors—Deliverables, Project Management, Quality Assurance, Process Improvement, Research and Development, Human Resource Development, and Customer Contact—through confirmatory factor analysis, based on the responses received to the questions relevant to the measurement model described in the previous subsection.

Then we estimate the overall SEE score each year by principal component analysis, i.e., SEE2005, SEE2006 and SEE2007. For example, a histogram of deviations of the SEE2006 score is shown in Fig. 2.2. Although there are several companies with outstanding SEE scores, we consider that the SEE analysis results are appropriate for further analyses since some scores of SEE are reasonable in light of the interviews with the individual respondents we conducted. Also, a scatter plot diagram matrix of the seven factors and the overall SEE score in the SEE2006 survey is shown in Fig. 2.3. The measurement model for 2007 was modified slightly based on: the response rate for each question item; the statistical significance of each observed response obtained in the 2005 and 2006 SEE surveys; and recent changes in technology and market trends.

Figure 2.4 contains box-and-whisker plots showing that the median SEE of the manufacturer spin-off vendors is higher than that of the user spin-off vendors, which, in turn, is higher than that of the independent vendors. However, the maxi-

Fig. 2.2 Histogram of deviations of SEE 2006

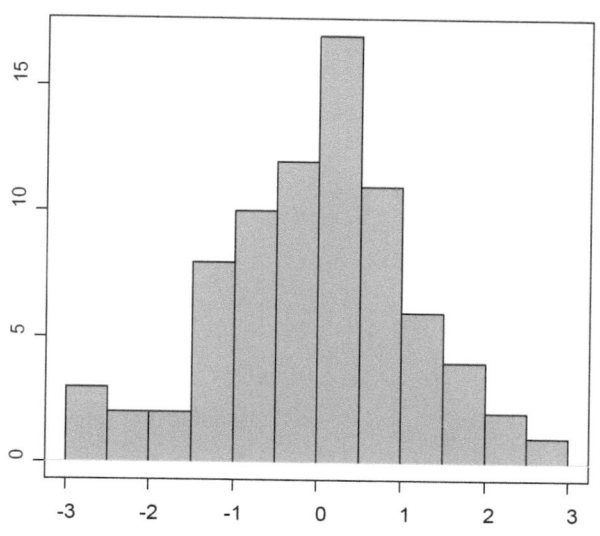

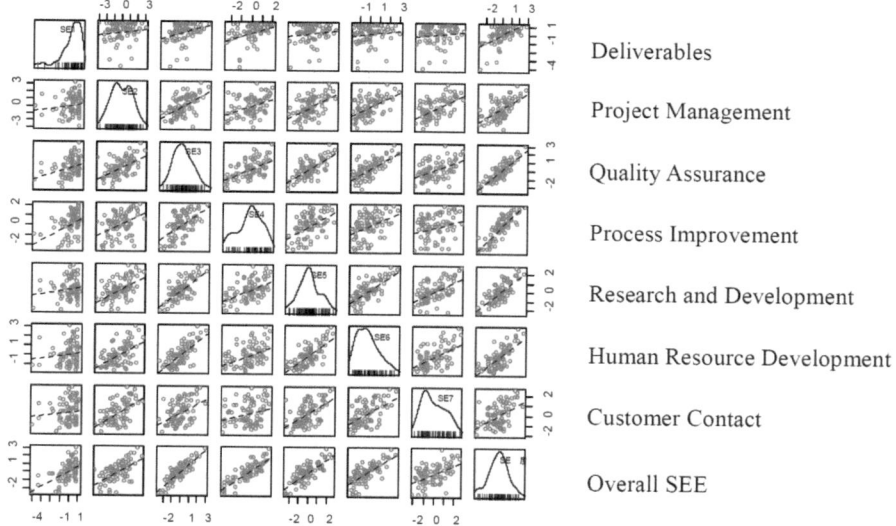

Deliverables

Project Management

Quality Assurance

Process Improvement

Research and Development

Human Resource Development

Customer Contact

Overall SEE

Fig. 2.3 Scatter plot diagram matrix of the seven SEE factors and over all SEE

mum SEE of the independent vendors is higher than that of the user spin-off vendors. This tendency in SEE2007 is the same as in SEE2005 and SEE2006. These findings suggest that IT user companies and IT vendors with subcontractors should select independent and manufacturer spin-off vendors through careful assessment of their software engineering capabilities.

Fig. 2.4 Deviations of SEE
by origin of vendors ($N = 100$)

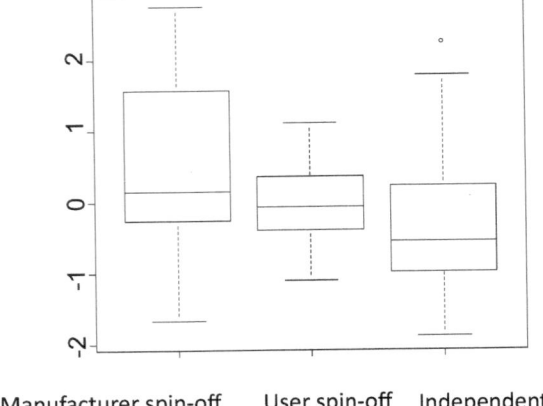

Manufacturer spin-off   User spin-off   Independent

2.4   Key Findings of SEE Surveys

In this section, key findings of the SEE surveys are shown from the view point of responses to questionnaires on SEE, responses to questionnaires on Business Environment, and implications from SEE relating analyses.

Since the SEE survey results are precious pieces of information in the study of the Japanese software industry, the figures relating to the observed responses to major questionnaires relevant to the seven SEE factors at the SEE2007 survey are shown in Appendix.

2.4.1   Responses to Questionnaires on SEE

First of all, the Deliverables score of SEE is estimated using responses to the relevant question items, such as achievement ratios of quality, cost, and delivery (QCD), and productivity, and understanding of project information.

The median QCD achievement ratios are over 70 % for all three types of vendor (Fig. 2.5). QCD achievement levels for user spin-off vendors tend to be higher than those for manufacturer spin-off vendors and independent vendors. This tendency was also observed in the previous study at SEE2005 and SEE2006. These findings might imply that parent companies of user spin-off vendors adequately agree with the subsidiary vendors on the quality of deliverables.

Second, the Project Management score of SEE is estimated using responses to the relevant question items: project planning capability, assistance to project managers, and project monitoring (scope, frequency).

For example, regarding project monitoring: frequency, most project monitoring operations are carried monthly or weekly (Fig. 2.6).

Third, the Quality Assurance score of SEE is estimated using responses to the relevant question items: review process, quality management organization (require-

Fig. 2.5 Quality, cost and delivery achievement ratios (%) for SEE survey respondents in 2007. (*N*=72)

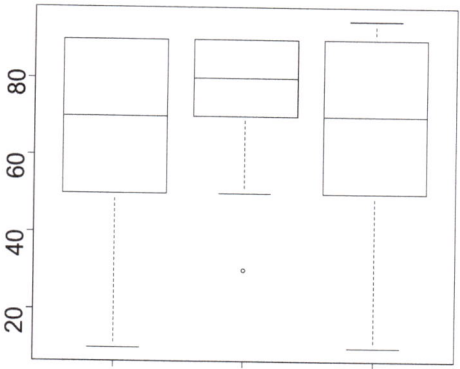

Manufacturer spin-off   User spin-off   Independent

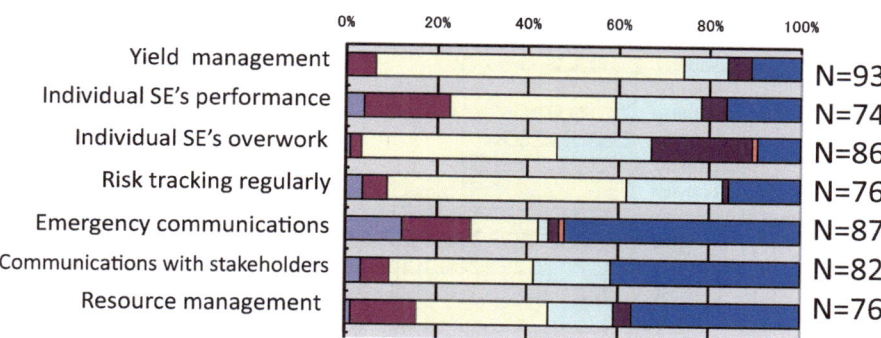

Fig. 2.6 Project monitoring: frequency. 1. annually, 2. 3/6-month period, 3. monthly, 4. weekly, 5. daily, 6. every few hours, 7. anytime

ment definition, schematic design, detail design, development, test, operation and manual), and management of outsources.

In terms of the Review process, almost half of IT vendors carry out quality reviews according to standard procedures of corporates through the project management process, i.e., requirement definition, schematic design, detail design, development, test, operation and manual (Fig. 2.7).

Fourth, the Process Improvement score of SEE is estimated using responses to the relevant question items: objectives management, data collection, data utilization, and improvement of estimation

With respect to Data collection for process improvement, some companies have collected data for process improvement on bugs, quality assurance, productivity, quality of life (QOL), technical skills, and cost for more than 20 years (Fig. 2.8).

Fifth, the Research and Development (R&D) score of SEE is estimated using responses to the relevant question items: strategy, organization, learning organiza-

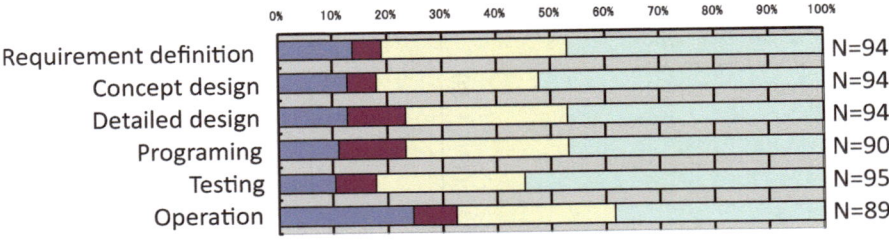

Fig. 2.7 Review process. 1.no review procedure, 2. little review with procedure, 3. half review with procedure, 4. almost review with procedure

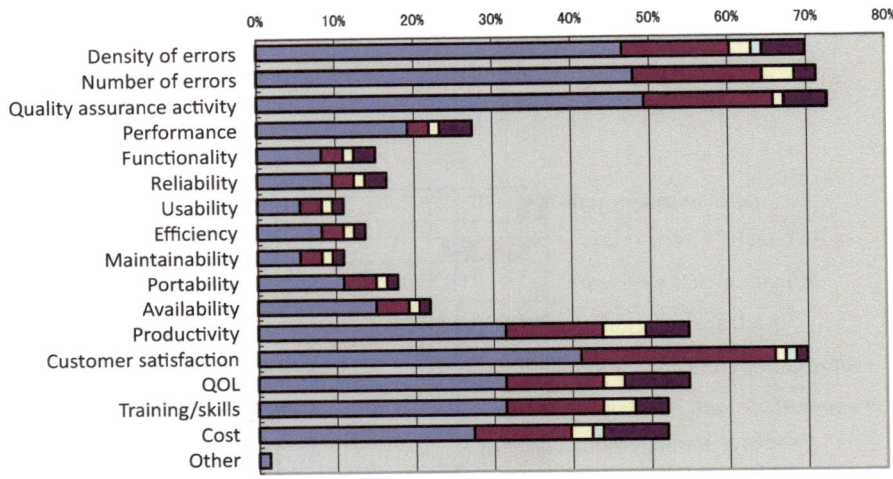

Fig. 2.8 Accumulated number of years of data collection for process improvement ($N = 73$). 1. –5 years, 2. 6–10 years, 3. 11–15 years, 4. 16–20 years, 5. 20– years

tion, readiness for state-of-the-art technology, development methodology, reuse of software resources, and effect of R&D.

Regarding Research and development (R&D) strategy, half of IT vendors have R&D strategies at least of a couple of years. On the other hand, 40 % of them have either no R&D strategies or single year R&D plans (Fig. 2.9).

Sixth, the Human Resource Development score of SEE is estimated using responses to the relevant question items: ratio of prime contracts, direct communication with customers' top management, understanding of proposal by vendors' top management, scope of services offered, clarification of user requirements, and prevention against unprofitable project.

One of the SEE questionnaires used to measure Human Resource Development asks about the number of training hours for new recruits. For new recruits, the median is over 400 training hours per year (Fig. 2.10), whereas for other experienced software engineers, another Human Resource Development measurement item queried in the survey, the median is almost 40 h per year (Fig. 2.11). This tendency

Fig. 2.9 Research and
development (R&D) strategy
($N = 100$)

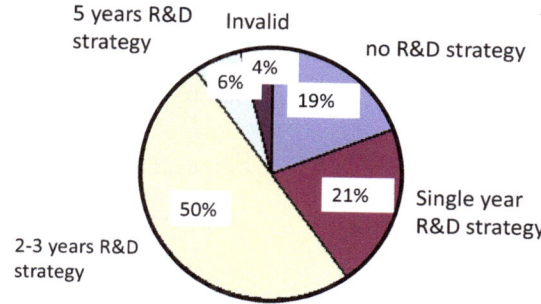

Fig. 2.10 Software engineer
training hours per year for
new recruits ($N=85$)

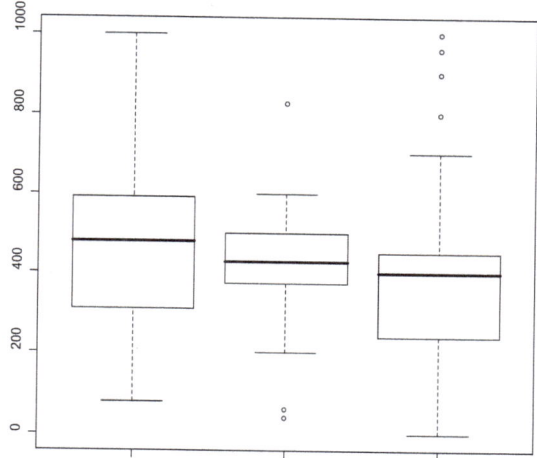

Fig. 2.11 Software engineer
training hours per year for
experienced workers ($N=86$)

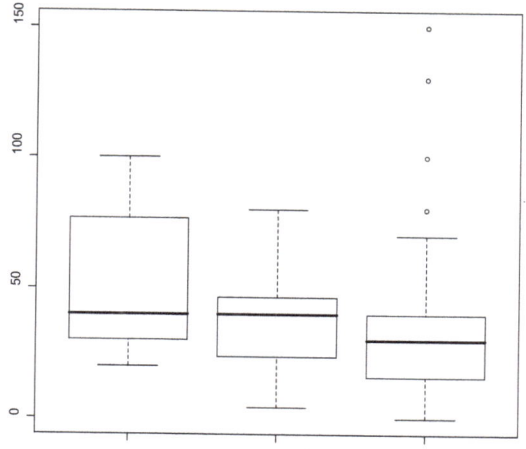

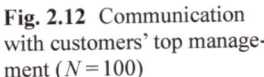 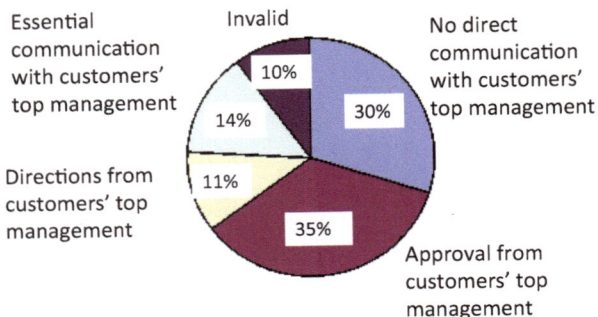

Fig. 2.12 Communication with customers' top management ($N = 100$)

observed in the 2007 survey results was also observed in the 2005 and 2006 results. Manufacturer spin-off vendors tend to invest relatively more time training engineers than do other types of vendors.

As discussed in Chap. 1, most IT vendors hire new recruits from universities and graduate schools every year, but many of them have not majored in computer science or software engineering, and seem under-qualified. In fact, most Japanese software engineers acquire practical skills through on-the-job training in projects, but tend to have limited opportunities to formally acquire professional skills based on computer science and software engineering disciplines. In other words, these results suggest that all types of vendors do not rely on the universities in Japan for the software engineering education.

In contrast, in the U.S., software engineering and computer science are scientific disciplines that develop the knowledge required for creating software professionally in the horizontally integrated software industry. Therefore, the U.S. provides sources of information on software engineering and computer science disciplines, e.g., SWEBOK, CMMI, and PMBOK, that we review in Chap. 1.

Seventh, the Customer Contact score of SEE is estimated using responses to the relevant question items: ratio of prime contracts, direct communication with customers' top management, understanding of proposal by vendors' top management, scope of services offered, clarification of user requirements, and prevention against unprofitable project.

In terms of Direct communication with customers' top management, one fourth of IT vendors have direct communication with customers' top management (Fig. 2.12).

2.4.2 Responses to Questionnaires on Business Environment

The salient characteristics of the enterprise software industry in Japan can be understood based on the responses to question items on Business Environment in the SEE surveys.

First of all, the medians of sales ratios of custom-made software in Fig. 2.13 are over 70 % in all types of vendors, which dovetailed with the recent fact in the

Fig. 2.13 Sales ratio of custom-made software (%)

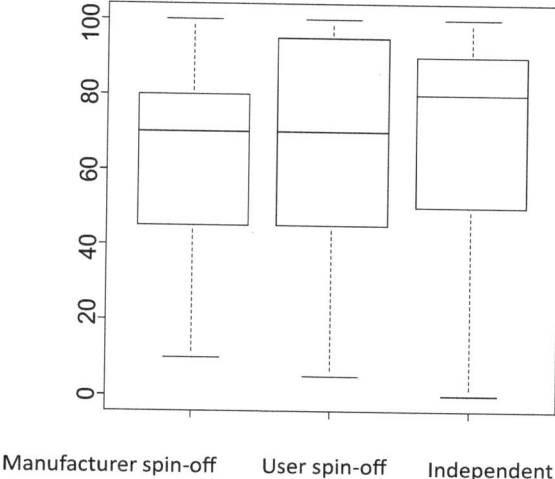

Manufacturer spin-off   User spin-off   Independent

METI report, as shown in Table 1.1 in Chap. 1, that the software development and programming market was 7,502,070 million yen, of which orders for software totaled 6,365,857 million yen in fiscal year 2013, (METI 2014). Since the dynamics of user-supplier interactions enables the development of finely tuned custom-made applications, and tends to establish long-lasting relationships between the user companies and IT vendors, the development of custom-made software can cause a high entry barrier for new comers from home and abroad.

Second, the ratios of prime contractors of manufacturer spin-off vendors and independent vendors are limited, compared with those of user spin-off vendors in Fig. 2.14.

Fig. 2.14 Ratio of prime contractor (%)

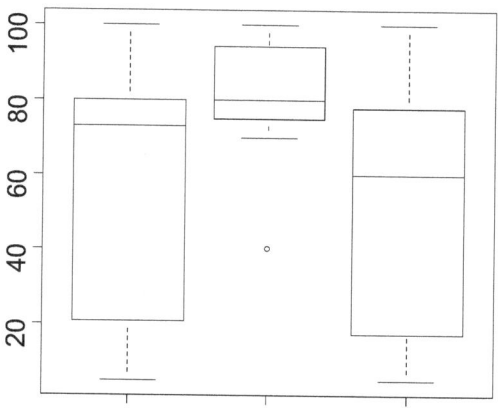

Manufacturer spin-off   User spin-off   Independent

Fig. 2.15 Ratio of outsourcing (%)

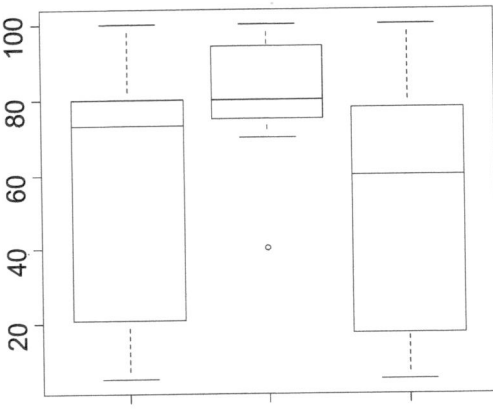

Manufacturer spin-off   User spin-off   Independent

Third, as shown in Fig. 2.15, the ratio of outsourcing cost account for around 40 % in each type of vendor. This implies that the Japanese software industry relies on the man-month-based multilayers subcontractors, as shown in Chap. 1.

In fact, most custom-made applications (Fig. 2.13) are developed jointly by the internal staff of the user company, and software engineers from IT vendors, as a team or individually. Thus, if necessary, software engineers may be dispatched from the man-month-based multilayer subcontractors. As a result, software engineers within the prime contractors (Fig. 2.14) tend to focus on dispatching engineers, and sometimes irresponsibly cede effective project management roles to the subcontractors.

This man-month-based multilayer-subcontractor structure in the Japanese software industry tends to inhibit the evolution of original Japanese innovations and innovators, such as new business models, e.g., packaged software, cloud computing, and entrepreneurs.

From the viewpoint of the demand-side, IT user companies in Japan seem to recuse themselves from adopting new technology at an early stage since sustaining shop-floor usability is given priority to introducing technological innovation when IT is deployed in user companies in Japan. In comparison, the U.S. software industry is highly packaged in that many large software development organizations, particularly in the area of ERP software, provide a specific set of software solutions, e.g., accounting, production management, sales management, logistics, etc. (SAP 2014). Also, a comparison of cloud network technology use rates among Japanese and U.S. enterprises in March 2013 shows that the rate in the United States reached 70.6 % against 42.4 % in Japan. There is a wide disparity between Japanese and U.S. enterprises in the use of cloud computing as a key ICT component (MIC 2013).

Consequently, the Japanese software industry experiences a vicious cycle in the factors such as sustaining shop-floor usability in IT user companies, university education in software disciplines, man-month-based multilayer subcontractors, senior management leadership of IT vendors, and introducing technological innovation.

2.4.3   Implications from SEE Relating Analyses

We have focused on the SEE and the Business Environment separately, but components of the Business Environment, such as the number of software engineers and the business model, and Business Performance, such as operating profit ratio, should also be brought into the account simultaneously so as to clarify the mechanism by which they leverage software engineering innovations. Then, we analyze the relationships among the SEE, the Business Environment, and Business Performance by the type of vendors: manufacturer spin-off, user spin-off, and independent vendors.

For example, Fig. 2.16 shows that any type vendors who have a larger number of software engineers tend to get a higher SEE score in the SEE2007 survey. This tendency is evident in the results of the three SEE surveys, 2005 through 2007, as shown in Fig. 2.17 for the SEE2006.

Equally, regardless of vendor type, vendors who have a larger number of software engineers tend to be less profitable (Fig. 2.18). This tendency also is evident in the results of the three SEE surveys, 2005 through 2007.

We need to investigate any trade-off between advantages of scale, notably, higher SEE scores, versus disadvantages, notably, lower profitability (Barney 2007). In other words, the causal relationships among the SEE factors, and Business Performance and Business Environment, including, e.g., the number of

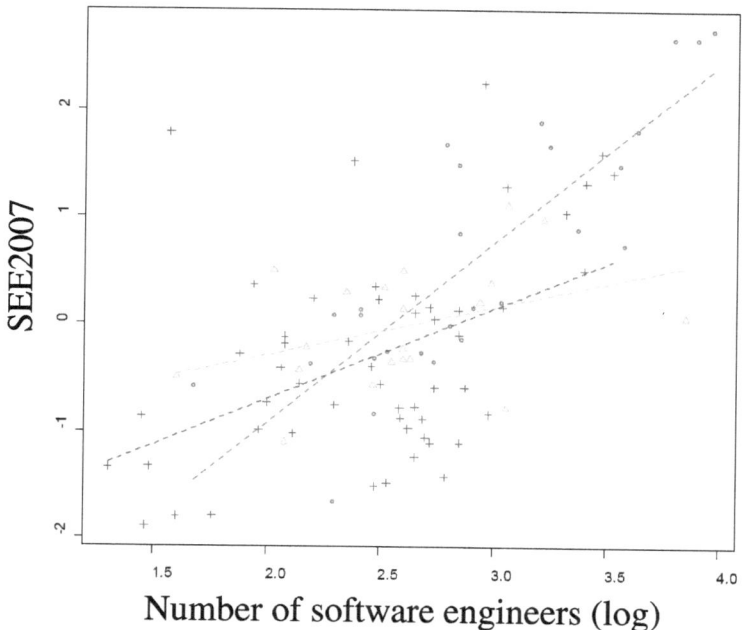

Fig. 2.16 Number of software engineers (log) and SEE2007 (*Circle* Manufacture spin-off, *triangle* user spin-off, + independent)

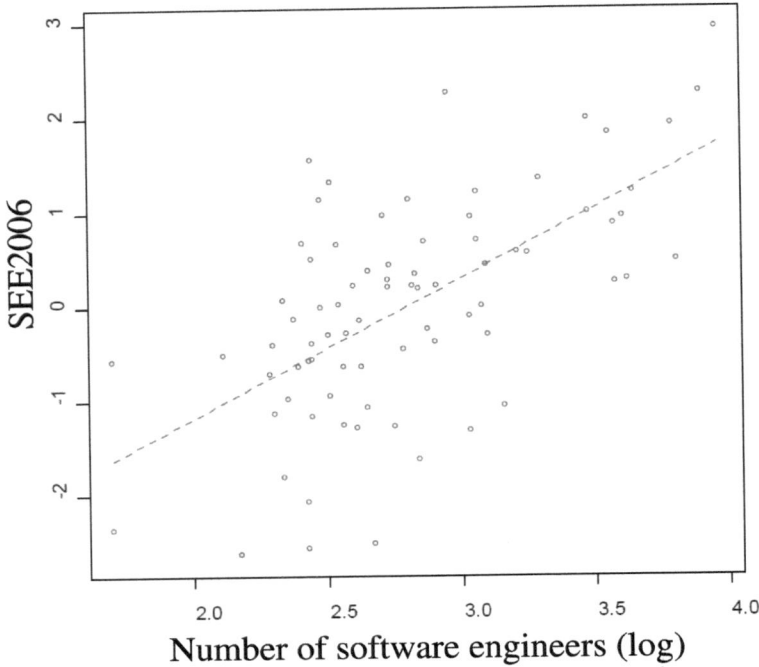

Fig. 2.17 Number of software engineers (log) and SEE2006

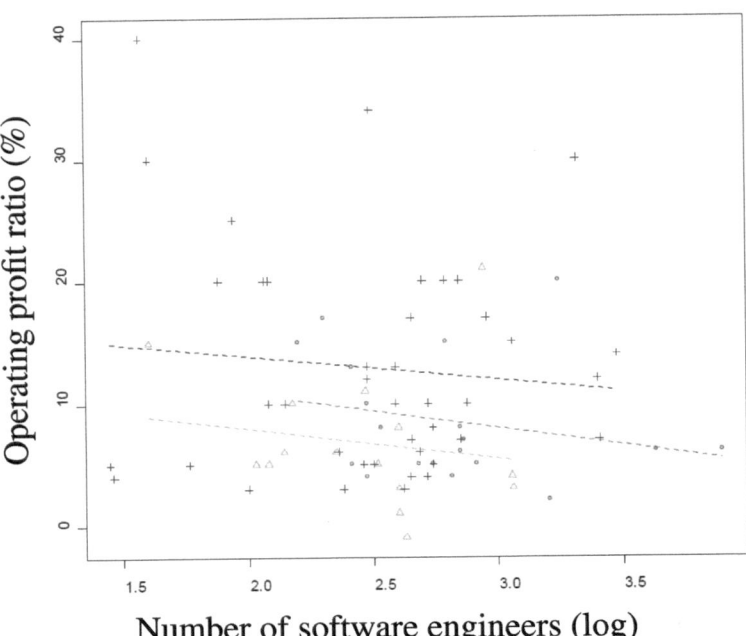

Fig. 2.18 Number of software engineers (log) and operating profit ratio (%) (*Circle* Manufacture spin-off, *triangle* user spin-off, + independent)

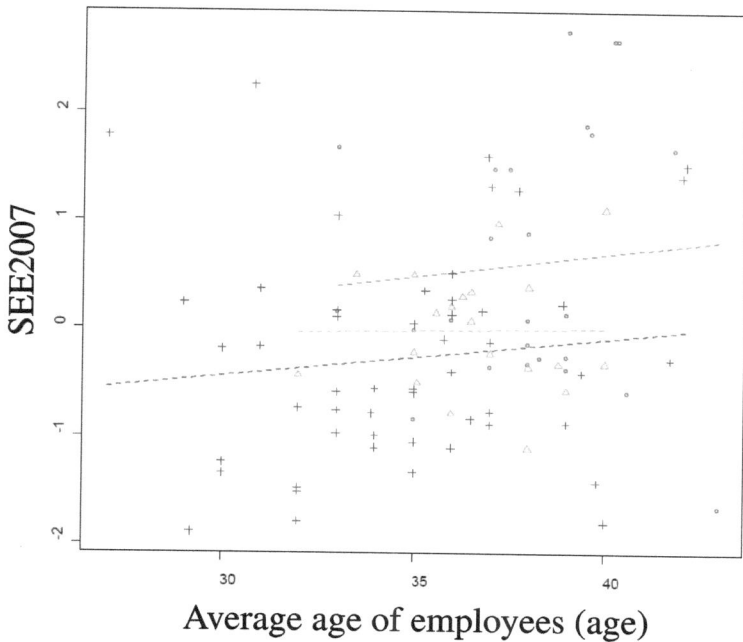

Average age of employees (age)

Fig. 2.19 Average age of employees (age) and SEE2007 (*Circle* Manufacture spin-off, *triangle* user spin-off, + independent)

software engineers, business model, and average age of employees, remain to be analyzed and understood in the future.

Figure 2.19 shows that vendors whose employees are older tend to score higher SEE, except the user spin-off vendors. The learning curve effect of senior engineers remains a matter of debate, particularly in the user spin-off vendors (Barney 2007). This tendency is evident in the results of the three SEE surveys, 2005 through 2007, as shown in Fig. 2.20 for the SEE2006, while vendors whose employees are older tend to be less profitable (Fig. 2.21).

Figure 2.22 shows the relationships between the ratio of custom-made software development, which does not utilize packaged software, and operating profit ratio. Only manufacturer spin-off vendors tend to be more profitable as they adopt a custom-made approach. In Japan, IT user companies prefer a custom-made approach to packaged software, as mentioned before. We need to further consider the pros and cons of utilization of packaged software in Japan, compared with the situations in the U.S., and other countries.

There is no significant relationship between the SEE and operating profit ratio, as shown in the SEE2006 survey (Fig. 2.23). However, in the SEE2007 survey, Fig. 2.24 shows that vendors who have a higher SEE tend to be slightly more profitable at independent vendors. By contrast, vendors who have a higher SEE tend to be less profitable at user spin-off vendors. In user spin-off vendors, indicators of

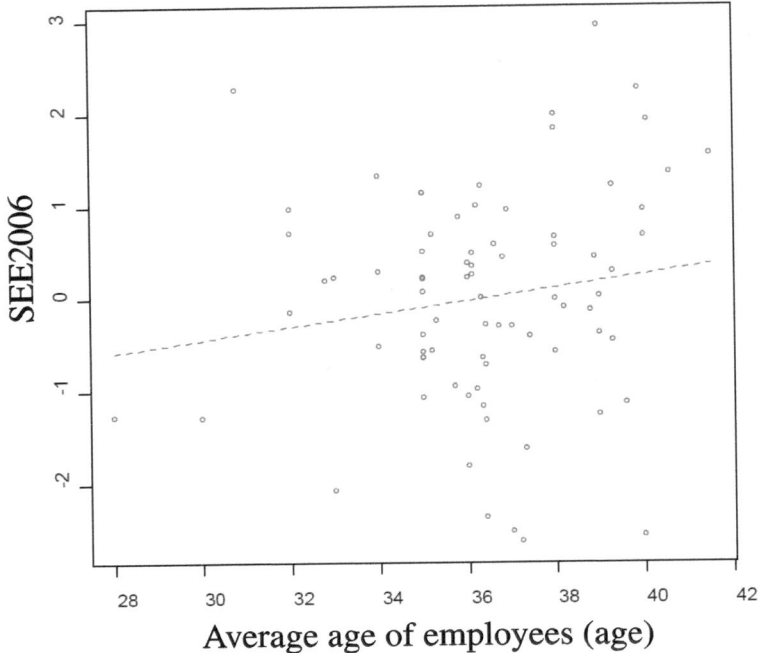

Fig. 2.20 Average age of employees (age) and SEE2006

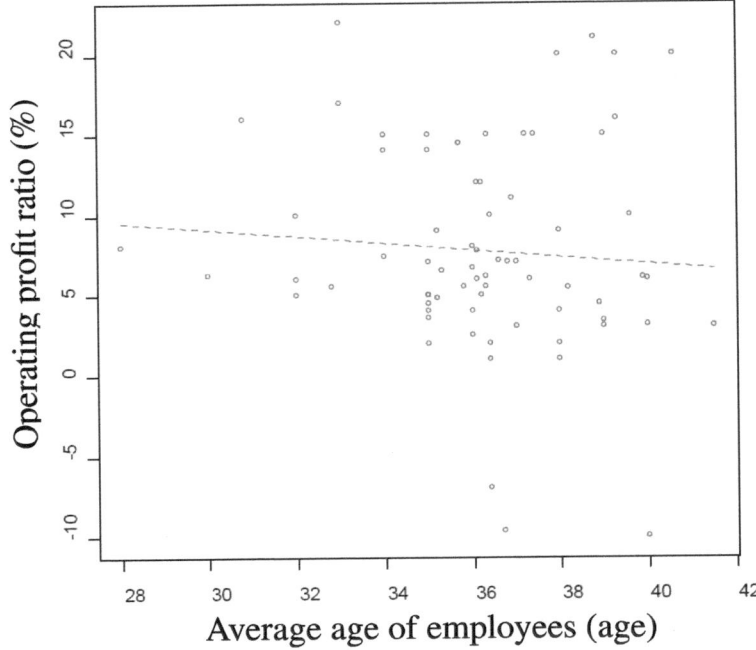

Fig. 2.21 Average age of employees (age) and operating profit ratio (%) (SEE2006)

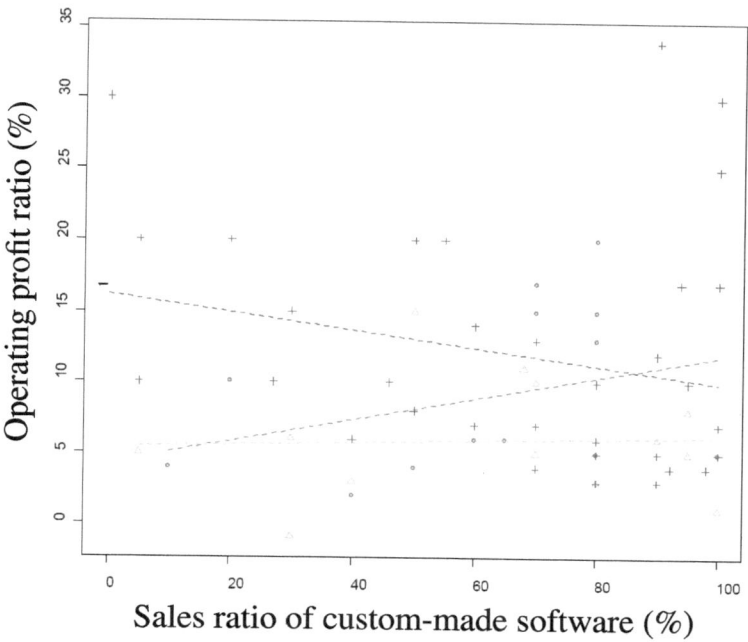

Fig. 2.22 Sales ratioo of custom-made soft ware (%) and operating profit ratio (%) (*Circle* manufacturer spin-off, *triangle* user spin-off, + independent)

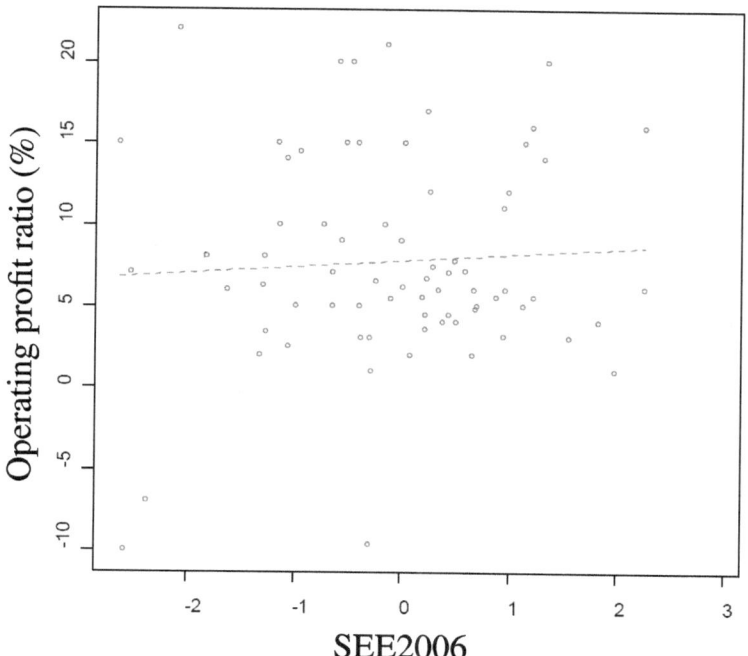

Fig. 2.23 SEE2006 and operating profit ratio (%)

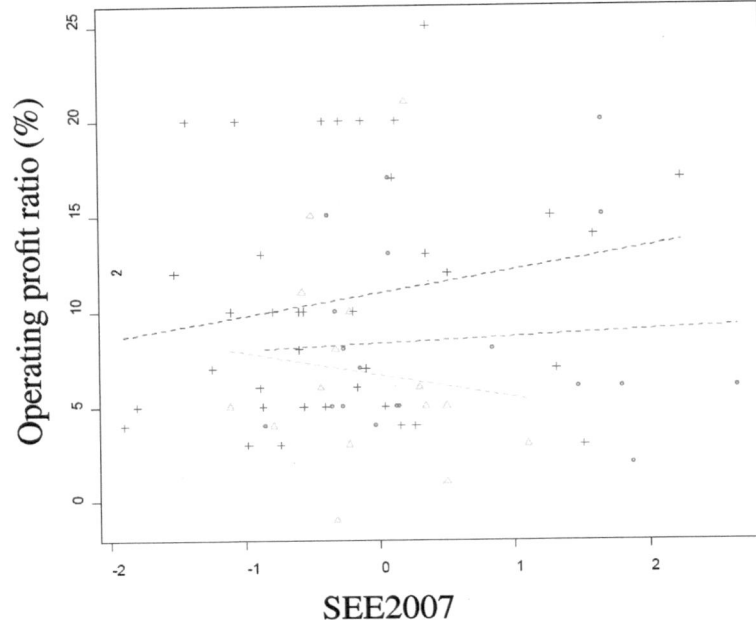

Fig. 2.24 SEE2007 and operating profit ratio (%) (*Circle* manufacturer spin-off, *triangle* user spin-off, + independent)

software engineering innovation might be attributable to a management policy of paying extra attention to business performance. Further analysis of causal relationships among the seven SEE factors would be conducted later in Chap. 3.

In summary, vendors who have a larger number of software engineers tend to get a higher SEE score. And, vendors whose employees are older tend to get a higher SEE score, while they tend to be less profitable. Finally, there is no significant relationship between the SEE score and operating profit ratio of the IT vendors in Japan. We will discuss the relationships among the SEE score, business performance, and business environment in more detail in the next Chapter.

References

Barney, J. B. (2007). *Gaining and sustaining competitive advantage*. New Jersey: Pearson Prentice Hall.

Carnegie Mellon University. (2014). Software engineering institute. http://www.sei.cmu.edu/cmmi/. Accessed 14 Aug 2014.

Dodgson, M., Gann, D., & Salter, A. (2008). *The management of technological innovation*. Oxford: Oxford University Press.

Fujimoto, T. (2003). Capability-building competition. Chuohkouronshinsya.

IEEE, Computer Society. (2013). SWEBOK V 3.0.

Japan Information Technology Service Industry Association (JISA). (2014). Research on IT human resources and training measures for globalization. http://itjobgate.jisa.or.jp/world/index.html. Accessed 14 Aug 2014.

ISO. (2010). ISO/IEC/IEEE 24765:2010 systems and software engineering–vocabulary.

Kadono, Y., Tsubaki. H., & Tsuruho, S. (2006). A study on the reality and economy of software development in Japan. In Proceedings of the sixth Asia Pacific Industrial Engineering Management Systems Conference, Bangkok, Thailand (pp. 1425–1433).

Kadono, Y., Tsubaki, H., & Tsuruho, S. (2012). Structural relationships among software engineering capabilities in Japan. *International Journal of Innovation and Learning, 12*(2), 217–227.

Ministry of Economy, Trade, and Industry (METI). (2014) Current survey on selected service industries: Information service industry.

Ministry of Economy, Trade and Industry, and Information-Technology Promotion Agency, Japan. (METI & IPA). (2007). Fact-finding investigation on software engineering capabilities of enterprise systems in Japan. (The responsibility for the investigation lies with Yasuo Kadono). sec.ipa.go.jp/reports/20071204/SE_level_research_2006_2.pdf.

Ministry of Internal Affairs and Communications (MIC). (2013). White paper—information and communications in Japan.

Prahalad, C. K., & Hamel, G. (1990). *The core competence of the corporation.* Harvard Business Review.

Pressman, R. S. (2010). *Software engineering: A practitioner's approach* (7th ed.). McGraw-Hill.

Project Management Institute. (2014). A guide to project management body of knowledge (PM-BOK). Project Management Institute. http://www.pmi.org/PMBOK-Guide-and-Standards/Standards-Library-of-PMI-Global-Standards.aspx. Accessed 14 Aug 2014.

SAP. Invester relations. (2014). http://www.sap.com/corporate-en/about/investors.html.

Stauss, B., Engelmann, K., Kremer, A., & Luhn, A. (2008). *Services science: Fundamentals, challenges and future developments.* Berlin: Springer-Verlag.

Tidd, J., & Bessant, J. (2013). *Managing innovation* (5th ed.). Wiley.

Chapter 3
Statistical Analysis Results and Practical Implications of the SEE Surveys

Abstract The objective of the research is to better understand the mechanisms of how software engineering capabilities relate to firms' business performance and business environment for the Japanese software industry. Based on the Software Engineering Excellence (SEE) survey results shown in Chap. 2, statistical analysis results are demonstrated using cross-section analysis, path analysis, stratified analysis, panel analysis, and longitudinal analysis. Focusing on management of software engineering innovation, we empirically verified the common order effects originating with human resource development and proceeding along the paths of service innovation, product innovation, and process innovation. Based on the panel analysis, we demonstrated several series correlations among the software engineering capabilities. The longitudinal analysis suggested positive relationships among software engineering capabilities and business performance in the long-term. However, the relationships between the software engineering capabilities and business performance vary significantly depending on the origin of a vendor: manufacturer or user spin-off or independent. Based on the analysis results, the several implications for managing innovation in software engineering in Japan, such as economies of scale and organizational inertia, are discussed in this chapter.

Keywords Industry policy · Empirical study · Management of technology · Innovation · Enterprise systems · Software engineering capability · Business performance · Business environment · Social research · Statistical analysis

In this chapter, the following research questions are discussed through statistical analysis methods based on the Software Engineering Excellence (SEE) survey results, the overall structural model (Fig. 2.1), and the measurement model introduced in Chap. 2.

The first research question relates to the base model of the relationships among software engineering factors and business performance.

Research Question 1 (RQ1) What are the common causal relationships among the seven SEE factors and business performance, discoverable from SEE2006 and SEE2007?

The second research question looks into the differences in the causal relationships depending on type of broken down by vendor—manufacturer spin-off, user spin-off and independent.

© Springer Japan 2015
Y. Kadono, *Management of Software Engineering Innovation in Japan*,
DOI 10.1007/978-4-431-55612-1_3

49

Research Question 2 (RQ2) What are the differences in the causal relationships among the seven SEE factors and business performance, discoverable from SEE2007, looking separately at each type of broken down by vendor, manufacturer spin-off, user spin-off and independent?

Third, we are interested in the series correlations among SEE factors using panel analysis.

Research Question 3 (RQ3) How does each SEE factor influence the other SEE factors within a given year; the same SEE factor in the future; and the other SEE factors in the future?

Fourth, we reconfirm the order effect of the seven software engineering capabilities based on the base model, using the 3 years data at the same time.

Research Question 4 (RQ4) What are the causal relationships among the seven SEE factors, discoverable from SEE2005, SEE2006, and SEE2007 looked at simultaneously?

Fifth, we look into the long-term relationships between SEE capabilities and business performance, based on the 10-year financial data of SEE respondents.

Research Question 5 (RQ5) Do IT firms with high software engineering capabilities tend to sustain and improve a high level of profitability in their business performance in the long-term?

In this section, we also investigate other relationships, including effects of business environment broken down by type of vendor.

Research Question 6 (RQ6) What causal effects does business environment exert on the seven SEE factors and on business performance, broken down by type of vendor?

3.1   Base Model and Cross-Section Analysis Results

The purpose of this section is to clarify, through cross-section analysis based on the 2006 and 2007 SEE survey results, the common mechanisms of how the management of software engineering innovation relates to the business performance of IT vendors. By analyzing data collected from 100 major IT vendors, we reproducibly observe that a higher effort level on Human Resource Development, Quality Assurance, and Project Management is associated with better performance in Customer Contact, Research and Development, Process Improvement, and Deliverables, consistent with the 2006 SEE survey results.

In this section, we think about the following research question to consider a base model of the relationships among the SEE factors.

Research Question 1 (RQ1) What are the common causal relationships among the seven SEE factors and Business Performance, discoverable from SEE2006 and SEE2007?

In order to answer this research question, we need to identify the causal relationships in SEE2006 and SEE2007, respectively. Specifically, we think about the following research questions.

Research Question 1-1 (RQ1-1) In SEE2006, what are the causal relationships among the seven SEE factors and business performance?

Research Question 1-2 (RQ1-2) In SEE2007, what are the common causal relationships among the seven SEE factors and business performance, as compared with SEE 2006?

3.1.1   Base Model and Hypothesis

To develop a base model for analyses in Chap. 3, we conducted interviews with over 50 experts in academic, business, and governmental circles in Japan and the U.S., and literature searches in the field of software engineering capabilities in a broad sense, as we reviewed in Chaps. 1 and 2. (ISO 2010; Pressman 2010; IEEE, Computer Society 2004; CMU 2014; PMI 2014; Barney 2007; Fujimoto 2003; Dodgson et al. 2008; Tidd and Bessant 2013).

Addressing RQ1-1, first, based on interviews with IT vendors and experts in Japan and the U.S., we identified three key factors for successful innovations: salesforce management, operational improvement, and R&D. Some vendors who manage their sales force effectively succeed in efficiently assigning their software engineers to upcoming customer projects. As a result, one such vendor operates at an average of 90 % capacity. Other profitable vendors have accumulated data on quality, cost, delivery, and productivity for more than 30 years in order to improve their operations (*kaizen*) (Ohno 1988). Most large-scale system integrators in Japan work earnestly on R&D activities, in addition to doing effective salesforce management and efficiently improving their operations. These three key factors are considered to be innovations in service, process, and product, respectively (Dodgson et al. 2008; Tidd and Bessant 2013).

Second, we conducted literature searches relating to innovation. The manufacturing capability model (Fujimoto 2003) for the automobile industry suggests that organizational routines finally influence business performance through both deep competitiveness, e.g., quality, productivity, product, and development lead-time; and superficial competitiveness, e.g., cost, delivery time, and product appeal power. Therefore, we considered the order effect on the three innovation paths in the structural model: IT vendor's routines and deep competitiveness, e.g., from Project Management to Customer Contact, and from Quality Assurance to Process Improvement; superficial competitiveness, i.e., Deliverables; and Business Performance, i.e., operating profit ratio.

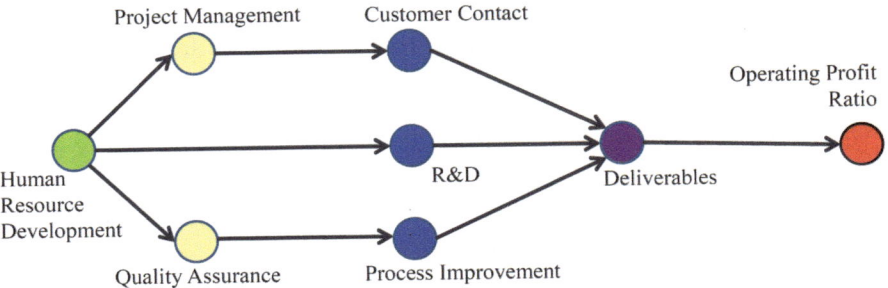

Fig. 3.1 Structural model hypothesis

As shown in Fig. 3.1, we assume the structural model hypothesis, proceeding from improved Human Resources Development through refinement of Deliverables toward improvement in Business Performance by leverage from the following three types of innovation in the management of software engineering:

- Service innovation: proceeding from Human Resource Development to Project Management and Customer Contact, as shown in the upper level;
- Product innovation: proceeding from Human Resource Development to Research and Development, as shown in the middle level; and
- Process innovation: proceeding from Human Resource Development to Quality Assurance and Process Improvement, as shown in the lower level.

3.1.2   Analysis Results and Implications

On the basis of the data collected from 78 firms in SEE2006, we succeeded, by a trial and error method, in constructing a well-fitted path model (CFI = 1.0), where all the existing path coefficients are significant at the 5 % level (Kadono et al. 2008a). As shown in Fig. 3.2, superior Deliverables and Business Performance correlate significantly with effort expended, particularly on Human Resource Development, Quality Assurance, Research and Development, and Process Improvement. In more detail, we found the following from SEE2006, through the use of a structural equation model (Bollen 1989).

Among the SEE factors, Human Resource Development is positioned as a point of origin. Human Resource Development has a positive impact on Quality Assurance, Project Management and Customer Contact. Quality Assurance and Customer Contact have direct negative impacts on the operating profit ratio. These paths suggest that the costs of Quality Assurance and Customer Contact do not pay off. However, indirectly, Quality Assurance and Customer Contact have positive impacts on the operating profit ratio via a positive influence on Process Improvement, Deliverables, and Research and Development. Research and Development has a direct positive impact on the operating profit ratio. Also, Process Improvement has

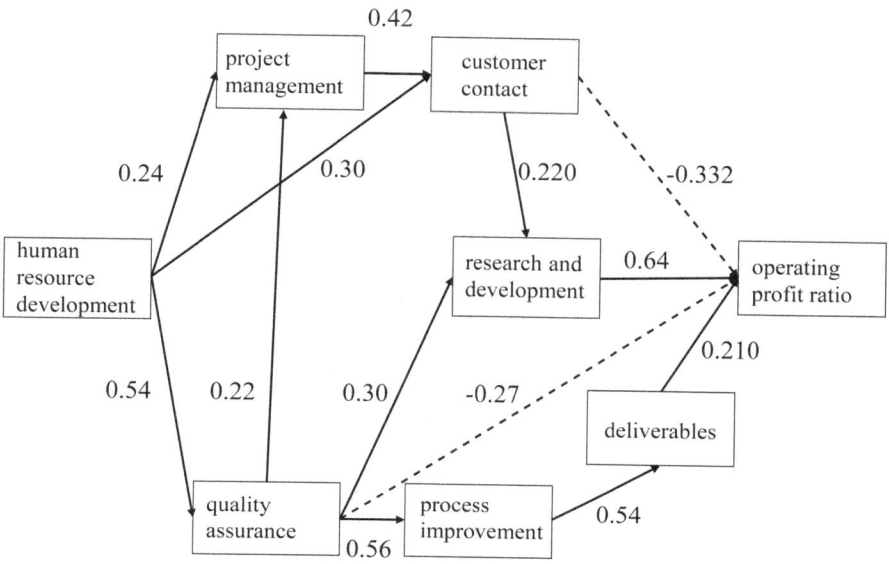

Fig. 3.2 Path analysis results from the 2006 SEE survey. 5 % significance

a positive impact on the operating profit ratio via Deliverables. These tendencies are similar to the results from the previous study, SEE2005 (Kadono et al. 2006).

Addressing RQ1-2, i.e., causal relationships discoverable from SEE2007: based on the structural model in Fig. 3.2 and the data collected from 100 major IT vendors in the 2007 SEE survey, we constructed a well-fitted path model by a trial and error method as shown in Fig. 3.3.

Addressing RQ1, i.e., causal relationships discoverable from SEE2007, compared with those from SEE2006 (Fig. 3.2), we reproducibly observed that a higher level of effort expended on Human Resource Development, Quality Assurance, and Project Management significantly improved the performance of IT vendors in Japan in Customer Contact, Research and Development, Process Improvement, and Deliverables, the same tendency that we had found in 2006. On the other hand, the paths are not significant that proceed towards operating profit ratio from Customer Contact, Research and Development, Quality Assurance, and Deliverables (Kadono 2013a).

Addressing the management of innovation (Dodgson et al. 2008) and the manufacturing model (Fujimoto 2003), the process innovation paths from Human Resource Development through Quality Assurance and Process Improvement, i.e., routines and deep competitiveness, do not reach operating profit ratio, i.e., Business Performance, but do significantly reach Deliverables, i.e., superficial competitiveness. However, the deep competitiveness paths of service and product innovations, relating to Project Management, Customer Contact, and Research and Development, reach neither superficial competitiveness nor Business Performance. Also,

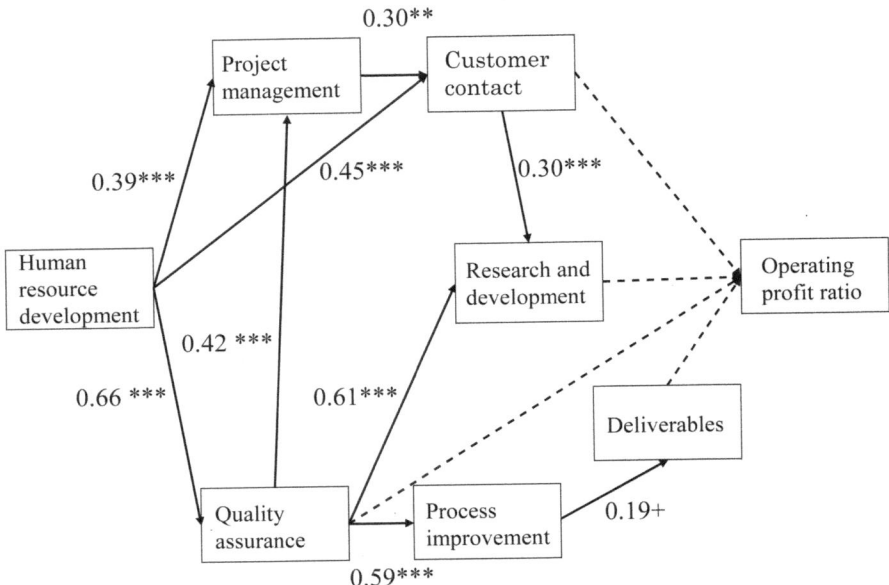

Fig. 3.3 Path analysis results from the 2007 SEE survey. ***$p<0.001$; **$p<0.01$; *$p<0.05$; +$p<0.10$

no relationship was observed between superficial competitiveness and Business Performance.

3.2   Differences by Vendor Type

The relationships among the SEE capabilities and business performance differ significantly by origin of vendor, i.e., manufacturer spin-off, user spin-off or independent. In manufacturer spin-off vendors, indicators of software engineering innovation, including service innovation, e.g., Project Management, and Customer Contact; process innovation, e.g., Quality Assurance, and Process Improvement; and product innovation, e.g., Research and Development; are all mutually interrelated, effectively originating with Human Resource Development. By contrast, in user spin-off vendors, indicators of innovation are extra attributable to a management policy of paying extra attention to business performance. Among independent vendors, Human Resource Development is the only factor that positively and significantly influences the other software engineering capabilities and business performance.

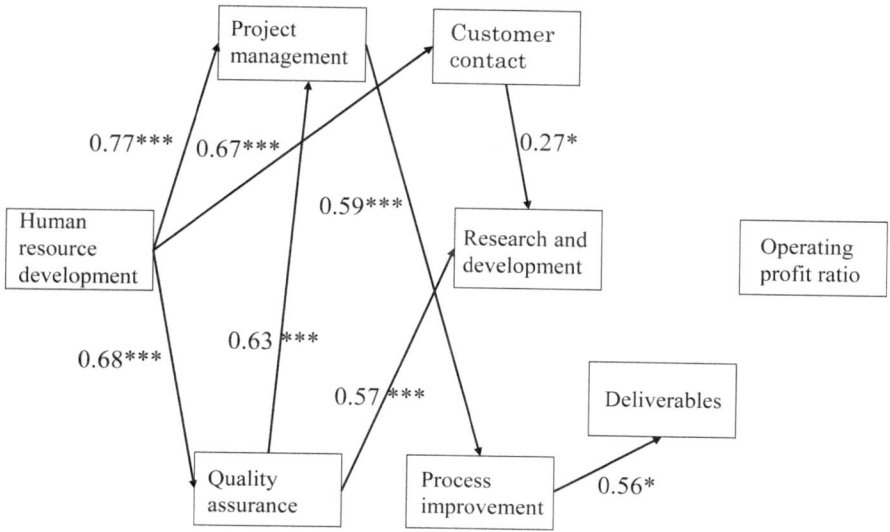

Fig. 3.4 Path analysis results for manufacturer spin-off vendors from SEE2007. ***$p<0.001$; **$p<0.01$; *$p<0.05$

Based on the analysis results for Research Question 1, we adopt Fig. 3.1 as the common causal model for our research, and proceed to Research Question 2, looking into the differences in the causal relationships by type of vendor—manufacturer spin-off, user spin-off and independent (Kadono 2013a).

Research Question 2 (RQ2) What are the differences in the causal relationships among the seven SEE factors and business performance, looking separately at each type of vendor, manufacturer spin-off, user spin-off, and independent?

3.2.1 Manufacturer Spin-off Vendors

First, proceeding from the base model in Fig. 3.1 and data relevant to manufacturer spin-off vendors discoverable from SEE2007 in Table 2.1, we constructed a well-fitted path model for the manufacturer spin-off vendors (CFI=1.0, p=0.84), where all the path coefficients are significantly positive at the 5% level. The causal relationships of the manufacturer spin-off vendors, shown in Fig. 3.4, are similar to the overall structure found in the 2007 SEE survey (Fig. 3.3) except for the following points. The path from Project Management to Process Improvement is significantly positive. Moreover, the path coefficient 0.56 from Process Improvement to Deliverables is much higher than that in the overall model (0.19). In addition, the paths from Human Resource Development to Research and Development through Quality Assurance and Customer Contact are significantly positive. However, the

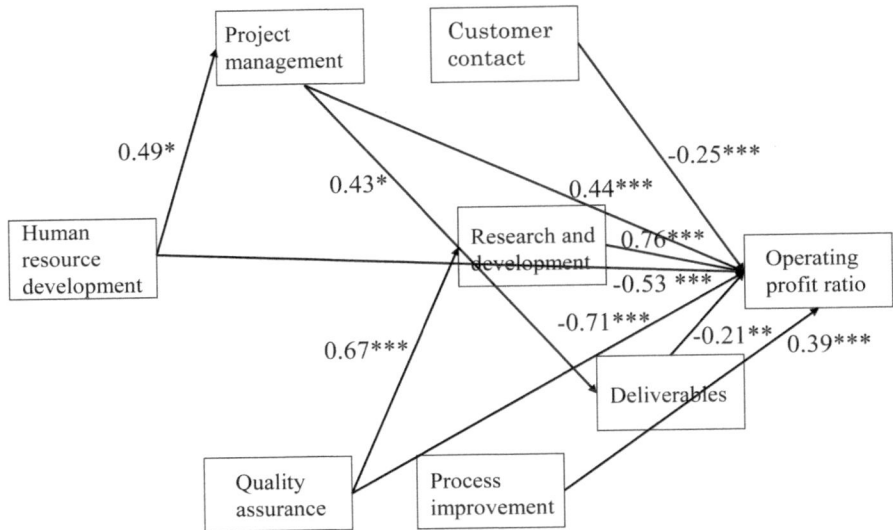

Fig. 3.5 Path analysis results for user spin-off vendors from SEE2007. ***$p<0.001$; **$p<0.01$; *$p<0.05$

path from Quality Assurance to Process Improvement and the path from Project Management to Customer Contact are not significant.

In the causal relationships for manufacturer spin-off vendors it is salient that the paths from Human Resource Development through Quality Assurance, Project Management and Process Improvement toward Deliverables are connected positively and highly significantly. Also, Human Resource Development has an overall positive impact on the other factors at the 15% significance (Kadono et al. 2009).

Focusing on the management of software engineering innovation, these results suggest that, in the manufacturer spin-off vendors, service innovation, process innovation and product innovation are mutually interrelated, effectively originating with Human Resource Development. However, these innovations do not lead to improvement in Business Performance, i.e., operating profit ratio, but reach superficial competitiveness, i.e., Deliverables, partially through Process Improvement.

3.2.2   User Spin-off Vendors

Second, proceeding from the base model in Fig. 3.1 and data relevant to the user spin-off vendors discoverable from SEE2007 in Table 2.1, we constructed a well-fitted path model for the user spin-off vendors (CFI=1.0, $p=0.89$), where all the path coefficients are significantly positive at the 5% level. As shown in Fig. 3.5, it is a salient feature of the user spin-off vendors that all of the seven SEE factors are connected to operating profit ratio either positively or negatively. The direct paths from Project Management, Research and Development, and Process Improvement to operating profit ratio are significantly positive. On the other hand, the direct paths from Human Resource Development, Quality Assurance, Customer Contact, and Deliverables to operating profit ratio are significantly negative.

In the case of the user spin-off vendors, a salient characteristic among the causal relationships is that all of the seven SEE factors exert an effect on the operating profit ratio, either positively, as with Project Management, Research and Development, and Process Improvement, or negatively, as with Human Resource Development, Quality Assurance, Customer Contact, and Deliverables. It is notable that only Project Management, as deep competitiveness, positively and significantly influences both superficial competitiveness, i.e., Deliverables; and business performance, i.e., operating profit ratio; as evaluated by standardized overall effects, including both direct and indirect effects.

Although the paths from Human Resource Development to operating profit ratio by way of Project Management are significantly positive, the direct path from Human Resource Development to operating profit ratio negates these positive effects overall. Similarly, although the paths from Quality Assurance to operating profit ratio by way of Research and Development are significantly positive, the direct path from Quality Assurance to operating profit ratio negates these positive effects overall. These results suggest that negative sources, such as Human Resource Development, Quality Assurance, Customer Contact, and Deliverables, do not pay off in the short-term, similar to the way in which the paths from Quality Assurance and Customer Contact to operating profit ratio are significantly negative in the 2006 SEE survey results. Even so, these efforts might possibly be expected to exert longer-term positive effects on other SEE factors.

Focusing on the management of software engineering innovation, each software engineering capability should be considered separately, without considering order effect of the innovations. In other words, if we focus on the operating profit ratio affected by each SEE factor, as shown in Fig. 3.5, it appears that the parent companies of user spin-off vendors might not care about the negative relationships, but do pay attention to their business performance attributable to management policy. This indicates that management focuses strongly on business performance and makes it a priority.

3.2.3 Independent Vendors

Third, proceeding from the base model in Fig. 3.1 and data relevant to the independent vendors discoverable from SEE2007 in Table 2.1, we constructed a well-fitted path model for the independent vendors (CFI = 1.0, $p = 0.79$), where all the path coefficients are significantly positive at the 5% level. It is remarkable in Fig. 3.6 that Human Resource Development significantly and positively influences all the

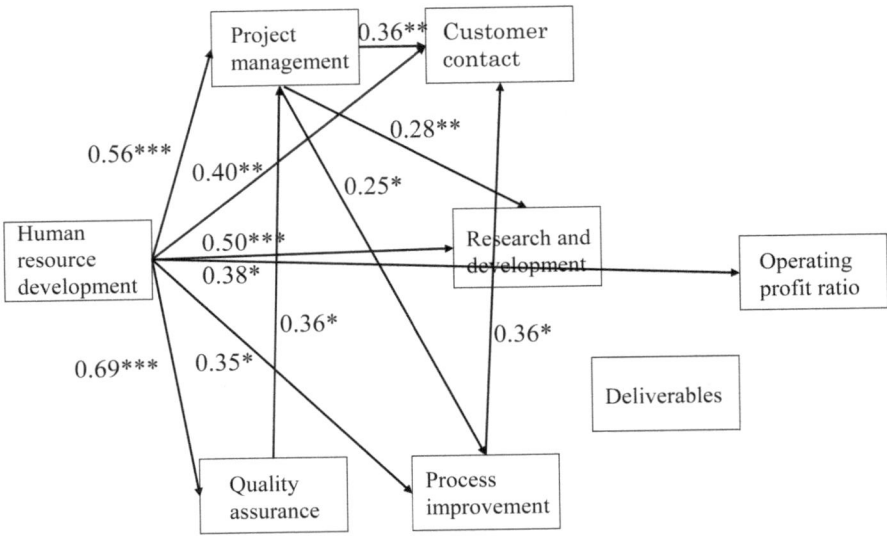

Fig. 3.6 Path analysis results for independent vendors from SEE2007. ***p<0.001; **p<0.01; *p<0.05

other factors of deep competitiveness, superficial competitiveness, and business performance, i.e., Project Management, Quality Assurance, Process Improvement, Customer Contact, Research and Development, operating profit ratio and Deliverables (at the 10% significance level), whereas the positive direct paths from Human Resource Development to Quality Assurance, Project Management, and Customer Contact are similar to those shown in the overall structure in Fig. 3.2. In addition, there are significant relationships from Quality Assurance to Project Management, from Project Management to Process Improvement, and from Process Improvement to Customer Contact.

In the case of the independent vendors, Human Resource Development significantly and positively influences all the other factors including deep competitiveness, superficial competitiveness, and business performance. Also, Human Resource Development is the only one of the seven SEE factors that has overall significantly positive impact on Deliverables, i.e. superficial competitiveness; and on operating profit ratio, i.e., business performance. These characteristics are unique to the independent vendors, distinguishing them from manufacturer spin-off vendors and user spin-off vendors.

Overall, Research and Development is positively and significantly influenced by Human Resource Development, Project Management, Quality Assurance, and Process Improvement; however, Research and Development does not exert significant influence on either Deliverables or operating profit ratio. It appears to be difficult for independent vendors to get a payoff in the short-term from Research and Development.

These results imply that Human Resource Development in particular is a key success factor for independent vendors. There are also significant relationships from Quality Assurance to Project Management, from Project Management to Process Improvement, and from Process Improvement to Customer Contact. These paths suggest that there are mutual connections between service innovation and process innovation, which has implications for the management of software engineering innovation.

3.2.4 Discussion

The purpose of the SEE surveys, carried out in collaboration with METI and IPA, was to clarify the mechanism of how the SEE factors are reflected in the Business Performance of IT vendors. In Sect. 1 and 2, we have investigated and compared the causal relationships among the seven SEE factors and Business Performance, paying attention to any differences between the 2006 and 2007 SEE survey results. Also, based on the 2007 survey, we have analyzed the differences in the causal relationships, broken down by origin of IT vendor, i.e., manufacturer spin-off, user spin-off, and independent.

We have analyzed the data collected from 100 major IT vendors in Japan in the 2007 SEE survey, and reproducibly observed that the more effort they put into Human Resource Development, Quality Assurance and Project Management, the better their performance in Customer Contact, Research and Development, Process Improvement, and Deliverables. This is consistent with a similar tendency that emerged from the 2006 SEE survey. In the context of Fujimoto's manufacturing model, we have found, through a cross-section analysis of the 2007 SEE survey results, that IT vendors' routines and deep competitiveness bring about improved superficial competitiveness, but they do not significantly improve Business Performance. However, we have also found that the relationships between the SEE factors and Business Performance factors vary significantly depending on vendor origin.

To better understand the relationships between the SEE factors and the business performance of Japanese IT vendors, panel analysis in the long-term should be an effective method. Beyond the cross-section analysis results presented in Sect. 1 and 2, first, we go on in the next section to perform a panel analysis on the software engineering capabilities of the uniquely identified firms that responded to the SEE surveys in 2005 through 2007. Then, in the following section, we conduct a panel analysis in which we include both the software engineering capabilities and the long-term financial data of the firms.

3.3   Panel Analysis Results of Software Engineering Capabilities

Based on the results of the panel analysis, our first observation is that most SEE factors in any 1 year have significant positive influences on the same factor the next year. Second, within a year, there are three paths to improving the level of Deliverables, i.e., through Project Management, through Quality Assurance and through Research and Development. Third, some SEE factors have significant positive influence diagonally on different SEE factors in the following year. Fourth, there are some negative paths, implying that efforts put toward a particular factor did not pay off within the duration of our research. Even so, these efforts might be expected to exert longer-term positive effects on other SEE factors. In comparison to the overall structure, stratified analysis of the relationships among the seven SEE factors for the 76 independent vendors suggests that year-to-year relationships for independent vendors tend to be strengthened due to enhancement of series correlation.

We first integrated 233 valid responses to the SEE surveys received over 3 years into a new database and identified 151 unique IT firms (Table 2.1). Then we conducted panel analyses on the seven SEE factors, using the 3 years of data, to clarify what influence SEE factors have within a year, year-to-year, and mid-term.

In this section, we think about the following research question.

Research Question 3 (RQ3) How does each SEE factor influence the other SEE factors within a given year; the same SEE factor in the future; and the other SEE factors in the future?

In other words, the research question here is how a SEE factor influences the other SEE factors horizontally, vertically or diagonally, as illustrated in Fig. 3.7.

3.3.1   Model and Hypothesis

As discussed in the previous section, based on interviews with successful IT vendors in Japan, we identified three key factors for successful vendors: salesforce management, operational improvement, and R&D. Some vendors who manage their salesforce effectively succeed in efficiently assigning their software engineers to upcoming customer projects. For example, a user spin-off vendor with successful salesforce management operates at an average of 90% capacity; and other profitable vendors have accumulated data on quality, cost, delivery, and productivity for more than 30 years, in order to improve their operations. Most large-

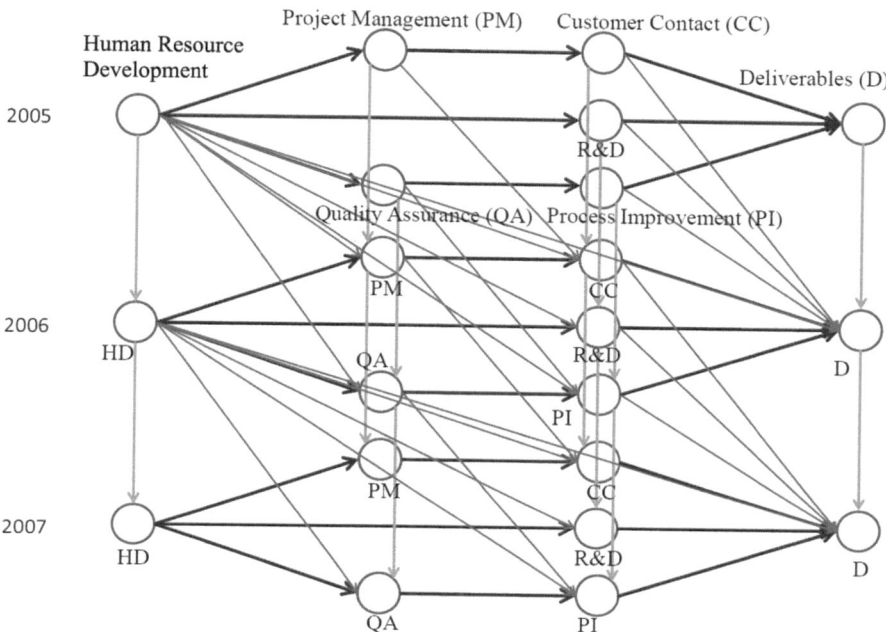

Fig. 3.7 Structural model hypothesis

scale system integrators in Japan emphasize the importance of R&D activities, in addition to doing effective salesforce management and efficiently improving their operations.

The hypothetical structure within each year (horizontally) is approximately consistent with the empirical results obtained from the SEE 2006 and the SEE 2007 surveys, as shown in the previous section. Therefore, within each year (horizontally), we assume three paths to improvement of Deliverables, e.g., quality, cost, and delivery, which relate to the management of technological innovation (Dodgson et al. 2008) as follows: in the upper level of Fig. 3.7, service innovation, proceeding from Human Resource Development through Project Management and Customer Contact; in the middle level, product innovation, proceeding from Human Resource Development through Research and Development; and, in the lower level, process innovation, proceeding from Human Resource Development through Quality Assurance and Process Improvement.

Also, vertically, year-to-year, we assume that each SEE factor at a firm has series correlation. For example, if a vendor has a high Human Resource Development factor score in 2005, it also has a high Human Resource Development factor score in 2006, and the tendency should continue in 2007. In addition, diagonally, we assume mid-term effects among SEE factors. For example, if a vendor invests in Human Resource Development in 2005, we look to see good R&D results in 2006.

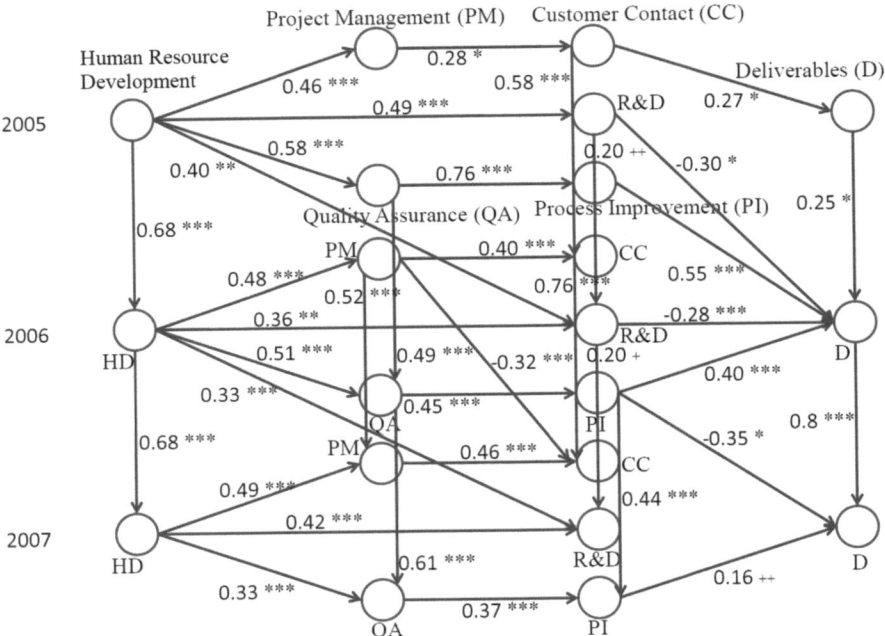

Fig. 3.8 Panel analysis results ($N=151$). ***$p<0.001$; ** $p<0.01$; * $p<0.05$; $+p<0.10$; $++p<0.15$

In this section, we also investigate the relationships among the seven factors from the viewpoint of service science (Stauss et al. 2008). Concepts of service science provide useful insights when considering users and vendors of IT. Out of the seven SEE factors, Project Management and Customer Contact are on the borderline between users and vendors of the software; and Deliverables are the common goal of both users and vendors. Vendors alone should be responsible for the other SEE factors, namely, Human Resource Development, Quality Assurance, Process Improvement, and R&D.

3.3.2   Analysis Results and Implications

Based on the structural model hypotheses, we conducted a panel analysis of the data from the 233 valid responses we had received from 151 unique firms in the 2005, 2006, and 2007 surveys. The results of the panel analysis are shown in Fig. 3.8 We found the following to be characteristics of the relationships among the seven SEE factors over the 3 years (Kadono et al. 2010).

Vertically, year by year, most SEE factors each have significant influence on the same factor in the following year. For example, Human Resource Development

(HD) in 2005 influenced HD in 2006, which, in turn, influenced HD in 2007. The same holds true for Quality Assurance (QA) and Deliverables (D). There are two exceptions. Project Management (PM) in 2005 did not seem to affect PM in 2006, nor did Process Improvement (PI) in 2005 seem to influence PI in 2006. Horizontally (within each year), most causal relationships are similar, and they are generally consistent with the results of the 2006 SEE survey. These results indicate that IT vendors build on the SEE factor levels that they have achieved thus far.

The structural consistency between different years implies that there are three paths to improving the level of Deliverables through service innovation (Project Management and Customer Contact), related to service science; through product innovation (R&D); and through process innovation (Quality Assurance and Process Improvement). These influences suggest medium-term positive effects.

Diagonally, some SEE factors have significant influence on different factors in the following year. Examples are Human Resource Development (HD) in 2005 and 2006, which influenced R&D in 2006 and 2007, respectively; and Process Improvement (PI) in 2005 which impacted Deliverables (D) in 2006. These influences suggest medium-term positive effects. However, there are some negative paths, such as R&D in 2005 and 2006, which negatively influenced Deliverables (D) in 2006; Process Improvement (PI) in 2006, which had a negative impact on Deliverables (D) in 2007; and Project Management (PM) in 2006, which negatively influenced Customer Contact (CC) in 2007 (Kadono 2011). The negative paths imply that effort expended on some factors does not pay off. Even so, these efforts might be expected to have positive long-term effects.

3.3.3   Additional Analysis Results for Independent Vendors

Since the characteristics of vendors vary significantly depending on the type and size of the vendor, we thought it important to conduct stratified analyses to inform the following discussion. Additionally, making full use of available data on independent vendors, we investigate the series correlations for independent vendors specifically.

Research Question 3-1 (RQ3-1)   Looking separately at independent vendors, what are the differences in the causal relationships among the seven SEE factors that were found in answering RQ3, and that are discoverable from SEE2007?

In order to investigate the differences by origin of vendor, we performed stratified analyses using the integrated 76 sets of data, based on the 112 valid responses from independent vendors who are pure-play firms focused on software engineering. On the basis of the hypothetical structural model that we introduced in Fig. 3.7, the panel analysis results are shown in Fig. 3.9 (Kadono 2011). In comparison with the overall structure shown in Fig. 3.8, we found additional characteristics of the relationships among the seven SEE factors for the independent vendors as follows.

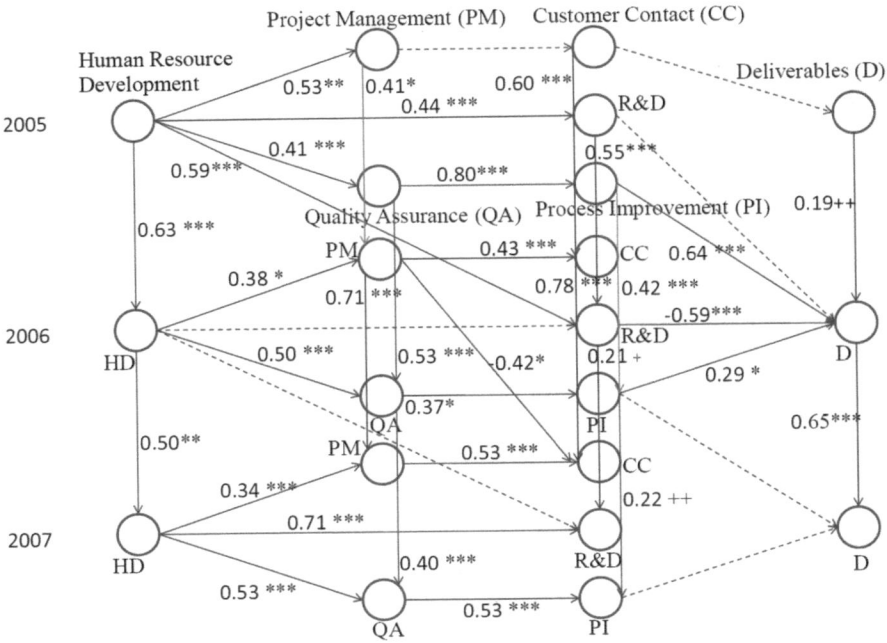

Fig. 3.9 Panel analysis results on independent vendors ($N=76$). ***$p<0.001$; **$p<0.01$; *$p<0.05$; + $p<0.10$; ++ $p<0.15$

Vertically, year by year, two paths become significant, i.e., Project Management (PM) in 2005 to PM in 2006, and Customer Contact (CC) in 2005 to CC in 2006. Horizontally (within each year), the dotted paths become insignificant, i.e., Project Management (PM) through Customer Contact (CC) to Deliverables (D) in 2005; Human Resource Development (HD) to R&D in 2006; and Process Improvement (PI) to Deliverables (D) in 2007. Also, diagonally, the dotted paths become insignificant, i.e., R&D in 2005 to Deliverables (D) in 2006; Human Resource Development (HD) in 2006 to R&D in 2007; and Process Improvement (PI) in 2006 to Deliverables (D) in 2007.

Although in general a smaller sample size tends to have less statistical significance, the above results of the stratified analyses on the relationships among the seven SEE factors for the 76 independent vendors do suggest that vertical year-to-year relationships for the independent pure-play software vendors tend to be strengthened in comparison to the overall structure shown in Fig. 3.8 ($N=151$), due to enhancement of series correlation, as we mentioned before.

In addition to these tracking features, the path coefficients for 2007 from Human Resource Development (HD) to R&D and Quality Assurance (QA), as shown in Fig. 3.9, are greater than those in Fig. 3.8 by 0.2 or more. These results are consistent with the cross-section analysis result, presented in the previous section, that in 2007 Human Resource Development (HD) was the most significant factor in the causal relationships for the independent vendors.

3.3.4   Discussion

In this section, we integrated 233 valid responses to three surveys on SEE into a new database and identified 151 unique IT vendors in Japan, of whom 42 were manufacturer spin-off vendors, 33 were user spin-off vendors and 76 were independent vendors. We investigated the relationships among the SEE factors over 3 years to clarify how they influence future SEE factors horizontally, vertically and diagonally. Within a year (horizontally), we assumed three paths toward improved Deliverables (quality, cost, and delivery): through service innovation, which includes Project Management and Customer Contact; through product innovation, including R&D; and through process innovations, including Quality Assurance and Process Improvement. Also, year-to-year (vertically), we assumed that each factor would be consistent due to series correlation. In addition, diagonally, we assumed mid-term effects, such as that vendors who invest in Human Resource Development in 2005 may be expected to see the results of that investment in their R&D in 2006.

Comparing with existing models, we empirically confirmed part of Fujimoto's manufacturing capability model for automobile companies (Fujimoto 2003). This model hypothesized that the organizational routines and deep competitiveness, e.g., quality, productivity, and product development lead-time, influence the superficial competitiveness, e.g., cost and delivery time, as well as business performance. In the context of the software industry, we have empirically proved in this section that superior Deliverables, e.g., QCD, an aspect of superficial competitiveness, has significant correlations with effort expended on routines and deep competitiveness, i.e., Human Resource Development, Project Management, Quality Assurance, Process Improvement, R&D, and Customer Contacts, as shown horizontally within a year in Fig. 3.8.

Statistically, we confirmed the series correlation. Once a factor loading of a certain SEE factor becomes high, it tracks itself in the next year and continues to be high. For example, we empirically proved high path coefficients among Human Resource Development (HD) factors in 2005 through 2007. Similar tracking phenomena were observed generally, except for the paths of Project Management (PM) between 2005 and 2006, and Process Improvement (PI) between 2005 and 2006.

From the viewpoint of service science, Project Management (PM) and Customer Contact (CC) are on the borderline between users and vendors of the software. In each year (horizontally), Project Management (PM) significantly influences Customer Contact (CC). And, vertically, year by year, Customer Contact (CC) in 2005 and 2006 exerts significant influence on the same factor in the following years. Also, Project Management (PM) in 2006 significantly influenced Project Management (PM) in 2007.

Regarding the Business Environment, we analyzed the relationships of threats, strengths/weaknesses and the number of software engineers, broken down by vendor type, i.e., manufacturer spin-off, user spin-off and independent vendors, as shown in Chap. 4 (Kadono et al. 2009). The results of analysis suggested that the manufacturer spin-off vendors significantly tend to expand business by, for example, new acquisition of patents, well-resourced R&D, offshore system development, and offshore client development. In contrast, the user spin-off vendors seem to depend heavily on demand from their parent companies; thereby, some of them are thought to gain inimitable capabilities, including knowhow on a specific function and inimitable products/services. In contrast again, many of the independent vendors, lacking specific strengths, merely supply temporary staff to principal contractors. However, some independent vendors that do have inimitable assets and are not threatened by industry stagnation seem to be role models for software vendors in Japan.

3.4 Results of Aggregation Analysis of Software Engineering Capabilities

Based on the results of path analyses on the data gathered in three surveys from 151 IT firms, we show that Human Resource Development and R&D are fundamental capabilities that significantly support improvement in the quality of deliverables. Also, improving capabilities in project management and process improvement significantly support an improvement in deliverables in the short term. By contrast, efforts to improve quality assurance and customer contacts might yield improvement only over the long term. Based on a data-centric approach, the results tend to confirm order effects among the software engineering capabilities.

In this section, we address Research Question 4:

Research Question 4 (RQ4) What are the causal relationships among the seven SEE factors, discoverable from SEE2005, SEE2006, and SEE2007 looked at simultaneously?

3.4.1 Research Model

In this section, we introduce the structural model and the measurement model of the research. First, following the base structural model already presented in Fig. 3.1, we assume the three innovation paths towards improvement in deliverables (quality, cost, delivery, etc.):

- From human resource development to project management and customer contact (service innovation),
- From human resource development to R&D (product innovation), and
- From human resource development to quality assurance and process improvement (process innovation).

The original structural model for the SEE surveys was developed by interviews with successful IT vendors and by literature searches. The structural model is con-

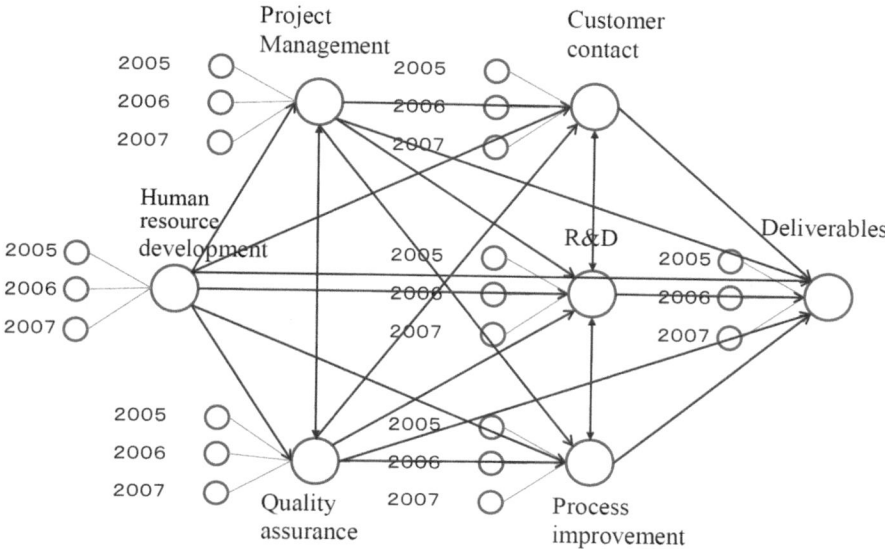

Fig. 3.10 Structural model

sistent with the empirical results obtained from the SEE 2006 and 2007 surveys, as shown in the previous sections.

Next, as introduced in the previous chapter, our measurement model for SEE was also originally developed through interviews with over 50 industry experts in Japan and the U.S. as well as through literature searches as shown in Chap. 1. It is an objective of this research to encourage innovation, so, to develop our measurement model, we surveyed state-of-the-art cases from the viewpoints of marketing, process, and product. Therefore, the scope of the survey includes a resource-based view of vendors (Barney 2007).

The SEE measurement model has a hierarchical structure with three layers: observed responses to question items, seven detailed factors, and SEE as a primary indicator. The measurement models for 2006 and 2007 were updated slightly based on the response rate for each question item, the statistical significance of each observed response to the 2005 and 2006 SEE surveys, and changes in technology and market trends.

SEE, as we have defined it in Sect. 2.2 in Chap. 2, consists of the following seven factors: Deliverables, Project Management, Quality Assurance, Process Improvement, Research and Development (R&D), Human Resource Development, and Customer Contact. In this section we aggregate each factor by conducting factor analysis of the factors for the 3 years, as shown in Fig. 3.10.

3.4.2   Analysis Results

As shown in Table 2.1 in Chap. 2, we integrated into a single database the data obtained from the 233 valid responses we received to the 2005, 2006, and 2007 sur-

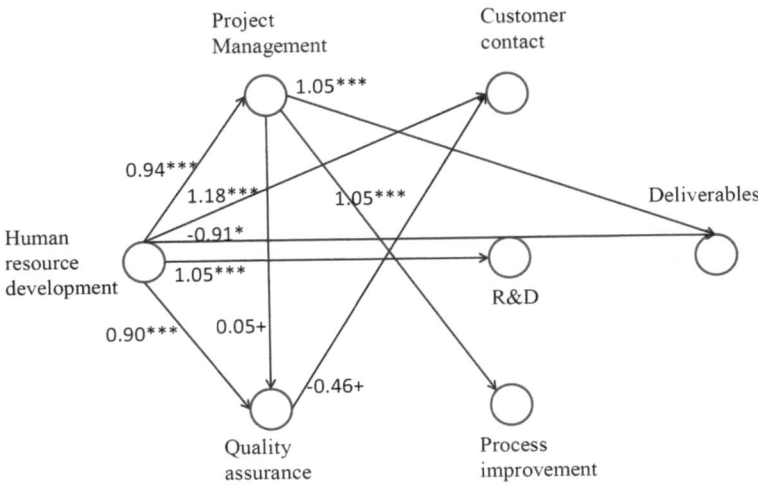

Fig. 3.11 Path analysis results. ***$p<0.001$; *$p<0.05$; +$p<0.10$

veys from 151 unique firms; we identified the 151 unique companies as consisting of 42 manufacturer spin-off vendors, 33 user spin-off vendors, and 76 independent vendors.

We then aggregated the scores of the seven SEE factors for the 3 years, and investigated the relationships among the seven SEE factors using path analysis based on the structural model hypotheses shown in Fig. 3.10.

The results of the path analysis are shown in Fig. 3.11. We found the following to be characteristics of the significant relationships among the seven SEE factors over the 3 years (Kadono et al. 2012):

- Human resource development has direct positive significant influence on project management, quality assurance, customer contact and R&D.
- Project management has direct positive significant influence on process improvement, deliverables and quality assurance.
- However, there are some negative paths, i.e., from quality assurance to customer contact, and from human resource development to deliverables.

3.4.3   Implications

Because the standardized effect from project management to process improvement is greater than 1 and process improvement is a terminal node in Fig. 3.11, project management and process improvement should be regarded as a single concept. The same aggregation as the above can be suggested for the relationship between human resource development and R&D. It follows that the above results could be simply interpreted as follows (Fig. 3.12):

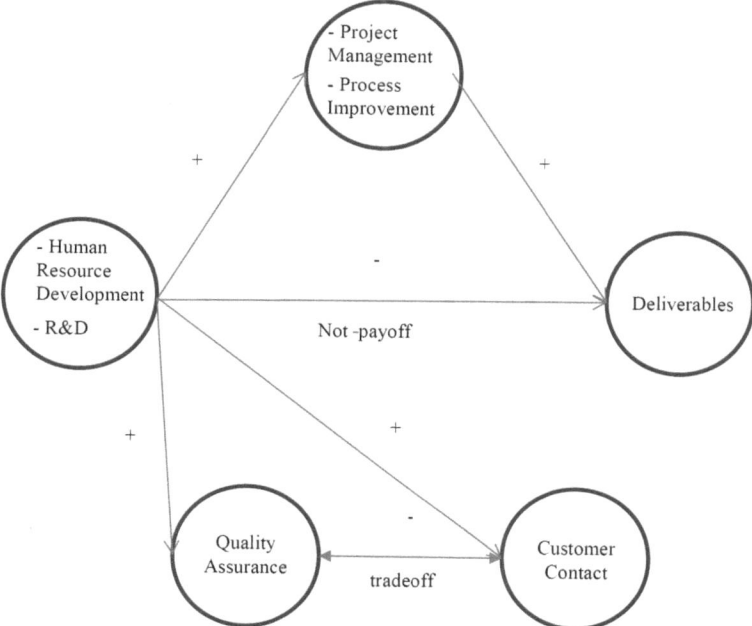

Fig. 3.12 Path analysis implications

- Human resource development and R&D are significantly influential factors on overall software engineering capabilities.
- Negative paths imply that effort invested in some factors did not pay off, at least during the duration of this research. It might, however, be expected to have long-term effects, e.g., from human resource development/R&D to deliverables. Otherwise, the negative paths might suggest a tradeoff between factors, e.g., quality assurance and customer contact.
- Downstream factors, such as deliverables, should be interpreted in relation to other factors such as business environment and business performance.

Based on the above findings, software engineering factors should be managed in the future in the following way. First, human resource development and R&D should be recognized as fundamental factors in efforts to improve the quality of deliverables. Second, among the seven software engineering capabilities, improving project management and process improvement can be expected to exert an immediate effect on deliverables. Third, by contrast, it might be necessary to invest efforts in quality assurance and customer contacts in the long term before achieving success.

In this way, the order effects among the seven software engineering capabilities contained in the base model have been further validated in this section, based on a bird's-eye and data-centric approach, using the 3-year SEE survey data.

Fig. 3.13 Research question

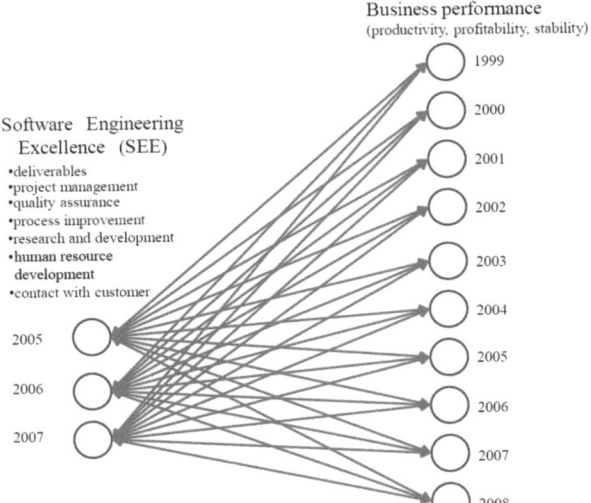

3.5   Long-term Relationships among Software Engineering Capabilities and Business Performance

In the panel analysis in the previous section we focused on software engineering capabilities in 2005, 2006, and 2007; however, the full range of relationships among capabilities, business environment, and business performance quantitatively, which are discussed qualitatively in Fujimoto's manufacturing capability model, are also fundamental issues in this book (Fig. 2.1).

As a next step, to expand the results of the research, it is important to better understand the long-term relationships between SEE factors and business performance of Japanese IT vendors. Simultaneously, we need to further investigate the series correlation we discussed in the previous section. Therefore, in the present section, we perform a panel analysis on the relationships between software engineering capabilities and business performance, i.e., long-term financial data of the 151 identified firms, based on longitudinal modeling.

In this section, we think about research questions looking into the relationships among the software engineering capabilities and business performance. More specifically, based on the previous analysis results and the literature search, the research questions in this section are to investigate the relationships among the seven SEE factors and business performance, e.g., productivity, profitability, and stability, in the long-term, as shown in Fig. 3.13. In other words, we aim to empirically verify the series correlation of the relationships between the seven SEE factors and the financial performance through a longitudinal analysis by making best use of the data obtained from the 151 unique IT firms who responded to the SEE surveys, i.e., the standardized seven SEE scores for 3 years and business performance for 10 years.

3.5.1   Long-Term Relationships between SEE and Profitability

In this subsection, we aim for a better understanding of the relationships among software engineering capabilities and profitability, as a component of, and representing, business performance, of software vendors in the long-term. To do so, by characterizing both intra-class and serial correlation among the repeated measurements of each firm, we apply a latent growth curve model including latent factors corresponding to the level and the improvement of long-term business performance in 1999 through 2008. Based on longitudinal modeling of the 3-year SEE data and 10-year operating profit ratio of the 151 respondents to the SEE surveys, we empirically verify that IT firms who have excellent software engineering capabilities tend to sustain and improve their business performance in the medium and long term.

The first research question in this section focuses on profitability as an indicator of business performance as follows:

Research Question 5 (RQ5) Do IT firms with high software engineering capabilities tend to sustain and improve a high level of profitability in their business performance in the long-term?

3.5.1.1   Model and Hypothesis

Recalling the empirical results obtained from the 2006 SEE survey, and in particular the finding that superior Deliverables and business performance correlated with the effort expended particularly on Human Resource Development, Quality Assurance, Research and Development, and Process Improvement at 5 % significance, and recalling also our interviews with successful IT vendors in Japan, we hypothesize that the firms that have excellent software engineering capabilities do tend to sustain and improve their business performance in the medium and long term.

Therefore, we assume a path model as shown in Fig. 3.14. Here, SEE consists of SEE2005, SEE2006 and SEE2007. Taking the operating profit ratio as a component of, and representing, business performance, we identified 151 unique IT firms that responded to the three SEE surveys, and calculated their operating profit ratios from 1999 through 2008, relying on accounting data supplied by a Japanese credit research firm. To better and more effectively characterize both intra-class and serial correlation among the repeated measurements of each firm, we adopted a latent growth curve model (Meredith and Tisak, 1990), including two latent factors corresponding to the level (intercept) and the growth (slope) of the operating profit ratio for 10 years.

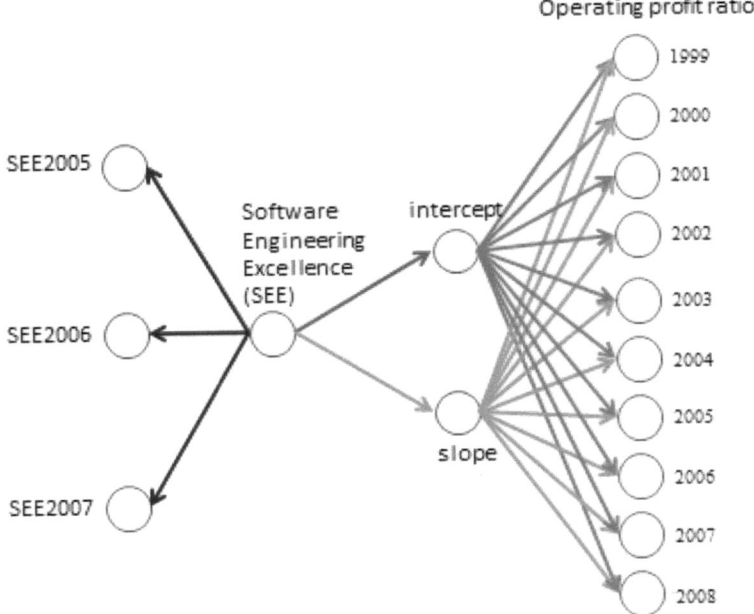

Fig. 3.14 Structural model hypothesis

3.5.1.2 Analysis Results

Based on the hypothetical structural model shown in Fig. 3.14, we conducted path analysis of the data from the 233 valid responses we had received to the 2005, 2006, and 2007 SEE surveys from 151 unique firms (Bollen 1989). The result of the path analysis is shown in Fig. 3.15 (Kadono et al. 2011). We found the following to be characteristics of the significant relationships among 3-year SEE scores and 10-year operating profit ratios (CFI=0.415). Regarding SEE, overall SEE is related to SEE2005, SEE2006 and SEE2007 at 0.1% significance. Overall SEE has a positive impact on the intercept of operating profit ratio for 10 years at 10% significance. Also, overall SEE has a positive impact on the slope of operating profit ratio for 10 years at 5% significance.

3.5.1.3 Implications and Discussion

In this section we significantly verified that firms that have excellent software engineering capabilities tend to sustain and improve their business performance, i.e., operating profit ratio, in the medium and long term. We arrived at this conclusion by longitudinal modeling, drawing on the data obtained from the three annual SEE surveys and 10 years of financial data obtained from IT vendors who responded to the SEE surveys. We focused on the relationship between an overall SEE score,

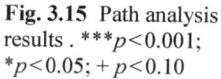

Fig. 3.15 Path analysis results . ***$p<0.001$; *$p<0.05$; +$p<0.10$

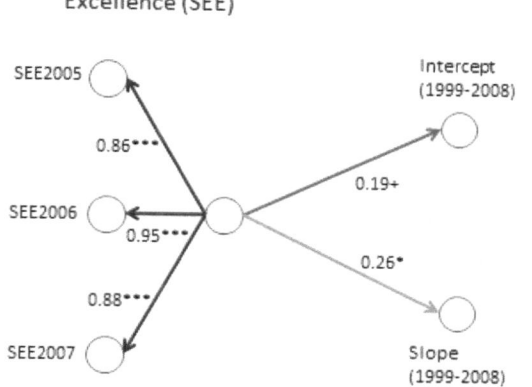

derived from the three surveys, and the 10-year operating profit ratio, as a component of, and representing, business performance. In other words, the contribution of the research was to empirically verify the relationship between the software engineering innovation level just before the cloud computing era began, and long-term financial data for the period just before Lehman's fall. However, it is a limitation of this research that SEE scores are available extending over only 3 years.

For a further study, we expand the initial longitudinal model that we considered in Fig. 3.14 so that we can analyze the relationships among the seven SEE factors, i.e., Deliverables, Project Management, Quality Assurance, Process Improvement, Research and Development, Human Resource Development, and Customer Contact, as against financial indicators such as productivity, and stability of management, in addition to profitability.

3.5.2 Long-Term Relationships among SEE factors and Business Performance

This study aims at better understanding the long-term relationships among the software engineering capabilities and business performance of representative IT firms in Japan. We conducted longitudinal analyses on standardized software engineering capability scores obtained from three surveys and the 10-year business performance of 151 firms. Through panel analyses using the best Akaike Information Criteria model, we found that IT firms sustaining high levels of deliverables, derived from high levels of Human Resource Development, Quality Assurance, Project Management and Process Improvement, tend to sustain high profitability, while IT firms with high levels of Project Management and Customer Contact tend to be highly productive and increasingly improve their productivity in the long-term. Concerning business performance, profitable IT firms tend to be stable and this tendency accelerates progressively due to the enhancement of Deliverables and R&D. However, productive IT firms are not necessarily profitable, likely because of the multi-layered industry structure in Japan.

In this subsection, we introduce the structural model and the measurement model for the following research question on the relationships among software engineering capabilities and business performance in the long-term.

Research Question 5-1 (RQ5-1) Do IT firms with high software engineering capabilities tend to sustain and improve a high level of productivity, profitability, and stability in their business performance in the long-term?

To effectively characterize both intra-class and serial correlation among the repeated measurements of each firm, we adopt a latent growth curve model (Meredith and Tisak 1990), including two latent factors corresponding to the level (intercept) and the growth (slope) of the seven standardized SEE factors over 3 years, and three indicators of financial performance over 10 years: productivity, profitability, and stability.

3.5.2.1   Research Model and Hypothesis

We assume a structural model of SEE and Business Performance as shown in Fig. 3.16. The SEE factors are measured by intercepts and slopes of the seven concepts, i.e., Human Resource Development, Project Management, Customer Contacts, R&D, Quality Management, Process Improvement, and Deliverables, from 2005 to 2007; and Business Performance is measured by intercepts and slopes of productivity, profitability, and stability, from 1999 through 2008.

Based on interviews with successful IT vendors in Japan, we hypothesize that firms that have excellent software engineering capabilities tend to improve their business performance in the medium- and long-term. More specifically, we assume the following three hypotheses, H1, H2, and H3, as shown in Fig. 3.16.

H1 Software firms with high level (intercept) and high growth (slope) of SEE, which are core competences for them, tend to improve the level (intercept) and growth (slope) of their business performance in the long-term.

H2 Regarding SEE, based on interviews with successful IT vendors in Japan, we identified three key factors for successful vendors efficient salesforce management, effective operational improvement, and excellent R&D.

First, vendors who manage their salesforce effectively succeed in efficiently assigning their software engineers to upcoming customer projects. As a result, one such vendor operates at an average of 90 % capacity. Second, some profitable vendors have accumulated data on quality, cost, delivery, and productivity for more

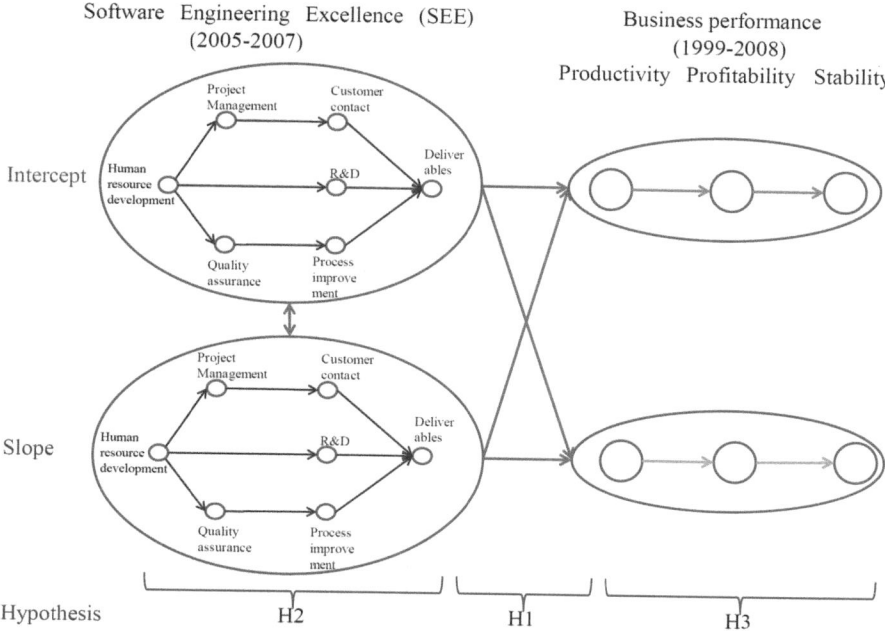

Fig. 3.16 Research model

than 30 years in order to improve their operations (*kaizen*). Third, most large-scale system integrators in Japan work very hard on R&D activities in addition to effectively managing their salesforce and efficiently improving their operations. The hypothetical structure is consistent with the base model in Fig. 3.1, and the panel analysis results based on the SEE 2006 and 2007 surveys.

Therefore, concerning the relationships among the seven SEE factors shown in Fig. 3.16, we assume three paths to improvement of Deliverables. In other words, there are three paths toward Deliverables: the upper path from Human Resource Development to Project Management and Customer Contact suggests service innovation; the middle path from Human Resource Development to R&D suggests product innovation; and the lower path from Human Resource Development to Quality Assurance and Process Improvement suggests process innovation.

H3 Within Business Performance, higher productivity leads to higher profitability and higher profitability leads to better stability in the long-term. In fact, the successful IT firms we interviewed tend to increase their capital gradually, based on their established high-profit structure and rising productivity.

3.5.2.2 Analysis Results

First, on the basis of the preliminary analyses of the intercepts and slopes of the seven SEE factors, the latent factors corresponding to the slopes of Human Resource

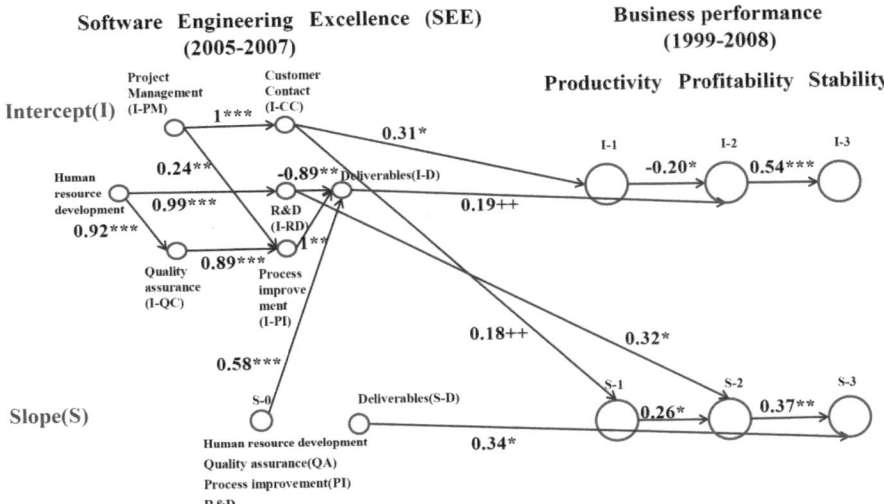

Fig. 3.17 Longitudinal analysis results. $***p<0.001$; $**p<0.01$; $*p<0.05$; $+p<0.10$; $++p<0.15$

Development (HD), Quality Assurance (QA), Process Improvement (PI), and R&D are considered to be single factor, and the slope factors of Project Management (PM) and Customer Contact (CC) can be ignored, since the variance components are not statistically significantly positive.

Then, based on the structural model hypothesis shown in Fig. 3.16 that is consistent with a series of empirical results, we adopted a latent growth curve model (Meredith and Tisak 1990) of the data from the 233 valid responses we had received to the 2005, 2006, and 2007 SEE surveys from 151 unique firms, and we selected the best panel model in terms of Akaike Information Criteria (AIC) (Akaike 1974), as shown in Fig. 3.17 (AIC=5945.81).

Based on the hypothetical model (H1, H2, H3) shown in Fig. 3.16 and the path analysis results shown in Fig. 3.17, we found the following to be characteristics of the relationships among the intercepts and the slopes of the seven SEE factors over the 3 years from 2005 to 2007 and the 10-year business performance from 1999 through 2008 (Kadono and Tsubaki 2012):

- Regarding the positive relationships among the intercepts of the SEE factors and the Business Performance (H1), the intercept path (H2) from Project Management (I-PM) to Customer Contact (I-CC) has significant influence on the intercept of productivity (I-1). Also, the intercept paths (H2) from Human Resource Development (I-HD) to Quality Assurance (I-QA), and from Project Management (I-PM) through Process Improvement (I-PI) toward Deliverables (I-D) significantly influence the intercept of profitability (I-2).

- Adding the positive interactions among the intercepts and the slopes to the above (H1), the intercept path (H2) from Project Management (I-PM) through Customer Contact (I-CC) has significant positive influence on both the intercept of productivity (I-1) and the slope of productivity (S-1). Also, the intercept path (H2) from Human Resource Development (I-HD) to R&D (I-RD) has significant positive influence on the slope of profitability (S-2).

- By contrast (H1), the slope of SEE factors (S-0) that consists of Human Resource Development (S-HD), Quality Assurance (S-QA), Process Improvement (S-PI) and R&D (S-RD), has a positive impact on the intercept of profitability (I-2) through the intercept of Deliverables (I-D).
- Regarding the positive slope relationship (H1), the slope of Deliverables (S-D) has a positive impact on the slope of stability (S-3).
- Within Business Performance (H3), productivity leads to profitability, and profitability leads to stability significantly positively, such as along the paths from the intercept of profitability (I-2) to the intercept of stability (I-3); from the slope of productivity (S-1) to the slope of profitability (S-2); and from the slope of profitability (S-2) to the slope of stability (S-3); but not along the negative path from the intercept of productivity (I-1) to the intercept of profitability (I-2).
- Regarding the relationships among the intercepts of the seven SEE factors (H2), there is another negative path from the intercept of R&D (I-RD) to the intercept of Deliverables (I-D).

These results suggest the following:
- From the viewpoint of Deliverables (D), IT firms that keep high levels of Deliverables (D), which is an outcome factor of the SEE factors and is related to Human Resource Development (HD), Quality Assurance (QA), Project Management (PM), and Process Improvement (PI), tend to maintain high profitability in the long-term, i.e., a high operating profit ratio.
- Improving Human Resource Development (HD), Quality Assurance (QA), Process Improvement (PI) and R&D has the effect of improving the level of Deliverables (D).
- Regarding Project Management (PM) and Customer Contact (CC), IT firms that are active in sales and marketing, i.e., having high levels of Project Management (PM) and Customer Contact (CC), tend to be at a high level of productivity, i.e., having high sales revenue per person; they also become increasingly likely to improve their productivity in the long-term.
- Although the level of R&D negatively influences the level of Deliverables (D), the level of R&D likely leads to the growth of profitability in the long-term.
- Regarding Business Performance, profitable IT firms tend to be stable, and this tendency accelerates, i.e., they achieve a higher capital adequacy ratio, due to higher levels of Deliverables (D) and R&D.
- Productive IT firms, i.e., those having a high level of sales revenue per person, are not necessarily more profitable, i.e., do not necessarily have a high operating profit ratio. This suggests that the established big IT firms tend to be less profitable due to the multi-layer subcontractor industry structure in Japan. By contrast, improving productivity does likely lead to higher profitability in emerging firms.

3.5.3   Discussion

Based on the structural model hypothesis in Fig. 3.16, which is consistent with a series of empirical results, our research question in this subsection is to investigate the relationships among the seven SEE factors and business performance in the long-term. Then, we conducted longitudinal analyses of the standardized data from the 233 valid responses we had received to the 2005, 2006, and 2007 surveys from 151 unique firms and newly introduced business performance data of the 151 firms, and selected the best panel model in terms of Akaike Information Criteria (AIC).

Through the panel analysis of the best longitudinal model, we found the following to be characteristics of the relationships among the intercepts and the slopes of the seven SEE factors over the 3 years from 2005 to 2007 and the 10-year business performance from 1999 through 2008. First, IT firms maintaining high levels of Deliverables, which are derived from high levels of Human Resource Development, Quality Assurance, Project Management and Process Improvement, tend to sustain high profitability in the long-term, e.g., operating profit ratio. Second, regarding the sales and marketing activities, IT firms with high levels of Project Management and Customer Contact tend to be highly productive, e.g., sales per person. Moreover, such firms increasingly improve the productivity in the long-term. Third, concerning Business Performance, the profitable IT firms tend to be stable and this tendency accelerates progressively due to the enhancement of the levels of Deliverables and R&D. The productive IT firms are not necessarily profitable since the established big IT firms in Japan tend to be less profitable because of the multi-layer subcontractor industry structure.

For future study, we suggest considering the relationship among the types of Japanese software vendors as representatives of the business environment, software engineering capabilities, and business performance of the firms.

3.6   Effects of Business Environment on Software Engineering Capabilities and Business Performance

We investigated causal relationships among business environment and software engineering capabilities, based on the business performance achieved by manufacturer/user spin-off vendors and independent vendors, as reflected in data collected from 100 major IT vendors in Japan in 2007. We found that both manufacturer/user spin-off vendors and independent vendors can get a head start from the scale factor, e.g., number of software engineers; that quality assurance is one of the key factors for successful business performance by manufacturer/user spin-off IT vendors; and that project management is one of the key factors for successful business performance by independent IT vendors.

Table 3.1 Result of principal factor analysis of business environment

Loadings	Factor1	Factor2	Factor3	Factor4	Factor5
Sales volume	0.751	−0.152			
Manufacturer		0.635	0.138	−0.951	
Financial institute	0.141	−1.033		0.145	
ICT			−0.280	0.181	
Public services			−0.205	0.396	0.110
Wholesale/retailer		0.120	0.207	0.268	−0.399
Services	−0.188			0.479	0.174
Utility			−0.503		
Construction		0.135	−0.391	−0.239	
Industry bias	−0.162		0.803		
Sales bias			0.430		0.144
Customer sales	0.275		0.167		0.258
Contract	0.213	0.256			0.129
Outsourcing		−0.217		−0.290	−0.196
MBA	−0.545		0.132	0.119	0.132
Technologist	0.150		−0.363		
# of SE	0.782		−0.211		0.272
Ratio of SE	0.178		0.174	0.170	1.001
Average age	0.317	0.203	0.137		−0.338
SS loadings	1.856	1.704	1.701	1.631	1.573
Proportion Var	0.098	0.090	0.090	0.086	0.083
Cumulative Var	0.098	0.187	0.277	0.363	0.446

Test of the hypothesis that 5 factors are sufficient
The chi square statistic is 95.61 on 86° of freedom
The p-value is 0.224

In this section, we investigate other relationships, including effects of business environment, broken down by type of vendor:

Research Question 6 (RQ6) What are the causal effects of business environment on the seven SEE factors and on business performance, broken down by type of vendor?

3.6.1 Research Model and Hypothesis

We conducted principal component analysis based on the following components of Business Environment presented in the previous chapter: annual sales volume; sales percentage by industry (manufacturer, financial institute, information and communication technology (ICT), public services, wholesale/retailer, services, utility, construction); industry bias; sales bias; customer sales; contract; outsourcing; board members with MBA or technologists; number of software engineers; ratio of software engineers; average age of employees.

Based on the results of the principal component analysis shown in Table 3.1, we identified the following five factors: scale (Factor 1), manufacturer-oriented

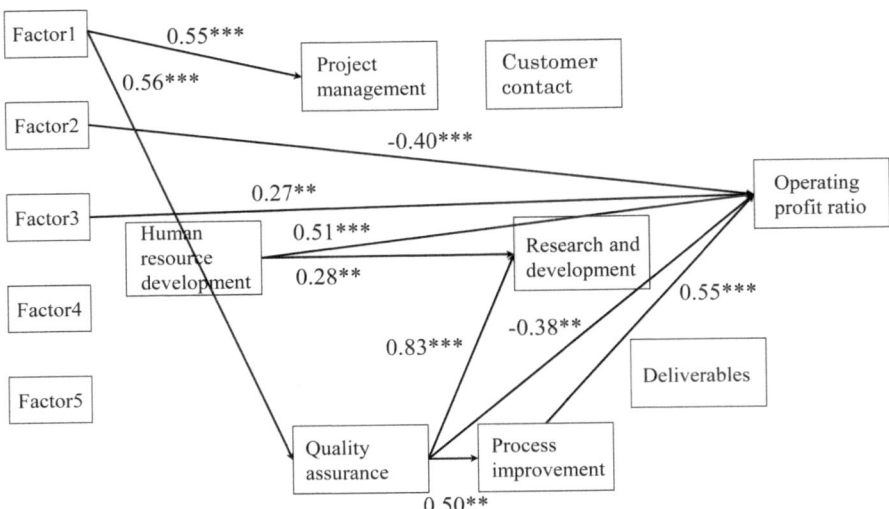

Fig. 3.18 Result of path analysis of manufacturer/user spin-off vendors. ***$p<0.001$; **$p<0.01$

(Factor 2), sales bias (Factor 3), service industry-oriented (Factor 4), software engineers-intensive (Factor 5).

Newly positioning the five factors of Business Environment in the left-side of the base model shown in Fig. 3.1, we constructed a path model that consists of all seven SEE factors, i.e., Deliverables, Project Management, Quality Assurance, Process Improvement, Research and Development, Human Resource Development and Customer Contact, and the operating profit ratio, together with the five factors of Business Environment. We then analyzed the causal relationships among Business Environment, the seven SEE factors, and Business Performance, broken down by manufacturer/user spin-off vendors and independent vendors.

Regarding the manufacturer/user spin-off vendors, we succeeded in constructing a well-fitted path model (p-value of chi square statistic is 0.05. CFI=0.81, GFI=0.70), where all the existing path coefficients are significant at the 1 % level. We found the following direct influences based on the paths shown in Fig. 3.18 (Kadono et al. 2008b).

- Regarding Business Environment, the scale factor (Factor 1), such as sales volume and the number of software engineers, positively affects Project Management and Quality Assurance.
- Also, manufacturer-oriented (Factor 2) exerts a negative impact on the operating profit ratio, while sales bias (Factor 3) exerts a positive impact on the operating profit ratio.
- Human Resource Development exerts a positive impact on Research and Development and on the operating profit ratio.
- Quality Assurance exerts a direct positive impact on Process Improvement and on Research and Development, just as in the case of independent vendors, as will appear below.

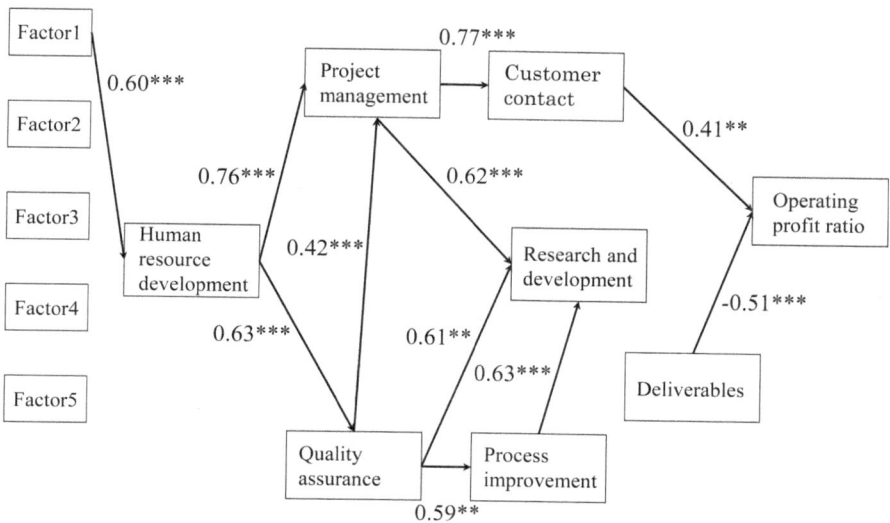

Fig. 3.19 Result of path analysis of independent vendors. ***$p<0.001$; **$p<0.01$

- However, Quality Assurance exerts a negative impact on the operating profit ratio; this could imply that effort invested in Quality Assurance does not pay off.
- Project Management exerts a direct positive impact on Customer Contact and on Research and Development.
- However, Research and Development exerts no direct impact on the operating profit ratio, a result which conflicts with the overall result obtained from the previous study on SEE2005 and SEE2006.
- Among the SEE factors, Customer Contact and Deliverables are isolated in the path model of manufacturer/user spin-off vendors.

Regarding the independent vendors, we succeeded in constructing a well-fitted path model (p-value of chi square statistic is 0.01. CFI=0.85, GFI=0.74), where all the existing path coefficients are significant at the 1 % level. We found the following direct influences as shown in Fig. 3.19 (Kadono et al. 2008b).

- Regarding Business Environment, only the scale factor (Factor 1), such as sales volume and the number of software engineers, positively affects Human Resource Development.
- Among the SEE factors, Human Resource Development is positioned in the topmost stream; the upper relationships discoverable from SEE2007 are similar to those from SEE2006, as shown in Figs. 3.2 and 3.3.
- Human Resource Development exerts a positive impact on Quality Assurance and on Project Management, which is consistent with the SEE2006 results.
- Quality Assurance exerts a direct positive impact on Process Improvement, Project Management, and Research and Development.
- Process Improvement exerts a positive impact on Research and Development.

- Project Management exerts a direct positive impact on Customer Contact and on Research and Development.
- However, for manufacturer/user spin-off vendors and independent vendors alike, Research and Development exerts no direct impact on the operating profit ratio, a result which conflicts with the overall result obtained from the previous study on SEE2005and SEE2006.
- On the other hand, Customer Contact does exert a direct positive impact on operating profit ratio.
- Finally, Deliverables exerts a direct negative impact on operating profit ratio; this could imply that effort invested in Deliverables does not pay off.

3.6.2 Implications

Both manufacturer/user spin-off vendors and independent vendors can get a head start from the scale factor (Factor 1), such as the number of software engineers. However, we found the relationships among the factors differ significantly depending on the origin of the vendor, i.e. whether manufacturer/user spin-off, or independent.

Regarding manufacturer/user spin-off vendors, the path coefficients from Factor 1, i.e., scale factor, through Quality Assurance, and Process Improvement to operating profit ratio are all positive, in addition to the direct positive path from Human Resource Development to operating profit ratio. Regarding independent vendors, the path coefficients from Factor 1 through Human Resource Development, Project Management, and Customer Contact to operating profit ratio are all positive.

In other words, Quality Assurance is a key factor for successful Business Performance in the Business Environment of manufacturer/user spin-off IT vendors, while Project Management is a key factor for successful Business Performance in the Business Environment of independent IT vendors. However, the paths to Research and Development are all positive for both manufacturer/user spin-off vendors and independent vendors, although they do not reach the operating profit ratio.

3.7 Lessons Learned from the Analysis Results

3.7.1 Summary of Statistical Analysis Results

The objective in Chap. 3 was to better understand the mechanisms of how software engineering capabilities relate to IT vendors' business performance and business environment in a challenging era for the Japanese software industry. To this end, in Chap. 2, we designed a research survey to look into software engineering capabilities, and administered it in 2005, 2006 and 2007, together with Japan's Ministry of Economy, Trade and Industry (METI) and Information-Technology Promotion

Agency (IPA). We received responses to the 2007 SEE survey from 117 companies, of which a total of 100 were valid, a response rate of 10%. There were 55 valid responses to the 2005 survey (a response rate of 24%), and 78 for 2006 (a response rate of 15%), including the largest class system integrators in Japan.

For further analysis, we integrated the 233 valid responses received over the 3 years into a database including 151 unique companies consisting of 42 manufacturer spin-off vendors, 33 user spin-off vendors and 76 independent vendors. Then we performed several statistical analyses upon the standardized software engineering capability scores for the 3 years and the financial data for 10 years, e.g., path analysis, cross-section analysis, panel analysis, longitudinal analysis, and stratified analysis.

Through the cross-section analysis on the 2007 survey, we reproducibly observe that a higher effort level on Human Resource Development, Quality Assurance, and Project Management brings about better performance in Customer Contact, Research and Development, Process Improvement, and Deliverables; this was consistent with the 2006 survey results. Focusing on management of software engineering innovation, the common order effects originating with Human Resource Development along the paths of service innovation, product innovation, and process innovation were empirically verified based on the data-centric approach.

Based on the panel analysis of the seven SEE factors, several series correlations among the software engineering capabilities were proved. Our first observation is that most SEE factors in 1 year had significant positive influences on the same factor the next year. Second, within a year, there were three paths to improving the level of Deliverables, i.e., through Project Management, Quality Assurance, and Research and Development. Third, some SEE factors exerted significant positive influence on different SEE factors in the following year diagonally. Fourth, there were some negative paths, implying that effort put toward a particular factor did not pay off. These results suggest that each IT vendor needs to know its own nature based on the path dependence and make the most of what it has.

The longitudinal analysis based on the latent growth model suggested positive relationships among software engineering capabilities and profitability, as a component of, and representing, business performance, in software vendors in the drastically changing IT industry in Japan. Based on the panel analysis of the 3-year SEE data and 10-year operating profit ratios of the 151 respondents to the SEE surveys, we significantly verified that IT firms that have excellent software engineering capabilities tend to maintain and improve their business performance in the medium and long term. Equally, the series correlations of a firm's financial performance were observed to correspond to those of its software engineering capabilities.

3.7.2 Implications for Technological Innovation and Industry Policy

These results imply the following contemporary perspectives on technological innovation, and industry policy (Hasegawa 2013). Based on the longitudinal analysis,

we verified that there are significant positive relationships between the sophistication of software engineering capabilities and the superior performance of IT vendors in the long-term. At the same time, through the panel analysis of the seven
SEE factors, several series correlations among the software engineering capabilities
were proved. For example, most SEE factors in 1 year had significant positive influences on the same factor the next year. It follows that the structure of the software
engineering capabilities and the financial results of IT vendors should be considered
to be entrenched in the long-term.

On the other hand, the relationships among the seven SEE factors and business
performance vary significantly depending on the origin of a vendor: manufacturer
spin-off, user spin-off or independent. If we focus on the management of innovation, then, in manufacturer spin-off vendors, service innovation, process innovation,
and product innovation are effectively connected. However, in user spin-off vendors, any indicated software engineering innovation is attributable to a management
policy of paying extra attention to business performance. In independent vendors,
Human Resource Development is the only factor that positively and significantly
influences the other capabilities and business performance. Also, having regard to
the size of vendors, we found that vendors who have a larger number of software
engineers tend to get a higher SEE score (METI and IPA 2007).

Therefore, in formulating industry policy proposals to promote software engineering innovation, we should consider both the individual characteristics and the
organizational inertia, broken down by type of vendor. For example, the government should encourage manufacturer spin-off vendors, especially large-scale system integrators, to accelerate state-of-the-art product innovations; to this end, the
government should commission huge nationwide IT projects. On the other hand,
the government should financially support small or medium-size independent vendors to help them develop human resources in software engineering. To help shape
sound industry policy, we think it crucial that (1) a stable measurement tool be
established, such as the SEE survey, by which to measure the management of innovation in the software industry in Japan, and (2) financial reporting standards be
adopted in common by corporate managers (Kadono 2013b).

3.7.3   Limitations and Future Research

Since the SEE surveys were a large-scale and costly research method, it was not
practical to continue administering the surveys routinely, year after year. Therefore,
we integrated the 233 valid responses received over the 3 years, 2005 through 2007,
into a database including 151 unique companies, the better to perform several statistical analyses, such as a longitudinal analysis of the relationships between the SEE
scores and the financial data from 1999 through 2008. We proved several findings
that are statistically significant; however, the amount of the SEE data is not necessarily sufficient to perform some other statistical analyses that would be desirable,
e.g., stratified analysis of the SEE scores by type of vendor for any given year.

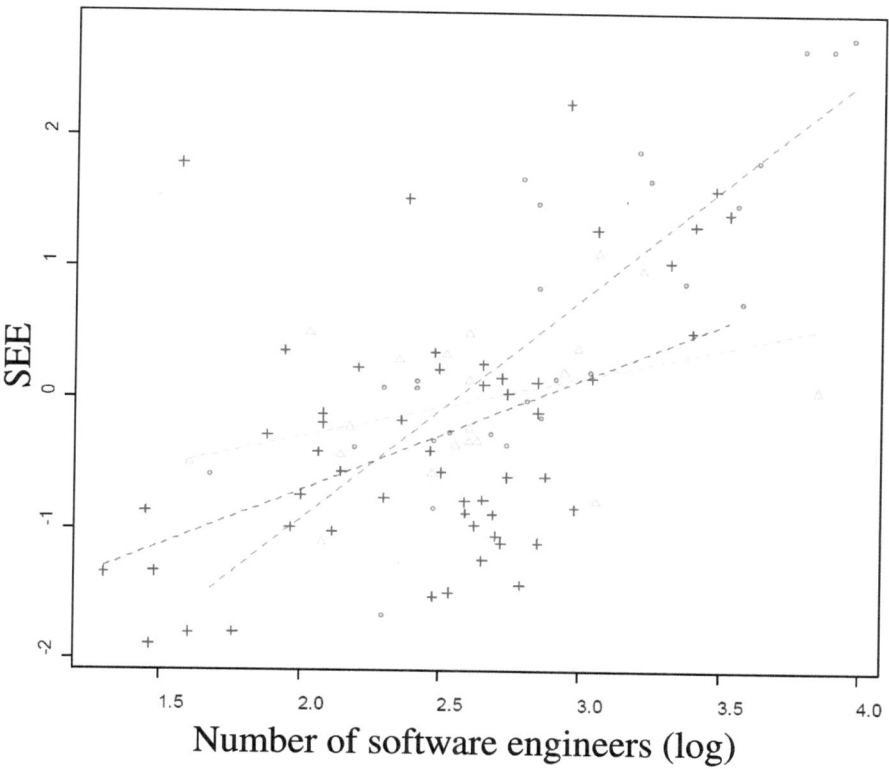

Fig. 3.20 Number of software engineers(log) and SEE (*Circle* Manufacture spin-off, *triangle* user spin-off, + independent)

Although the research in Chaps. 2 and 3 is intended to cover issues relating to IT management and software engineering innovation in the broadest sense, the research approach—using social surveys, and statistical analyses based on the resource-based view—has limitations. For example, if the rules of the game in the Japanese software industry change in a rapid and unpredictable manner, e.g., Schumpeterian revolutions, or a paradigm shift caused by a breakthrough in technology, then it will be difficult to adapt the findings discovered by the approach to a new business environment. However, the current business environment is entrenched in the Japanese software industry and is likely unchangeable for good or bad, just as in other industries in Japan and other cultures.

In the present chapter, we have focused on the three types of vendor, but components of the Business Environment, such as the number of software engineers and the business model, should also be brought into the account so as to clarify the mechanism by which they leverage software engineering innovations. For example, as noted earlier in Chap. 2, vendors who have a larger number of software engineers tend to get a higher SEE score (Fig. 3.20). This tendency is evident in the results of the three SEE surveys, 2005 through 2007. Equally, regardless of

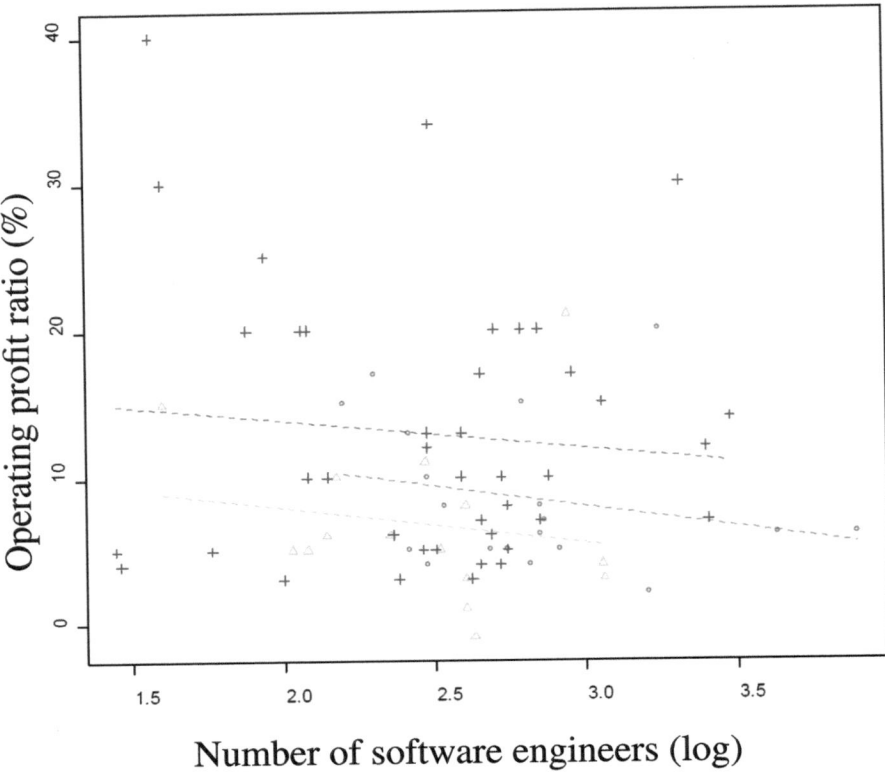

Fig. 3.21 Number of software engineers (log) and operating profit ratio (%) (*Circle* Manufacturer spin-off, *triangle* user-turned, + independent)

vendor type, vendors who have a larger number of software engineers tend to be less profitable (Fig. 3.21). This tendency also is evident in the results of the three SEE surveys, 2005 through 2007. We need to investigate any trade-off between the advantages of scale, notably, higher SEE scores, versus the disadvantages, notably, lower profitability. In other words, the causal relationships among the SEE factors, and Business Performance and Business Environment, including, e.g., the number of software engineers, business model, and average age of employees, remain to be analyzed and understood in the future (Fig. 2.1).

In the global cloud computing era, to further study issues associated with the management of software engineering innovation in the Japanese IT industry, we suggest doing global comparisons of IT industry architecture; in particular, we suggest comparing the multilayered subcontractor industry in Japan with the industries in the United States, and other Asian countries, such as China, India, and others. Also, we think it important to simulate the future possible industry architecture in more detail, based on a data-centric approach and continuing fact-finding surveys, such as the SEE surveys, so as to formulate an effective industry policy for the software industry in Japan. These issues will be discussed in Chaps. 7 and 8.

References

Akaike, H. (1974). A new look at the statistical model identification. *IEEE Transactions on Automatic Control, 19,* 716–723.

Barney J. B. (2007). *Gaining and sustaining competitive advantage.* New Jersey: Pearson Prentice Hall.

Bollen, K. A. (1989). *Structural equation with latent variables.* New York: Wiley-Interscience Publication.

Carnegie Mellon University (CMU). (2014). Software engineering institute. http://www.sei.cmu.edu/cmmi/. Accessed 14 Aug 2014.

Dodgson, M., Gann, D., & Salter, A. (2008). *The management of technological innovation.* Oxford: Oxford University Press.

Fujimoto, T. (2003). *Capability-building competition.* Tokyo: Chuohkouronshinsya.

Hasegawa, S. (Ed.). (2013). *History of Japan's trade and industry policy (7) machinery and information industries.* Tokyo: Keizai Sangyo Chosakai.

IEEE, Computer Society. (2004). *SWEBOK 2004.*

ISO. (2010). ISO/IEC/IEEE 24765:2010 Systems and software engineering–Vocabulary.

Kadono, Y. (2011). A study on management of software engineering capability in Japan using panel analysis. *International Journal of Service Science, Management, Engineering, Technology, 2*(3), 20–32.

Kadono, Y. (2013a). The differences in structural relationships among software engineering capabilities and business performance depending on origin of IT firm in Japan. *International Journal of Innovation and Learning, 14*(3/4), 308–328.

Kadono, Y. (2013b). Scenario prediction of Japanese software industry through hybrid method (Best Research Award). Proceedings of Technology Innovation and Industrial Management, 2013.

Kadono, Y., & Tsubaki, H. (2012). A study on the relationships between software engineering capabilities and business performance of Japanese it firms through longitudinal modeling. Proceedings of the 16th Pacific Asia conference on information systems (PACIS2012), Ho Chi Minh, Vietnam, 2012. (AIS-relating international conference award by JASMIN).

Kadono, Y., Tsubaki, H., & Tsuruho, S. (2006). A study on the reality and economy of software development in Japan. Proceedings of the sixth Asia Pacific Industrial Engineering Management Systems Conference, Bangkok, Thailand (pp. 1425–1433).

Kadono, Y., Tsubaki, H., & Tsuruho, S. (2008a). A survey on management of software engineering in Japan. In A. Sio-long, et al. (Ed.), *Current thems in engineering technologies.* American Institution of Physics.

Kadono, Y., Tsubaki, H., & Tsuruho, S. (2008b). A study on reality and issues on management of enterprise software engineering in Japan: Causal relationships by maker/user-turned vendors and independent vendors. Proc. The 9th Asia Pacific Industrial Engineering Management Systems Conference (APIEMS), Bali, Indonesia (pp. 1234–1243).

Kadono, Y., Tsubaki, H., & Tsuruho, S. (2009). A study on characteristics of software vendors in Japan: From environmental threats and resource-based view. Proc. the 13th Pacific Asia Conference on Information Systems.

Kadono, Y., Tsubaki, H., & Tsuruho, S. (2010). A study on management of software engineering capability in Japan through panel analysis. Proceedings of 5th Mediterranean Conference on Information Systems (MCIS).

Kadono, Y., Tsubaki, H., & Tsuruho, S. (2011). Longitudinal modeling of the software engineering capabilities and profitability of software companies in Japan. Proceedings of Technology Innovation and Industrial Management (TIIM).

Kadono, Y., Tsubaki, H., & Tsuruho, S. (2012). Structural relationships among software engineering capabilities in Japan. *International Journal of Innovation and Learning, 12*(2), 217–227.

Meredith, W., & Tisak, J. (1990). Latent curve analysis. *Psychometrika, 55,* 107–122.

Ministry of Economy, Trade and Industry, & Information-Technology Promotion Agency, Japan (METI & IPA). (2007). *Fact-finding investigation on software engineering capabilities of enterprise systems in Japan.* (The responsibility for the investigation lies with Yasuo Kadono). sec.ipa.go.jp/reports/20071204/SE_level_research_2006_2.pdf. Accessed 14 Aug 2014.

Ohno, T. (1988). *Toyota production system: Beyond large-scale production.* Productivity Press.

Pressman, R. S. (2010). *Software engineering: A practitioner's approach* (7th ed.). McGraw-Hill.

Stauss, B., Engelmann, K., Kremer, A., & Luhn, A. (2008). *Services science: Fundamentals, challenges and future developments.* Berlin: Springer-Verlag.

Tidd, J., & Bessant, J. (2013). *Managing innovation* (5th ed.). New York: Wiley.

Part II
Research Relevant to Managing
Innovation in Software Engineering
in the Broader Sense

Chapter 4
A Study into Characteristics of Software Vendors in Japan from a Competitive Environment and Resource-Based Viewpoint

Abstract The objectives of this research are to describe the competitive environment in the software industry in Japan and to understand the characteristic differences among manufacturer spin-offs, user spin-offs and independent vendors. Based on management frameworks such as Porter's five forces and Barney's resource-based view, we developed a model to measure environmental threats and competitive strengths/weaknesses. We then conducted factor analysis of the data collected from 100 major IT vendors in Japan. On this basis, we extracted eight threat factors, e.g., industry stagnation, difficulty in recruiting bright people, ROI/quality demands from clients, price cutting/quick delivery demands from clients, and adoption of new technology. We also identified six strength/weakness factors, e.g., human capital, advantage of scale, expansive business, inimitability, and stability. Regression tree analysis suggested that manufacturer spin-off vendors tend to significantly expand their business with well-resourced R&D, while user spin-off vendors seem to depend heavily on demand from parent companies, as a result of which some of them are thought to gain inimitable capabilities. On the other hand, many independent vendors supply temporary staff to principal contractors and do not show specific strengths; even so, some independent vendors with inimitable assets are thought to be role models for software vendors in Japan.

Keywords Types of software vendors · Software industry in Japan · Environmental threats · Five forces · Resource-based view · Statistical analysis · Regression tree analysis

4.1 Introduction

IT vendors in Japan are facing drastic changes in their business environment, such as technology innovations, new entrants from China and India, and recent business stagnation. Also, issues peculiar to the IT industry in Japan have been pointed out, such as man-month-based multilayer subcontractors, and business models depending on custom-made applications for the domestic market, as shown in Chap. 1 (METI 2014; Cusumano 2004; Kadono 2007; Kadono et al. 2009; Kimura 2014). In order to assist the IT industry in Japan in meeting these challenges and clients'

Y. Kadono, *Management of Software Engineering Innovation in Japan*,
DOI 10.1007/978-4-431-55612-1_4

rising expectations, especially as to quality, cost and delivery, and to understand key factors for medium- and long-term success, we designed a survey of the software industry and conducted it in collaboration with the Ministry of Economy, Trade and Industry (METI) in 2005, 2006 and 2007.

In designing the survey, we developed a measurement tool called Software Engineering Excellence (SEE), by which to evaluate the overall software engineering capabilities of IT vendors from the viewpoints of deliverables, project management, quality assurance, process improvement, research and development, human resource development, and contact with customers. We also introduced two other indicators: business performance and competitive environment, as shown in Chap. 2. We found that the competitive environment complemented the relationship between SEE and the business performance of the software vendors.

In the SEE2006 survey, we modified the measurement model used for SEE2005, and increased the number of surveyed IT vendors from 55 to 78, in order to more deeply investigate both the impact of software engineering on business performance, and the competitive environment. In particular, in this study we focused on the relationships among the SEE factors; the competitive environment; and business performance, as measured by operating profit ratio. By analyzing the data collected from 78 major IT vendors, we found that superior deliverables and business performance were correlated with the effort expended particularly on human resource development, quality assurance, research and development, and process improvement.

In SEE2007, we modified the measurement model again, and analysed the data collected from 100 major IT vendors. We repeatedly observed that the level of effort put into human resource development, quality assurance, and project management resulted in better performance in customer contact, research and development, and process improvement on the part of the IT vendors, all consistent with the results of SEE2006.

However, the causal relationships differ significantly depending on type of vendor, i.e., whether manufacturer spin-off, user spin-off or independent vendor, where manufacturer (user) spin-off vendors are affiliate companies of computer makers (users), while independent vendors are not affiliate companies of either computer makers or computer users, as shown in Chap. 3 (Kadono 2013).

These findings motivated us to focus more strongly on the industry structure, the competitive environment, and the characteristics of each type of vendor. Therefore, the objectives of this research were:

- To describe the competitive environment in the IT industry in Japan; and
- To understand the characteristic differences between manufacturer spin-off vendors, user spin-off vendors, and independent vendors in the competitive environment.

To achieve these objectives, we statistically analysed the data collected from 100 major IT vendors in SEE2007. In the following sections, we present our research method, our survey of the software industry in Japan, our analysis, our results and discussion, our conclusions, and opportunities for future work.

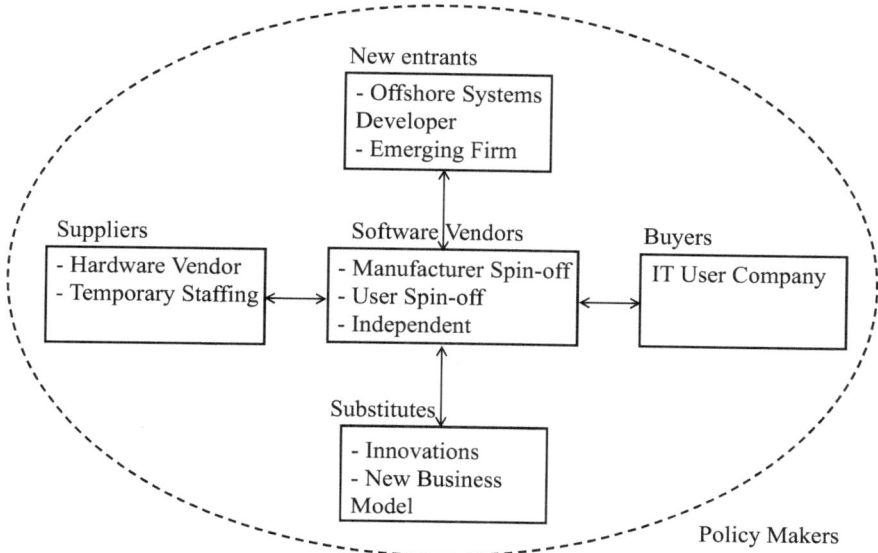

Fig. 4.1 The five forces model of the software industry in Japan

4.2 Research Method

The measurement model for our survey was originally developed through inter-
views with over 50 experts in the IT industry in Japan as well as in the U.S., and
through literature searches under the topic of software engineering and management (Porter 1980; Porter 1985; Barney 2007; Barney 1986; Besanko et al. 2007;
Lippman and Rumelt 1982; Dodgson et al. 2008; Mongomery and Wernerfelt 1991;
Prahalad and Hamel 1990; Arthur 1989; Dierickx and Cool 1989; Selznick 1957;
Penrose 1959; IEEE 2004; ISO 2010; CMU 2014; Fujimoto 2003; METI 2014;
MIC 2014; JISA 2014; SAP 2014; McKinsey et al. 2013; Kadono 2004; Kadono
2007; Kadono 2009).

In this research, we investigate firms in the IT industry in Japan from two viewpoints: the five forces model, and the resource-based view.

First, in Fig. 4.1, we introduce the structure of the software industry in Japan
by means of the five forces model (Porter 1980). In the central box, there are three
types of software vendor, depending on the origin of a company: manufacturer spin-
off, user spin-off, or independent vendor. The buyers in the right-side box include
IT user companies. The suppliers in the left-side box include hardware vendors and
temporary staffing as a variable cost. The upper box shows that offshore IT vendors
from China and India are emerging as new entrants in the Japanese market. The
lower box shows that Japanese customers increasingly expect delivery of software
as a package or software as a service (SaaS), rather than custom-made software.
Policymakers, such as the government and IT industry groups, are considered as a

sixth player that used to be active in the era of high-speed growth in the Japanese economy.

Consistent with the five forces model, we came up with questionnaire items regarding environmental threats, based on interviews with experts in the IT industry as well as literature searches above-mentioned.

The questionnaires postulated the following environmental threats: T.1: new entrants, e.g., China, India; T.2: US/EU vendors; T.3: difficulties in recruiting bright people; T.4: low-profitability industry; T.5: low-growth industry; T.6: mature oligopoly; T.7: packaged software, e.g., Enterprise Resource Planning (ERP); T.8: decline in demand for IT; T.9: clients demanding quick delivery; T.10: clients demanding price cutting; T.11: clients particular as to quality; T.12: clients demanding ROI; T.13: low IT literacy of clients; T.14: self-development by clients; T.15: shortage of subcontractors; T.16: adoption of new technology; T.17: product differentiations; T.18: clients switching vendors; T.19: erosion of software engineering capability; T.20: falling supply of bright IT students; T.21: turnover problems; T.22: M&A; T.23: retirement of senior software engineers; T.24: stagnation rather than innovation in IT.

These questionnaire items were ranked by the following four criteria: short-term threat; mid- to long-term threat; not applicable; no threat.

Second, from the resource-based view (Barney 2007), we came up with questionnaire items looking into competitiveness, i.e., the strengths/weaknesses of the firms, through interviews with experts in the IT industry as well as literary searches. More precisely, we applied Barney's VRIO framework, i.e., the factors of value, rarity, imitability and organization, which involve important management concepts such as sustained competitive advantage, unique historical conditions, path dependence, causal ambiguity, social complexity, complementary resources, and capability.

As a result, the questionnaires looked into the following competitive strengths and weaknesses: C.1: state-of-the-art technology; C.2: mainframe technology; C.3: software product development; C.4: development capability on ERP; C.5: large scale systems development; C.6: knowhow on specific function; C.7: specification description; C.8: inimitable products/services; C.9: scale of human resources; C.10: quality of human resources; C.11: high productivity of employees; C.12: challenge orientation; C.13: stability orientation; C.14: collaborators network; C.15: sales/ services coverage; C.16: sales volume; C.17: system integration capability; C.18: business diversification; C.19: new acquisition of patent; C.20: brand equity; C.21: customer base; C.22: lump-sum contract capability; C.23: sales efficiency; C.24: customer satisfaction; C.25: well-resourced research and development; C.26: cost competitiveness; C.27: repeat order; C.28: stable revenue sources; C.29: market share in strong segment; C.30: proposal capability; C.31: new client development; C.32: new business/services development; C.33: offshore systems development; C.34: offshore client development; C.35: financial characteristics; C.36: capability to respond to client's requests; C.37: leadership provided by management; C.38: government or industry group contacts.

These questionnaire items were ranked by the following four criteria: not applicable; weak; strong; strong and sustainable.

Table 4.1 Software Engineering Excellence surveys

Fiscal year	2005	2006	2007
Questionnaires sent	230	537	1000
Valid responses	55	78	100
Manufacturer spin-off	17	27	27
User spin-off	15	15	20
Independent	23	36	53
Response rate (%)	24	15	10

Finally, in the following sections, we statistically extract the characteristics of each type of vendor, i.e., manufacturer spin-off vendor, user spin-off vendor and independent vendor, based on the information on environmental threats and competitive strengths and weaknesses, obtained as above from the data collected from 100 major IT vendors in Japan.

4.3 Surveys of the Software Industry in Japan

To achieve the research objectives explained in the Introduction, above, we conducted a survey on Software Engineering Excellence in 2007 (SEE2007). For this survey, we designed a questionnaire on the practice of software engineering and the competitive environment of companies. This questionnaire was sent to the CEOs of 1000 major Japanese IT vendors, each with over 300 employees, as well as to the member firms of the Japan Information Technology Services Industry Association (JISA), from December 2007 through January 2008. Responses were received from 117 companies; valid responses totaled 100 for SEE2007 (response rate of 10%). Valid responses had numbered 55 (response rate of 23%) for SEE2005 and 78 (response rate of 15%) for SEE2006, as shown in Table 4.1.

4.4 Analysis, Results, and Discussion

First, we conducted factor analysis of the items looking into environmental threats based on the five forces, i.e., T.1 through T.24 in Table 4.2. From the results, we significantly identified the following 8 factors: TF1: industry stagnation; TF2: difficulties in recruiting bright people; TF3: ROI/quality demanded by clients; TF4: new entrants; TF5: price cutting/quick delivery demanded by clients; TF6: Software Engineering capability erosion; TF7: stagnating IT innovation; TF8: new technology adoption.

Second, we conducted factor analysis of the items looking into competitiveness, i.e., strengths and weaknesses, C.1 through C.38 in Table 4.3. From the results, we significantly identified the following 6 factors. CF1: human capital; CF2: advantage of scale; CF3: expansive business; CF4: new client/services development; CF5: inimitability; CF6: stability.

Table 4.2 Results of factor analysis on environmental threats

	TF1	TF2	TF3	TF4	TF5	TF6	TF7	TF8
T.1 new entrants (China, India etc.)		-0.143				0.148	0.162	
T.2 US/EU vendors	0.323	0.138		0.939				0.132
T.3 recruiting bright people	0.16	0.645	0.126	0.527	0.192	0.173	0.137	
T.4 low-profitability industry	0.701	0.149		0.12				
T.5 low-growth industry	0.854	0.323	0.12					
T.6 mature oligopoly	0.405	0.135		0.183		-0.188	-0.462	0.186
T.7 packaged software (ERP)	0.379	0.394		0.318		0.108		
T.8 decline in demand for IT	0.15	0.255		0.179	0.124	0.104		-0.117
T.9 clients demanding quick delivery			0.33		0.554			0.163
T.10 clients demanding price cutting			0.194		0.954	0.138		0.12
T.11 clients particular as to quality			0.712		0.168			0.118
T.12 clients demanding ROI		0.19	0.897		0.188	0.111	0.189	-0.17
T.13 low IT literacy of clients	0.21	-0.233	0.122	-0.174	0.128	0.159	0.205	
T.14 self-development by clients		0.22	-0.136	0.118	0.199	-0.226	0.389	
T.15 shortage of subcontractors		0.385		0.369		0.238	0.243	0.936
T.16 adoption of new technology		0.207	0.228	0.138		0.206	-0.129	0.412
T.17 product differentiations		0.451	0.162				0.145	
T.18 clients switching vendors	0.128	0.402	0.129	-0.12	0.185		0.172	
T.19 erosion of SE capability	0.107	0.183	0.18			0.944	0.354	
T.20 fewer bright IT students	0.147	0.137		0.16		0.482		
T.21 turnover problems		0.496					0.432	
T.22 M&A	0.201		-0.135	0.202				

Table 4.2 (continued)

	TF1	TF2	TF3	TF4	TF5	TF6	TF7	TF8
T.23 retirement of senior SEs						0.162	0.388	
T.24 stagnating IT innovations		0.109					0.484	
SS loadings	1.874	1.804	1.758	1.604	1.498	1.496	1.354	1.256
Proportion Var	0.078	0.075	0.073	0.067	0.062	0.062	0.056	0.052
Cumulative Var	0.078	0.153	0.227	0.293	0.356	0.418	0.475	0.527

A blank in table denotes a number less than 0.1
Test of the hypothesis that eight factors are sufficient:
the chi square statistic is 116.53 on 112 degrees of freedom
the *p*-value is 0.366

Table 4.3 Results of factor analysis on competitiveness

	CF1	CF2	CF3	CF4	CF5	CF6
C.1 state-of-the-art technology	0.424	0.195	0.46	0.213	0.42	
C.2 mainframe technology	0.152	0.103	0.26	−0.118	0.249	0.328
C.3 SW product development	0.314	0.298	0.265	0.366	0.106	
C.4 development capability on ERP	0.351		0.396	0.151	0.159	
C.5 large scale systems development	0.425	0.265	0.414		0.37	0.152
C.6 knowhow on specific function	0.229				0.626	0.185
C.7 specification description	0.565		0.212	0.115	0.234	0.169
C.8 inimitable products/services	0.189		0.3		0.573	
C.9 scale of human resources	0.32	0.719	0.317		0.107	
C.10 quality of human resources	0.654	0.357	0.307		0.128	0.1
C.11 high productivity of employees	0.502	0.115	0.235	0.329	0.162	0.304
C.12 challenge orientation	0.636	0.125		0.286	0.111	−0.115
C.13 stability orientation		0.241				0.563
C.14 collaborators network	0.329	0.503		0.151	0.173	0.202
C.15 sales/services coverage	0.237	0.465	0.127	0.539		0.155
C.16 sales volume	0.29	0.637	0.294	0.187	0.196	0.297
C.17 system integration capability		0.42	0.112	0.177	0.438	0.206
C.18 business diversification		0.402	0.32	0.127	0.179	0.154
C.19 new acquisition of patent	0.173	0.345	0.702	0.162	0.243	0.111
C.20 brand equity	0.151	0.608	0.204	0.181	0.25	
C.21 customer base	0.237	0.188	0.271	0.205	0.348	0.27
C.22 lump-sum contract capability	0.345	0.212		0.179	0.355	
C.23 sales efficiency	0.527	0.251		0.34		0.299
C.24 customer satisfaction	0.657	0.143	0.121	0.256		0.17
C.25 well-resourced R&D	0.262	0.348	0.557	0.305	0.298	0.115
C.26 cost competitiveness	0.196		0.136	0.581		0.405
C.27 repeat order	0.236			0.161	0.337	0.562
C.28 stable revenue sources				0.144	0.253	0.678
C.29 market share in strong segment		0.313			0.461	0.241
C.30 proposal capability	0.531	0.217	0.169	0.49	0.233	
C.31 new client development	0.327	0.252	0.152	0.767	0.209	
C.32 new business/services development	0.291	0.279	0.223	0.572	0.18	
C.33 offshore systems development	0.275	0.351	0.633	0.134	−0.159	0.13
C.34 offshore client development	0.187	0.347	0.598	0.258		0.186
C.35 financial characteristics	0.403	0.114	0.297			0.376
C.36 can respond to client's requests	0.55	0.332	0.281	0.178	0.16	0.262
C.37 leadership from management	0.543	0.193	0.226	0.379		0.328
C.38 government/industry group contacts	0.336	0.42	0.272	0.223	0.185	
SS loadings	5.019	3.824	3.437	3.102	2.633	2.475
Proportion Var	0.132	0.101	0.09	0.082	0.069	0.065
Cumulative Var	0.132	0.233	0.323	0.405	0.474	0.539

A blank in table denotes a number less than 0.1
Test of the hypothesis that six factors are sufficient:
the chi square statistic is 517.01 on 490 degrees of freedom
the p-value is 0.193

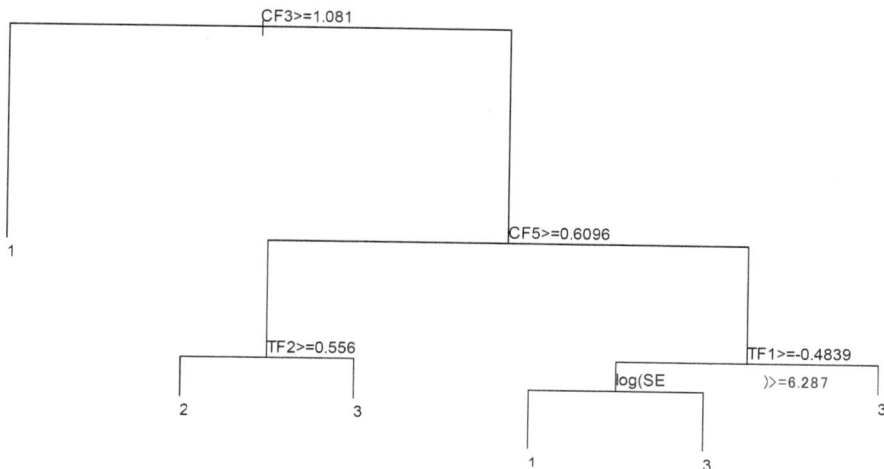

Fig. 4.2 Result of recursive partition analysis
(1) root 78 40 3 (0.29487179 0.21794872 0.48717949) (2) CF3>=1.08058 13 2 1 (0.84615385 0.15384615 0.00000000)* (3) CF3<1.08058 65 27 3 (0.1846 1538 0.23076923 0.58461538) (6) CF5>=0.60963 20 9 2 (0.20000000 0.55000000 0.25000000) (12) TF2>=0.5559618 8 0 2 (0.00000000 1.00000000 0.00000000)* (13) TF2<0.5559618 12 7 3 (0.33333333 0.25000000 0.41666667) (7) CF5<0.60963 45 12 3 (0.17777778 0.08888889 0.73333333) (14) TF1>=−0.483853 28 12 3 (0.28571429 0.14285714 0.57142857) (28) log(SE#)>=6.286658 9 3 1 (0.66666667 0.00000000 0.33333333)* (29) log(SE#)<6.286658 19 6 3 (0.10526316 0.21052632 0.68421053)* (15) TF1<−0.483853 17 0 3 (0.00000000 0.00000000 1.00000000)*.
Note: *denotes terminal node. For example, in (2), the *left* most terminal node includes 13 nodes with CF3>=1.08058, 11 of which are manufacturer spin-off (*1*) and two of which are either user spin-off (*2*) or independent vendors (*3*). More precisely, manufacturer spin-off vendors (*1*) makes up 84.615385%, user spin-off vendors (*2*) makes up15.384615%, and independent vendors (*3*) makes up 0.00000000%

Finally, in order to extract the characteristics of each type of vendor, i.e., (1) manufacturer spin-off vendors; (2) user spin-off vendors; (3) independent vendors; we fit a tree-based model by rpart (Recursive Partition) in R with Zini criteria, using competitiveness factors (CFs), threat factors (TFs), and the number of software engineers (log (SE#)). The research showed that the number of software engineers is one of the key parameters. Based on the analysis results in Fig. 4.2, we found the characteristics of each type of vendor to be as follows (Kadono et al. 2009).

- We identified five factors to effectively explain the different results among types of vendors as follows: CF3: expansive business; CF5: inimitability; TF1: industry stagnation; TF2: difficulties in recruiting bright people; and the number of software engineers (log (SE#)).
- Manufacturer spin-off vendors significantly tend to expand their business (CF3>=1.081), e.g., C.19: new acquisition of patent; C.25: well-resourced R&D; C.33: offshore systems development; C.34 offshore client development.
- User spin-off vendors significantly tend to be less expansive (CF3<1.081) and less inimitable (CF5>=0.6096), e.g., C.6: knowhow on specific function; C.8:

inimitable products/services. However, difficulty in recruiting bright people is not identified as a threat (TF2 >= 0.556).

- Another type of manufacturer spin-off vendor tends to be less expansive (CF3 < 1.081) and less inimitable (CF5 < 0.6096). However, industry stagnation (TF1 >= 0.4839), e.g., T.4: low-profitability industry, and T.5: low-growth industry, is not identified as a threat; and these firms tend to be a large (log (SE#) >= 6.287, i.e., SE# >= 538).
- Independent vendors tend not to satisfy the above conditions. i.e. they may be:

  - less expansive (CF3 < 1.081), less inimitable (CF5 >= 0.6096), and have difficulties recruiting bright people s
  - less expansive (CF3 < 1.081), less inimitable (CF5 < 0.6096), but without threat of industry stagnation (TF1 >= 0.4839), and relatively small-sized (log(SE#) < 6.287, i.e., SE# < 538).
  - less expansive (CF3 < 1.081), less inimitable (CF5 < 0.6096), and with threat of industry stagnation (TF1 < 0.4839).

We consider the implications of the above results as follows.

Some manufacturer spin-off vendors are leading the IT industry in Japan by pursuing state-of-the art technology as well as new patent acquisition on the basis of well-resourced research and development. Simultaneously they try to develop clients and systems abroad, even though offshore systems and client development are relatively limited among Japanese IT vendors in general (METI and IPA 2007). Others are relatively less expansive and less inimitable, despite having a relatively large number of software engineers (>= 538). These need to utilize human resources more effectively, e.g., capability building, effective posting.

Some user spin-off vendors seem to depend heavily on demand from the parent company. Therefore, they do not need to be expansive or careful about recruiting people. All they need to do is focus on the business of the parent company. As a result, they are thought to gain inimitable skills, e.g., knowhow on specific functions, and inimitable products/services.

Independent vendors are a wide variety. Many of them supply temporary staff to principal contractors (Fig. 4.1). However, their revenue base could be fragile, particularly in the recent business depression. Therefore, they might not be able to afford to train people sufficiently, as shown in Fig. 4.3. The role model for independent vendors should be the first type of independent vendor shown in Fig. 4.2, i.e., inimitable (CF5 >= 0.6096), or the second type in Fig. 4.2, i.e., no threat of industry stagnation (TF1 >= 0.4839), even if they are relatively small-sized (log (SE#) < 6.287, i.e., SE# < 538).

4.5 Conclusions and Future Work

The objectives of this research were to describe the competitive environment in the software industry in Japan and to understand the characteristic differences between manufacturer spin-off vendors, user spin-off vendors and independent vendors in

Fig. 4.3 Boxplot of training hours for software engineers by types of vendors (hours)

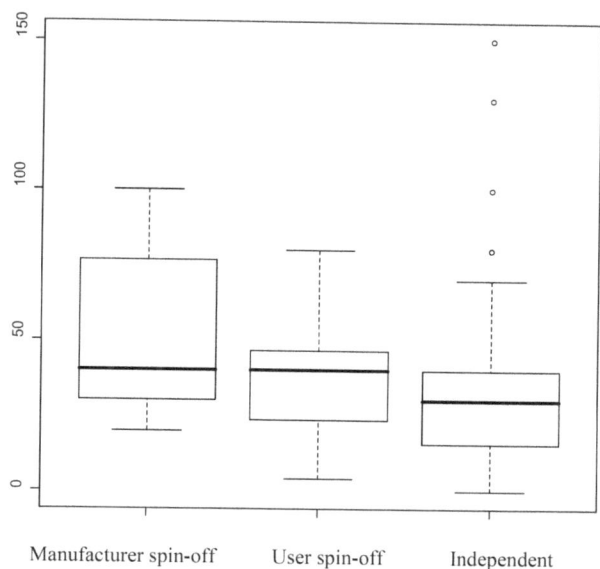

that environment. To do so, we statistically analysed the data collected from 100 major IT vendors in SEE2007.

On the basis of management frameworks such as Porter's five forces and Barney's resource-based view, we developed a model to measure environmental threats and competitiveness, i.e., strengths and weaknesses. We conducted factor analysis of data collected from the 100 IT vendors. We then extracted eight threat factors: industry stagnation, difficulties in recruiting bright people, ROI/quality demands from clients, new entrants, price cutting/quick delivery demands from clients, software engineering capability erosion, stagnating IT innovation, and new technology adoption. We also identified six competitive strength/weakness factors: human capital, advantage of scale, expansive business, new client/services development, inimitability, and stability.

The regression tree analysis of threats, strengths/weaknesses, and the number of software engineers suggests that manufacturer spin-off vendors significantly tend to expand business by, e.g., acquisition of new patents, well-resourced R&D, offshore systems development, and offshore client development.

User spin-off vendors seem to depend heavily on demand from the parent company. Therefore, some of them are thought to gain inimitable capabilities, e.g., knowhow on specific functions, and inimitable products/services.

Many independent vendors supply temporary staff to principal contractors and have no specific strengths. However, some independent vendors that have inimitable assets and are not threatened by industry stagnation seem to be a role model for software vendors in Japan.

To expand this research, it is desirable to investigate how vendors can better make use of their unique strengths and protect themselves from revealed weaknesses from the viewpoint of competitive environment. Additionally, in this research we

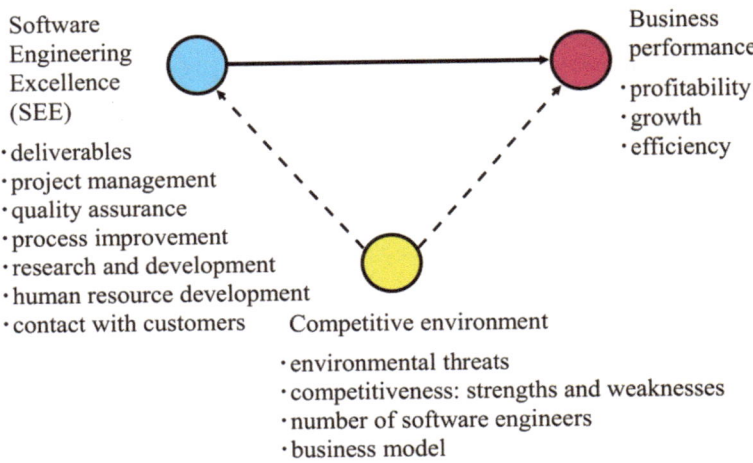

Fig. 4.4 Structural model for a future study

have focused on the competitive environment; analyses of the relationships between software engineering capability (SEE), business performance, and the competitive environment (Fig. 4.4) remain to be done in other chapters.

Finally, to better understand the reality and issues facing the IT industry in the medium- and long-term, we suggest that future studies be carried out as follows:

- further refinement of the measurement model and analysis;
- data collection from a wider range of IT vendors;
- global benchmarking, e.g., China, India, and the U.S.; and
- time series analysis.

References

Arthur, W. B. (1989). Competing technologies, increasing returns, and lock-in historical events. *Economic Journal, 99,* 116–131.

Barney, J. B. (2007). *Gaining and sustaining competitive advantage.* New Jersey: Pearson Prentice Hall.

Barney, J. B. (1986). Organizational culture: Can it be a source of sustained competitive advantage? *Academy of Management Review, 11,* 656–665

Besanko, D., Dranove, D., Shanley, M., & Schaefer, S. (2007). *Economics of starategy.* New York: Willey.

Carnegie Mellon University. (2014). Software Engineering Institute. http://www.sei.cmu.edu/cmmi/

Cusumano, M. (2004). *The business of software.* New York: Free Press.

Dierickx, I., & Cool, K. (1989). Asset stock accumulation and sustainability of competitive advantage. *Management Science, 35*(12), 1504–1511 (Winter).

Dodgson, M., Gann, D., & Salter, A. (2008). The management of technological innovation. Oxford University Press.

Fujimoto, T. (2003). *Nouryoku Kouchiku Kyousou*. Tokyo: Chuohkouronshinsya.

IEEE Computer Society. (2004). *SWEBOK 2004*.

ISO. (2010). ISO/IEC/IEEE 24765:2010 Systems and software engineering–Vocabulary.

Japan Information Technology Service Industry Association (JISA). (2014). Research on IT human resources and training measures for globalization. http://itjobgate.jisa.or.jp/world/index.html. Accessed 14 Aug 2014.

Kadono, Y. (2004). *Evolution of IT management creating business value*. Tokyo: Nikkagiren.

Kadono, Y. (2007). "The Issues on IT Industry in Japan," *Nikkei Net*. http://it.nikkei.co.jp/business/news/index.aspx?n=MMITac000017122007.

Kadono, Y., Tsubaki, H., & Tsuruho, S. (2009). A study on characteristics of software vendors in Japan: From environmental threats and resource-based view. Proc., the 13th Pacific Asia Conference on Information Systems.

Kadono, Y. (2013). The differences in structural relationships among software engineering capabilities and business performance depending on origin of IT firm in Japan. *International Journal of Innovation and Learning, 14*(3/4), 308–328.

Kimura, T. (2014). The forty five evils brought by man-moth based business, and multilayer subcontractors in IT industry. *Nikkei Computer*.

Lippman, S., & Rumelt, R. (1982). Uncertain imitability: An analysis of interfirm differences in efficiency under competition. *Bell Journal of Economics, 13*, 418–438.

McKinsey & Company, Bughin, J., Chui, M., & Manyika, J. (2013). Ten IT-enabled business trends for the decade ahead. *McKinsey Quarterly*.

Ministry of Economy, Trade and Industry. (2008). Report on software industry.

Ministry of Economy, Trade and Industry, & Information-Technology Promotion Agency, Japan (METI & IPA). (2007). *Fact-finding investigation on software engineering capabilities of enterprise systems in Japan*. (The responsibility for the investigation lies with Yasuo Kadono). sec.ipa.go.jp/reports/20071204/SE_level_research_2006_2.pdf. Accessed 14 Aug 2014.

Ministry of Economy, Trade, and Industry (METI). (2014). *Current survey on selected service industries: Information service industry*.

Ministry of Internal Affairs and Communications (MIC). (2014). White Paper: The Information and Communications in Japan. http://itpro.nikkeibp.co.jp/atcl/watcher/14/334361/072100007/?ST=ittrend&P=1. Accessed 14 Aug 2014.

Mongomery, C. A., & Wernerfelt, B. (1991). Source of superior performance: Market share versus industry effects in the U.S. brewing industry. *Management Science, 37*, 954–959.

Penrose, E. T. (1959). *The theory of the growth of the firm*. New York: Wiley.

Porter, M. (1980). *Competitive strategy*. New York: Free Press.

Porter, M. (1985). *Competitive advantage*. New York: Free Press.

Prahalad, C. K., & Hamel, G. (1990). *The core competence of the corporation*. Harvard Business Review.

SAP. (2014). Invester relations. http://www.sap.com/corporate-en/about/investors.html. Accessed 14 Aug 2014.

Selznick, P. (1957). *Leadership in administration*. NewYork: Harper & Row.

Chapter 5
IT Management Effectiveness: An Empirical Study in Japanese Companies

Abstract The purpose of this study is to clarify the mechanism of how information technology (IT) creates business value, particularly from the viewpoint of IT management in individual companies. To do this, we developed a hypothetical structural model that consists of six performance indicators, namely: awareness and actions of top management, linkage between management and IT, IT development capability, IT investment and deployment, IT readiness, and business value creation from IT. Based on analyses of data collected from 509 major companies comprising various types of business in Japan, we found that awareness and actions of top management lead to business value creation from IT via other intermediate factors, such as linkage between management and IT, etc. Based on the structural model, we propose a framework called "IT management effectiveness", by which the overall effectiveness of IT management is measurable.

Keywords Social research · Performance measures · IT management · Corporate management · Empirical study · Covariance analysis · Size factor

5.1 Introduction

Although the IT revolution shifted into full gear around 2000, many Japanese managements were not fully convinced that IT was a powerful management tool, partly because the relationship between IT and its business value had not been sufficiently analyzed or evaluated on a data basis. We therefore conducted an empirical study on representative Japanese companies to measure "IT management effectiveness", a framework which reflects both management and IT viewpoints and measures the performance of IT in business management, extending through all levels from management to operations. This measurement framework also contributes to clarifying the mechanism of how IT management is effective in the creation of business value through IT.

Several studies had already been conducted on the relationship between business organization and business value creation from IT; these included studies on a direct comparison between IT investments and business value (Strassman 1990; Tam 1998); strategic alignment based on IT (Earl 1996; Henderson et al. 1993);

© Springer Japan 2015
Y. Kadono, *Management of Software Engineering Innovation in Japan,*
DOI 10.1007/978-4-431-55612-1_5

information economics (Parker and Benson 1988); the relationship between organization and IT (Bensaou and Earl 1998; Orlikowski and Hofman 1997); and others (Porter 1980; Shapiro and Varian 1998; Sproull and Kiesler 1993; U.S.A. Department of Commerce 2000; Kohili and Grover 2008). However, not many studies had investigated the links between top management's awareness of IT, IT investment and deployment, and business value creation from IT. Moreover, very few studies had quantitatively analyzed business value with a main focus on the linkage between management and IT (Brynjolfsson and Hitt 1998). Particularly in Japan, it was not practical to rely on past studies, as the amount of data available was insufficient to analyze the differences broken down according to the size and business category of companies.

For this study, "IT management effectiveness" is defined as a set of organizational activities aimed at effectively utilizing IT as a management tool. Its measurement framework is composed of four layers with different degrees of abstractness. The measurement method is based on statistical methods such as factor analysis and principal component analysis, which are used to summarize the information obtained from the lower layers.

Through our interviews with the top managements of companies in Japan as well as in the U.S. over a period of more than 10 years, we have developed the following hypotheses: top management's awareness of and actions relating to IT influence the overall operational activities using IT in a company; and those activities result in the creation of business value from IT. In the next section, we discuss these hypotheses from the viewpoint of linkage between management and IT. To confirm these hypotheses, we identify the following six major performance indicators in this Chapter:

1) Top management's awareness of and actions relating to IT
2) Linkage between management and IT
3) IT development capability
4) IT investment and deployment
5) IT readiness,
6) Business value creation from IT.

We analyze the data gathered in this research to verify the hypotheses on the causal structures of the six indicators to obtain a comprehensive framework with which to evaluate the overall relationship between IT and management.

Finally, we derive "IT management effectiveness" as an overall performance indicator based on the six primary indicators by applying principal component analysis to identify companies that have successfully established effective linkage between their businesses and IT. The overall performance measurement is evaluated by an appropriate weighted average of management, operation, and performance indicators, since the sustainable competitiveness of a company is dependent on the management and operation levels rather than the bottom-line performance in the short term. Such consensus is attained in several performance investigations of companies, including the self-measurement system for the Malcom Baldrige National Quality Award developed by the National Institute of Standards and Technology (NIST)in the U.S.

We also utilize the 2nd principal component analysis to distinguish between "IT management styles" , since in the real business world, we often observe some companies successfully investing in IT initiatives in an infrastructure-led fashion, whereas other companies effectively invest in IT in an application-led way. Finally, we rank 509 Japanese companies by applying the proposed "IT management effectiveness" framework and discuss the current situation of IT in Japan.

In the next section, we introduce the structural and measurement models to clarify our hypotheses, and explain the outline of the survey. In Sect. 5.3, we explain the derivation of the primary indicators and the confirmation of the structural model, including the measurement process of the indicators, the measurement of the primary indicators, and the results of testing hypotheses on the structural model. In Sect. 5.4, we construct the overall performance measures such as the "IT management effectiveness" framework. In Sect. 5.5, we discuss the results of the survey, conclusions, and future work.

5.2   Research Methods

In this section, we describe our structural model and the hypotheses with the measurement models; we also explain data collected for this research from previous research on IT management effectiveness.

5.2.1   Structural Model and Hypotheses

To carry out our research, we referred to several previous studies on the relationship between business organization and business value creation through the use of IT. For example, the strategic alignment of IT (Earl 1996; Henderson et al. 1993) gave us suggestions on the management level-operational level adoption axis as well as on business-IT. Also, information economics (Parker and Benson 1988) showed us the importance of the output levels of both IT and business performance.

Based on these previous studies, Fig. 5.1 shows the relationship between business and IT, based on the six major performance indicators.

The horizontal axis of Fig. 5.1 represents two decision-making domains: business and IT. The vertical axis represents three decision-making levels: management, operation, and performance i.e., output. The area enclosed by these two axes represents organizations or divisions that correspond to domains and levels of decision-making. Here, they correspond to Chief Executive Officer (CEO), Chief Information Officer (CIO), user divisions, and IT divisions. "Top management's awareness and actions on IT" means the extent to which the top management participates in IT adoption. "Linkage between management and IT" means the overall linkage between the above-stated four organizations/divisions, including user divisions. "IT development capability" means the development skills of the IT division. "IT

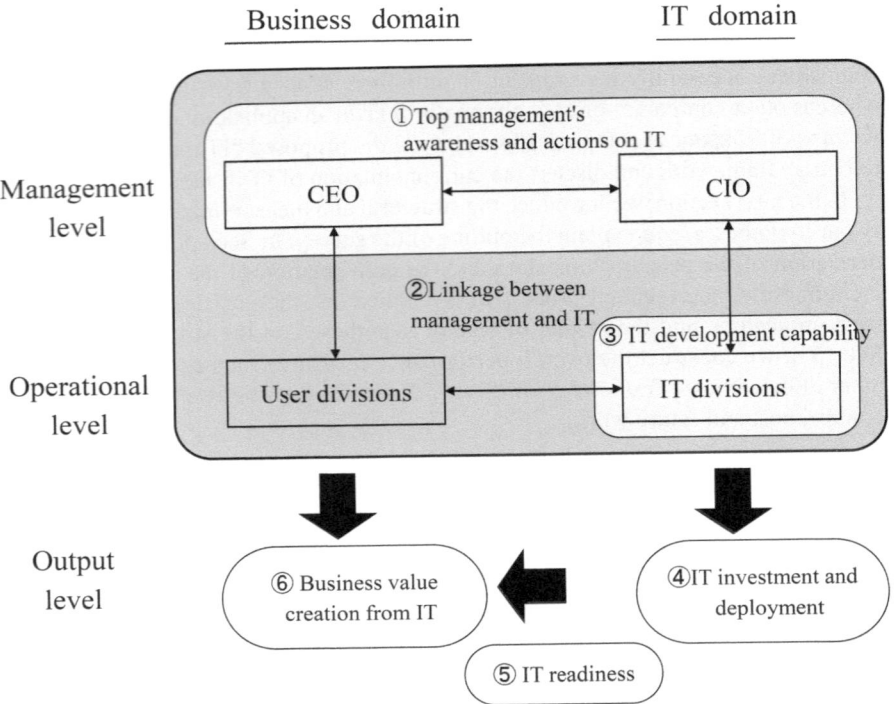

Fig. 5.1 Relationships between business and IT

investment and deployment" means IT outputs, such as the situation of IT infrastructure and IT investments. "Business value creation from IT" means a management output, namely, business value created from IT. "IT readiness" means the possibility that "IT investment and deployment" can effectively create business value. As described above, we have defined the six performance indicators to compose "IT management effectiveness" in a top-down approach.

Moreover, a causal relationship is assumed, as described in Fig. 5.2. Here, the management indicator means "Top management's awareness and actions on IT", operational indicators are "Linkage between management and IT" and "IT development capability", and performance indicators are "IT investment and deployment", "IT readiness", and "Business value creation from IT".

Hypothesis 1 "Top management's awareness and actions on IT", as a management indicator, has a direct impact on the other five indicators (i.e., "Linkage between management and IT", "IT development capability", "IT investment and deployment", "IT management effectiveness", and "IT readiness").

Hypothesis 2 Operational indicators (e.g., "Linkage between management and IT" and "IT development capability") directly affect output indicators (e.g., "IT investment and deployment", "IT management effectiveness", and "IT readiness").

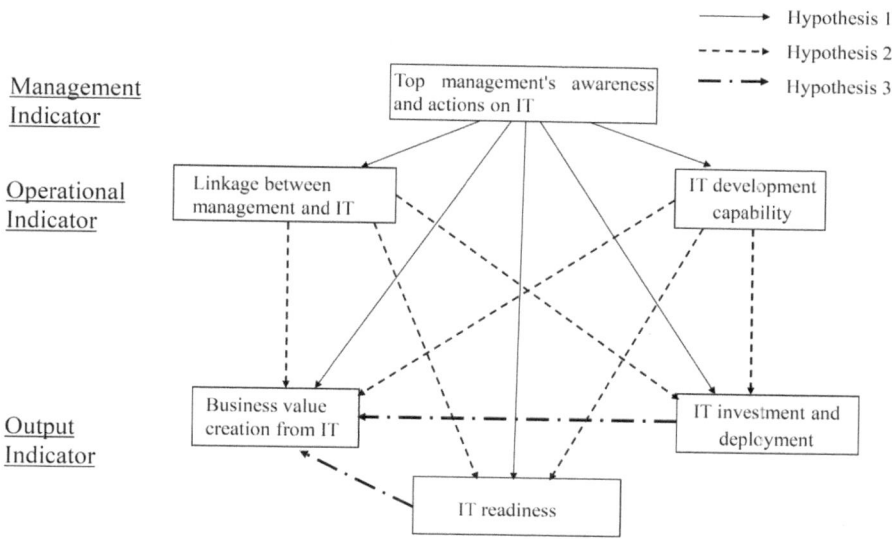

Fig. 5.2 Working hypotheses

Hypothesis 3 Within performance indicators, "IT investment and deployment" and "IT readiness" directly influence "IT management effectiveness".

In the following section, we verify these hypotheses based on the data gathered in this research.

5.2.2   Outline of the Measurement Model

In this subsection, we introduce the measurement model for the indicators introduced in 2.1. Our measurement framework has a hierarchical structure with four layers (Fig. 5.3):

1) observed responses to 495 items in questionnaires related to management, operation, and performance concepts, and basic attributes including the business environment of the investigated organizations;
2) 28 detailed concepts to evaluate the level of management, operation, and performance of organizations, which aggregate observed responses to related items by fitting mostly confirmatory one-factor models;
3) six primary indicators, namely, "Top management's awareness and actions on IT", "Linkage between management and IT", "IT development capability", "IT investment and deployment", "IT readiness", and "Business value creation from IT", which aggregate factor scores of the related detailed concepts by fitting confirmatory one-factor models (details will be described in Sect. 5.3);

Overall Evaluation	Primary Indicator	Detailed Concept	Question Item

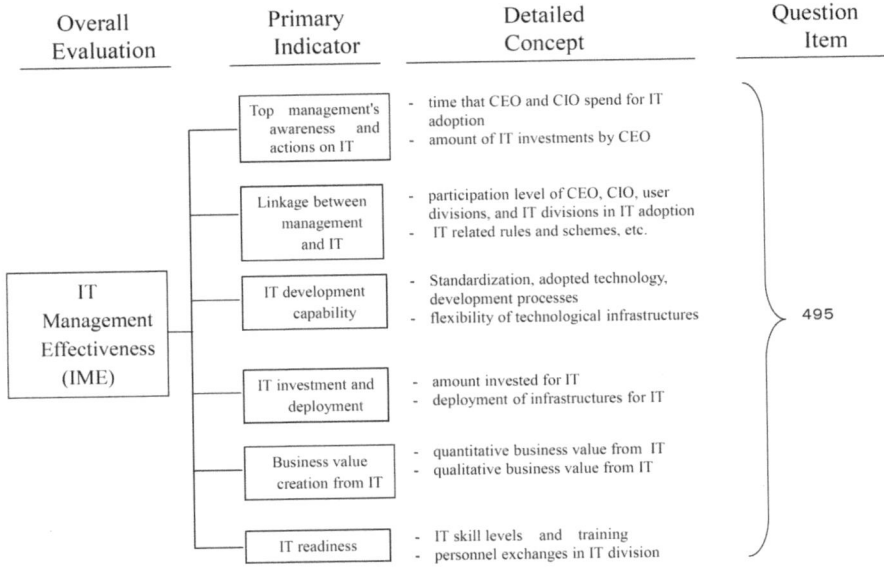

Fig. 5.3 Measurement model: hierarchical structure with four layers

4) two overall performance measures to evaluate "IT management effectiveness" and to characterize "IT management style", which aggregate the primary indicators statistically by principal component analysis (details will be given in Sect. 5.4).

In the above series of measurement procedures, the construction of the six primary indicators from the 28 detailed concepts is particularly important since these six primary indicators are directly related to the main objective of our research; therefore, we describe the detailed concepts that characterize the six primary indicators concretely as follows:

1. "Top management's awareness and actions on IT"

   – Amount of time that CEO and CIO spend on IT adoption
   – Amount of IT investment that CEO can make at his/her discretion
   – Authority of CIO
   – Gaps in IT awareness among top management, etc.

2. "Linkage between management and IT"

   – Participation levels of CEO, CIO, user divisions, and IT divisions in IT adoption
   – IT strategy as a common language
   – IT-related rules and schemes shared among divisions (such as investment verification and user satisfaction), etc.

3. "IT development capability"
  − Standardization of adopted technologies
  − Standardization of development processes and infrastructures
  − Flexibility of technological infrastructures
  − Compliance with delivery period and budget, etc.

4. "IT investment and deployment"
  − Amount invested in IT
  − Deployment of infrastructures for IT and Electronic Commerce (EC), etc.

5. "IT readiness"
  − IT skill levels
  − Training
  − Personnel exchanges in IT division
  − Capability to adapt to strategic changes, etc.

6. "Business value creation from IT"
  − Quantitative business value created from IT (such as speeding-up of business processes and cost savings)
  − Qualitative business value created from IT (such as improved customer services)
  − Innovation in business processes or business models through IT
  − Effectiveness of packaged software, etc.

5.2.3   Outline of the Survey

The first IT management level investigation was planned based on the measurement and structural framework introduced in the previous subsections, and was executed in 2000. In this subsection, we outline the survey and the characteristics of the data.

We invited 3068 Japanese companies to respond to a questionnaire survey. First, from the database of a major credit agency, we selected 3007 companies based on the criteria that the number of employees was more than 500 and the sales revenue was more than 30 billion yen (for the nearest ended year as of April 2000). Then, we deliberately selected and added a further 61 advanced IT-related companies that frequently appeared in IT-related magazines from 1997 through 1999.

The questionnaires were sent to the public relations department of each company and distributed to the CEO, CIO, IT planning department, and IT development department.

Valid responses were obtained from 509 companies (17%). Table 5.1 shows the distribution of the responding companies by industry and size (head count), which clarified that the data were sufficient for appropriate stratified analyses (Kadono 2004).

Table 5.1 Distribution of the responding companies by industry and size (head count)

Industry	Headcount					Total by industry
	Less than 500	500–999	1000–1999	2000–4999	5000 and over	
Construction companies	0	10	16	8	6	40
Drink, food, and feed manufacturers	0	6	5	12	3	26
Chemical manufacturers	0	8	7	15	7	37
Electronic and electrical manufacturers	1	5	13	13	17	49
Machines and transportation manufacturers	0	12	17	9	13	51
Other manufacturers	2	13	13	19	14	61
Wholesalers	0	21	20	8	4	53
Retailers	0	26	15	6	7	54
Banking	0	20	15	4	2	41
Insurance, other financial institutions	2	5	3	6	8	24
Services industries	1	11	17	17	12	58
Others	0	3	10	1	1	15
Total by head count	6	140	151	118	94	509

5.3   Derivation of Primary Indicators and Confirmation of Structural Model

In this section, we confirm the hypotheses on the structural model of the six primary indicators shown in Fig. 5.2 by using covariance structure analyses as the path analysis or graphical modeling after the measurement of the six indicators by estimating the factor or principal component scores corresponding to the detailed concepts.

5.3.1   Process of Measuring Indicators

Scoring Detailed Concepts

Our survey was designed to present at least three questionnaire items aimed at estimating each detailed concept level; therefore, in principle, we could estimate a concept by fitting a confirmatory factor model using the maximum likelihood estimation procedure. However, some concepts were measured as principal component scores of only two questionnaire items or standardized variables of a single questionnaire item, since we excluded some items whose factor loading was too small and could not be considered as an appropriate attribute related to the corresponding detailed concept.

Further, to review the content validity of the detailed concepts after the exclusion of the items, we modified a few original concepts by splitting them into two or three more detailed concepts, by accounting for the results of exploratory factor analyses through the use of promax rotation. For example, concerning the management concept "Time that CEO spends on IT adoption", one question item to the CEO and two question items for the IT planning department were used to measure the concept, and their factor loadings were 0.489, 0.513 and 0.943, respectively. Although the last item might be too heavily weighted, all the loadings were more than 0.4; therefore, the content validity was satisfied and the last item was considered to be a variable criterion for the corresponding concept. Then we adopted the factor score obtained as a measurement result of the detailed concept, which aggregates the management level evaluation of both the CEO and the others. As a result, the obtained level was a function of cross-check among the management into account.

Measurement of the Primary Indicators
We selected the potential composition concepts of each primary indicator exclusively from among the detailed concepts to satisfy content validity, which we verified from previous research or by interviews with top management, etc. We then fitted the corresponding one-factor model to check the internal validity of the measurement by checking the sign condition on the factor loadings as shown in Table 5.2, the goodness of fit, and Cronbach's reliability coefficient. As a result, we deleted the concept, "Time that CIO spends on IT adoption" from the measurement attributes of the indicator "Top management's awareness and actions on IT". Thus, the six primary indicators were estimated as the standardized factor scores of the final one-factor model after the internal validity check. All the distributions of the estimated indicators were unimodal and not extremely skewed, making them applicable to our structural modeling (Fig. 5.4). Prior to testing the hypotheses presented in section 2, above, we calculated the correlations among the six indicators, and the results are shown in Table 5.3. It should be noted that "Business value creation from IT" as a performance criterion indicator is significantly strongly correlated to the other management, operation and performance indicators, aside from the several other strong correlations between the indicators.

We should note here that we have non-parametrically imputed the estimates of the missing concepts with second nearest neighborhood averaging in order to obtain all indicators from all responders (Kadono and Tsubaki 2002).

5.3.2 Results of Hypotheses Testing for the Structural Model

We fitted a path model for the six estimated indicators corresponding to Fig. 5.2 to test the structural hypotheses introduced in Sect. 5.2 by checking the statistical significance of the corresponding path coefficients. The results are as follows:

Table 5.2 Measurement results of primary indicators from detailed concepts

Primary indicator	Detailed concept	Factor loading
Top management's awareness and actions on IT	CEO'S awareness on IT	0.51
	CEO's time	0.52
	CEO's involvement in discussion on IT	0.69
	CEO's commitment on IT investment	0.46
	CIO's involvement in discussion on IT	0.55
Linkage between management and IT	IT strategy as a common language	0.62
	Participation level of business and IT	0.73
	Codification of IT investment policy	0.49
	Standard procedure before IT development	0.9
	Standard procedure after IT development	0.48
IT development capability	Completion of IT planned	0.17
	Standardization of technologies	0.26
	Standardization of methodologies	0.99
IT investment and deployment	IT deployment	0.81
	EC deployment	0.87
	IT investment	0.2
IT readiness	IT relating training	0.59
	Business literacy training	0.5
	Research on new technologies and cases	0.58
	Carrier path in IT division	0.43
	Motivation in IT division	0.45
	Flexibility in IT infrastructure	0.47
Business value creation from IT	Qualitative business value from IT	0.29
	Business value from EC	0.49
	Business value from packaged software	0.71
	Business value from IT in human resource	0.42
	Satisfaction in IT investment/projects	0.38

Hypothesis 1 is partially confirmed at a 5 % statistically significant level; that is, the management indicator "Top management's awareness and actions on IT", affects not all of the operation and performance indicators but only three of them: "Linkage between management and IT", "Business value creation from IT", and "IT readiness". In other words, the direct effects of the management indicators "IT development capability" and "IT investment and deployment" are not significant at the 5 % level.

Hypothesis 2 on the effect of operation indicators is also partially confirmed: "Linkage between management and IT" directly affects only "IT readiness", while "IT development capability" affects only "Business value creation from IT".

Hypothesis 3 is fully supported by the data; that is, both "IT readiness" and "IT investment and deployment" directly and positively affect "Business value creation from IT". Therefore, it is confirmed that "IT investment and deployment" is useful to create business value.

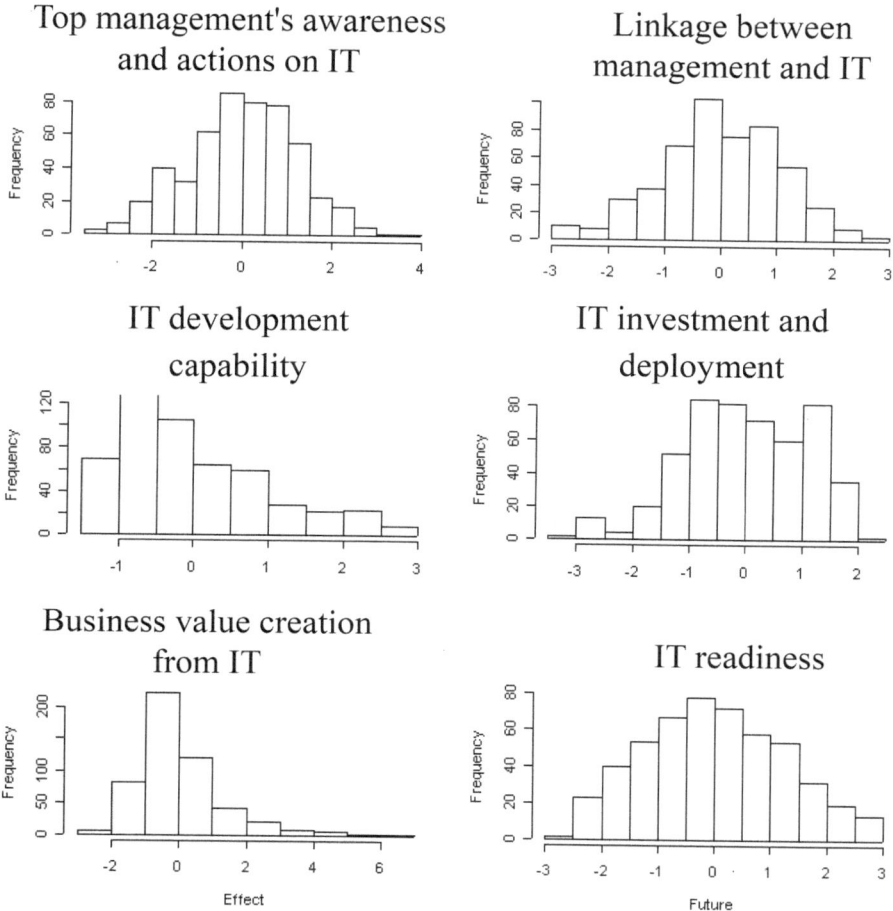

Fig. 5.4 Histograms of the six primary indicators

The goodness of fit of the path model is not so satisfying. Therefore, we explored an appropriate structural model by using graphical modeling to obtain a significant partial correlation structure as shown in Fig. 5.5, where the significant partial correlation relationships between the indicators are indicated by the edges of the graph as follows:

1) From "Top management's awareness and actions on IT" to "Linkage between management and IT";
2) Between the operation indicators "Linkage between management and IT" and "IT development capability";
3) From the operation indicators to "IT readiness";

Table 5.3 Correlation coefficients matrix of the six primary indicators

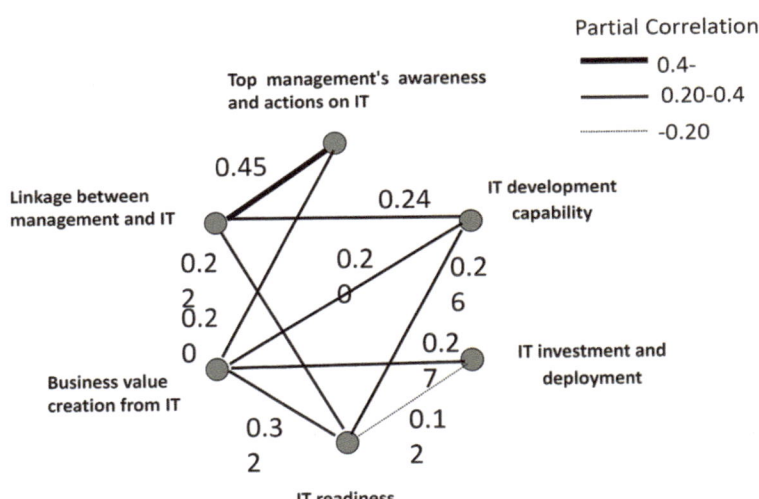

Fig. 5.5 Results of graphical modeling

4) From "IT development capability" to "Business value creation from IT";
5) Among the performance indicators, "IT readiness" and "IT investment and deployment" affect "Business value creation from IT".

Based on hypothesis testing and additional findings by graphical modeling, we reconstructed a well-fitted path model (*p*-value of the goodness of fit=0.243,

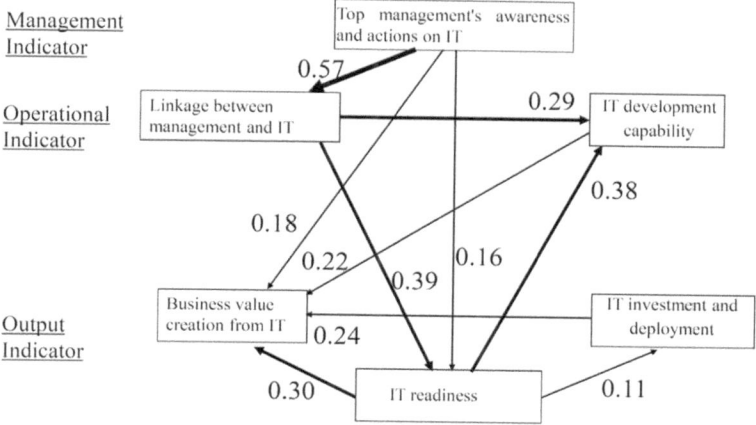

Fig. 5.6 Results of hypotheses testing on the structural model. *p*-value=0.243, GFI=0.996, AGFI=0.982

GFI=0.996, and AGFI=0.982) as shown in Fig. 5.6, all the existing path coefficients of which are positive and significant (Kadono and Tsubaki 2002).

This modified model encourages the expectation that the following new hypotheses will prove significant, although final confirmation can be realized only by accumulating more data:

- "IT readiness" can be considered to be partially an operation indicator that will directly affect both "IT development capability" and "IT investment and deployment". This is reasonable because an element of "IT readiness", i.e. "IT training", is considered to be a mid/long-term investment that is expected to affect "IT development capability".
- There will be a significant relationship between the operation indicators; that is, "IT development capability" will also be directly affected by "Linkage between management and IT".
- Finally, we can expect that "Top management's awareness and actions", "Linkage between management and IT", and "IT readiness" will each indirectly affect "Business value creation from IT" through improvement in "IT development capability" and other performance indicators.

5.3.3   Conclusions of the Analyses

In this section, we have clarified the mechanism or series of causal relationships for creating business value from IT, as shown in Fig. 5.6 (Bollen 1989; Kadono and Tsubaki 2002). "Top management's awareness and actions on IT" has a positive effect on the operation system, as measured by "Linkage between management and IT", "IT development capability", and "IT readiness"; therefore, business value is created from IT through "IT investment and deployment".

5.4   Derivation of Overall Performance Measures

As was introduced in Sects. 5.1 and 5.3, we calculated the overall performance criteria based on the six primary indicators simply by applying principal component analysis to identify the overall performance level and approaches of the IT management; we did so since we recognize that such overall performance measures will be useful to identify enterprises that will successfully establish an effective linkage between the business and IT. We should also point out that because there are so many different approaches to IT management, it is also useful to develop a measure of the types of approach.

An overall performance measure should not itself be a current performance indicator or even an appropriate weighted average of such performance indicators; it should, however, be an appropriate weighted average of the management, operation and performance indicators, since the sustainable development of an enterprise is ensured by the management and operation levels rather than by the real observed performance in the short term.

This has been proven in several performance investigations of enterprises, including the self-measurement system for the Malcom Baldrige National Quality Award developed by the National Institute of Standards and Technology (NIST) in the U.S. in 1987; Malcolm Baldrige served as Secretary of Commerce, and his managerial excellence contributed to long-term improvement in efficiency and effectiveness of government (NIST 2014). The Award Program, responsive to the purposes of Public Law 100–107, i.e., quality improvement of product and process, led to the creation of a new public-private partnership.

In Japan, Nihon Keizai Shimbun's NICES is a private-sector multi-evaluation system to pursue the image of an excellent company from the viewpoint of an investor, consumer, business partner, employee, society, and of its potential; it includes responses to questionnaires and public financial data (Nihon Keizai Shimbun 2013). NICES conducts a large-scale survey of over 500 companies and performs a statistical analysis, such as using a structural equation model (Bollen 1989), to evaluate the priorities of the respondents.

However, we should verify the criterion validity of a derived overall performance measure by checking whether the correlations between primary performance indicators and the derived overall measure are higher than those between other indicators and the derived measure.

In order to construct such a measure, we could subjectively determine the weights of the indicators to attain the content validity as adopted in the Malcom Baldrige National Quality Award; however, in this research, as the initial step, we simply apply principal component analysis to the six primary indicators. The proportion of total variation explained by the first principal component is 50%; and all the principal component loadings, which are equal to the correlation between the principal component score and the indicators, are positive. Thus, the first principal component is interpreted as a size factor to most effectively differentiate between the performances of enterprises; it has a content validity for overall measures and also a criterion validity, in that the principal component loadings on "Business value creation from IT" and "IT readiness, " which are typical performance measures, are the highest and the second highest, respectively. Therefore, the derived first principal component can be regarded as an overall performance measure called "IT management effectiveness."

The proportion of total variation explained by the second principal component is 16%; it is interpreted not as an overall measure but as a measure of "IT management style", since the loading on "IT investment and deployment" is positive, the loadings on the management and operation indicators are negative, and those on the other performance indicators are nearly equal to zero. Thus the second principal component tends to be negative in the case that a company takes a management-oriented approach in IT adoption.

Figure 5.7 is Gauer's Bi-plot representation, which summarizes our principal component analysis. The horizontal axis indicates "IT management effectiveness" (the first principal component) while the vertical axis indicates "IT management style" (the second principal component).

A company is mapped as a point at the coordinate values of the principal component scores. The scales on the left and the bottom correspond to principal component scores where the mean value is 0, and the standard deviations are standardized to the corresponding eigenvalues. The arrows from the origin indicate the directions of the eigenvectors. The length of the vectors represents the magnitude of influence. The cosine of the angle between two vectors approximately represents the correlation between the two criteria, and a smaller angle indicates a stronger correlation.

On the horizontal axis, companies ranking higher in "IT management effectiveness" are placed towards the right, while companies ranking lower are placed to-

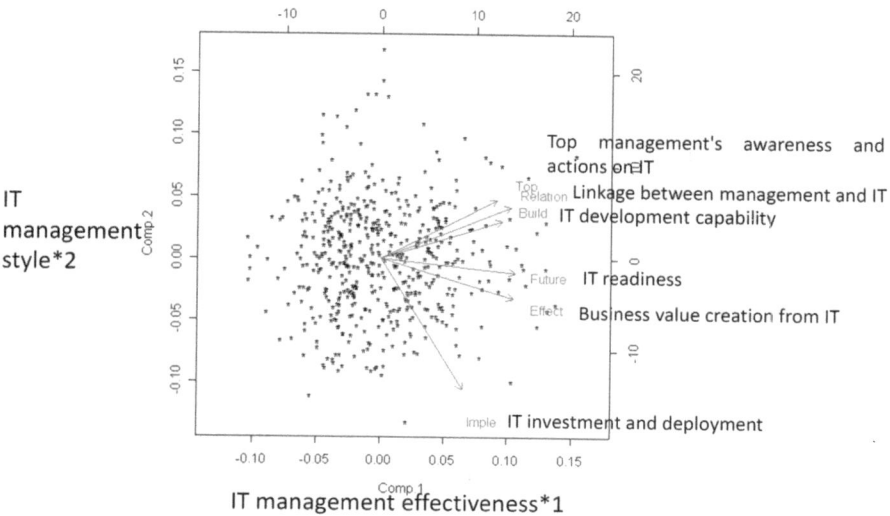

Fig. 5.7 Bi-plot mapping of overall performance measures. *1 the proportion of total variation explained by first principal component is 50 %, *2 the proportion of total variation explained by second principal component is 16 %

wards the left. From the viewpoint of "IT management style", which is indicated on the vertical axis, the companies on the upper side tend to attach importance to "IT investment and deployment". By contrast, the companies on the lower side tend to attach importance to "IT adoption scheme" from management to IT development, such as "Top management's awareness and actions on IT", "Linkage between management and IT", and "IT development capability".

By splitting the map into four quadrants (two in horizontal and two in vertical), the companies are characterized into the following four types:

- Type A (lower right quadrant): high "IT management effectiveness"; attaches importance to "IT investment and deployment";
- Type B (upper right quadrant): high "IT management effectiveness"; attaches importance to "IT adoption scheme";
- Type C (upper left quadrant): low "IT management effectiveness"; attaches importance to "IT adoption scheme"; and
- Type D (lower left quadrant): low "IT management effectiveness"; attaches importance to "IT investment and deployment".

These classifications indicate that a company needs to enhance "IT management effectiveness" by selecting an "IT management style" suitable for it.

5.5   Conclusions and Future Work

We have discussed "IT management effectiveness", which aims at clarifying the mechanism of how IT creates business value from the viewpoint of management and IT. To do this, first, we developed a hypothetical structural model that consists of six performance indicators, namely, "Awareness and actions of top management", "Linkage between management and IT", "IT development capability", "IT investment and deployment", "IT readiness", and "Business value creation from IT". Based on analysis of data collected from 509 major companies comprising various types of businesses in Japan, we found that the awareness and actions of top management lead to business value creation from IT via other intermediate factors, such as "Linkage between management and IT", etc. Based on the structural model, we propose a framework called "IT management effectiveness", which is an instrument to measure the overall effectiveness of IT management.

Through this study, we found that the leadership of top management is one of the most critical issues in large traditional Japanese companies that need to adopt next-generation business models in the Internet era. Some companies require decision and leadership to constructively scrap existing business models; they also require creative thinking and decisions on strategy, to improve their chances to survive and prosper. The CEO is the person who makes such strategic decisions. We consider, therefore, that the role of the CIO, who supports the CEO from the viewpoint of IT as well as business, will become increasingly important in the coming era.

However, based on the results of this research, we found that most CIOs in Japan are not necessarily sufficiently experienced in both business and IT.

Based on the above observations, we would like to extend our research to include the following future endeavors:

- detailed analysis of the cause-effect relation between concept levels,
- comparison of the profiles of companies, e.g., industries and sizes of companies,
- comparison with overseas companies, and
- evaluation of time-series data.

In particular, in our analysis of the cause-effect relationship, we will focus on the structure between the concepts of companies that successfully achieve "Business value creation from IT". To do this, we must identify more concepts, such as the business environment and the attributes of the CIO, in addition to the 28 concepts that were identified herein.

References

Bensaou, M., & Earl, M. (1998). The right mind-set for managing information technology. *Harvard Business Review, 76*(5), 118–128.

Bollen, K. (1989). *Structural equation with latent variables*. New York: Wiley-Interscience Publication.

Brynjolfsson, E., & Hitt, L. (1998). Beyond the productivity paradox: Computers are the catalyst for bigger changes. *Communications of the ACM, 41*(8), 49–55.

Earl, M. J. (1996). Integrating IS and the organization: A framework of organizational fit. In M. J. Earl (Ed.), *Information management*. New York: Oxford University Press.

Henderson, J. C., Venkatraman, N., & Oldach, S. (1993). Continuous strategic alignment. *European Management Journal, 11*(2), 193–149.

Kadono, Y., & Tsubaki, H. (2002). How IT create business value. Proceedings of Pacific Asia Conference on Information Systems (PACIS).

Kadono, Y. (2004). *Evolution of IT management creating business value*. Tokyo: Nikkagiren.

Kohili, R., & Grover, V. (2008). Business value of IT: An essay on research directions to keep up with the times. *Journal of the Association for Information Systems, 9*(1), 23–39.

National Institute of Standards and Technology (NIST). (2014). Malcom Baldrige National Quality Award. http://www.nist.gov/baldrige/about/improvement_act.cfm. Accessed 14 Aug 2014.

Orlikowski, W., & Hofman, J. D. (winter 1997). An improvisational model for change management: the case of group technologies. *Sloan Management Review*.

Parker, M. M., & Benson, R. J. (1988). *Information economics: Linking business performance to information technology*. New Jersey: Prentice Hall.

Porter, M. E. (1980). *Competitive strategy*. New York: Free Press.

Shapiro, C., & Varian, H. (1998). *Information rules*. Boston, MA: Harvard Business Publishing.

Nihon Keizai Shimbun. (2013). NICES. http://www.nikkei-r.co.jp/domestic/management/nices/. Accessed 14 Aug 2014.

Sproull, L., & Kiesler, S. (1993). *Connections: New ways of working in the networked organization*. Cambridge, MA: MIT Press.

Strassman, P. (1990). *Business value of computers*. Information Economic Press.

Tam, K. Y. (1998). The impact of information technology investments on firm performance and evaluation: Evidence from newly industrialized economies. *Information Systems Research, 9*(1), 58–98.

U.S.A. Department of Commerce. (2000). *The emerging digital economy*.

Chapter 6
Social Research on IT Management Innovation Towards Service Science and Science for Society

Abstract The stakeholders in IT management of enterprise systems include not only the demand side, i.e., IT user companies, but also the supply side, i.e., IT vendors. We attempt to design a new social research scheme including both the demand side and the supply side to accelerate innovation in IT management. To do so, we first analyze the processes and results of the five surveys we have administered, researching into IT management effectiveness on the demand side and Software Engineering Excellence on the supply side. Second, based on service dominant logic, we construct a new social research scheme for IT management innovation that is more dynamic and interactive between IT user companies and IT vendors than traditional social research schemes. One advantage of the new social research scheme is to be able to pursue management sophistication in the use of IT through three stages: Quality, Cost, and Delivery (QCD) assessment, potential growth factor analysis, and benchmarking with world-class cases. Another advantage is to be able to construct an information circulation platform to accumulate information and knowledge on cases of management sophistication in the use of IT.

Furthermore, through a case in the information service industry, we consider the role of science for society in a future-oriented manner that co-creates value beyond the border, i.e., aufheben, between the supply side and the demand side.

Keywords IT management · Enterprise systems · Innovation · Learning · Social research · Service science · Science for society

6.1 Introduction

We started to consider conducting a survey on IT management effectiveness in the middle of the IT revolution in Japan, around 2000, when personal computers and Internet access became widespread and IT startups were emerging. From the viewpoint of macroeconomic statistics, the productivity paradox, to do with the contribution of IT investment to business performance, was almost resolved (Brynjolfsson and Hitt 1998). However, in the reality of corporate management, senior managers of individual firms became increasingly skeptical about the return on IT investment, and from a social point of view it was becoming more urgent to resolve the IT paradox.

© Springer Japan 2015

Y. Kadono, *Management of Software Engineering Innovation in Japan*,
DOI 10.1007/978-4-431-55612-1_6

Fig. 6.1 Stakeholders in IT management

		IT user companies		
		Business	IT	IT vendors
Management		CEO	CIO	
Operation		User divisions	IT divisions	

Therefore, in the survey on IT management effectiveness, we defined IT management as the integrated organizational activities undertaken to effectively manage the use of IT for better business performance.

The stakeholders in enterprise IT systems include not only IT user companies as the demand side but also IT vendors as the supply side. Furthermore, the business environment surrounding IT user companies includes customers, competitors, industrial structure, states, and society as a whole.

Figure 6.1 indicates the stakeholders in IT management. The horizontal axis of Fig. 6.1 represents two decision-making domains of IT user companies: business and IT, besides IT vendors. Besides these stakeholders, we can also imagine policymakers and academia in the horizontal axis. The vertical axis represents two decision-making levels: management and operation. From the viewpoint of user companies, the area enclosed by these two axes represents organizations or divisions that correspond to domains and levels of decision making. Here, they correspond to Chief Executive Officer (CEO), Chief Information Officer (CIO), user divisions, and IT divisions.

The essential issue in enterprise IT management is to answer the question of senior managers, such as the CEO and CIO: How does the company create business value from the use of IT? Many companies in Japan that use enterprise software have not been satisfied with the quality, cost, and productivity of software that IT vendors deliver, or with the speed of delivery. Meanwhile, IT vendors in Japan are facing drastic changes in their business environment, such as technological innovations and new entrants from emerging countries, e.g., China, and India. Also, there are issues that are special to the IT industry in Japan, such as vendors relying on multilayer subcontractors and on business models that depend on supplying custom-made applications for the domestic market.

In general, IT user companies are not monolithic organizations. The user division of an IT user company tends to demand many changes in current IT systems, which do not necessarily bring about a favorable business impact for the company. On the other hand, the IT division of an IT user company tends to focus on discussing the use of new technology. Therefore, the CIO needs to take active responsibility for aligning the business impact and the IT usage of the company.

In order to research into the above-mentioned issues on enterprise IT management, we administered the IT Management Effectiveness (IME) surveys in 2000 and 2002, to gather data from IT user companies' perspective, and the Software Engineering Excellence (SEE) surveys in 2005, 2006, and 2007, to gather data from the IT vendors' perspective, both as shown in Table 6.1 (Kadono 2004; METI and IPA 2007).

Table 6.1 Surveys on IT management from user side and vendor side

Survey	IT Management Effectiveness (IME)		Software Engineering Excellence (SEE)		
Fiscal year	2000	2002	2005	2006	2007
Questionnaires sent	3068	3200	230	537	1000
Valid responses	509	413	55	78	100
Response rate (%)	17	13	24	15	10

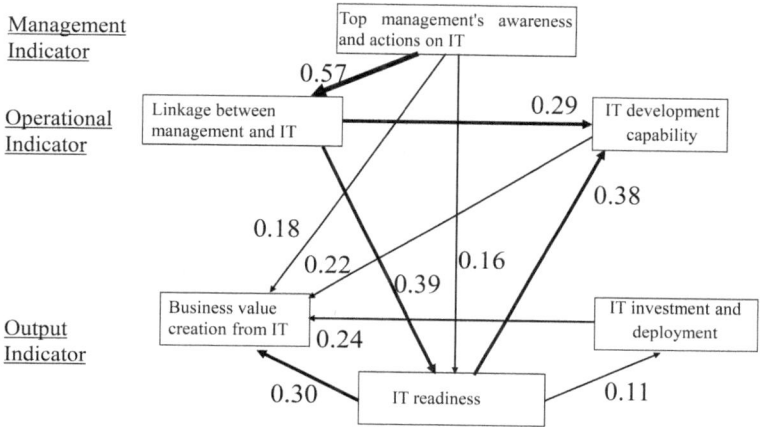

Fig. 6.2 Causal relationships among the *six* factors in the IME study

At that time, from a macroeconomic viewpoint, the positive economic effects resulting from the use of IT in business management had almost been proved, against the opposing view, i.e., the productivity paradox (Brynjolfsson and Hitt 1998). However, in individual companies in Japan, senior managers increasingly became skeptical about the return on IT investment, since enterprise systems were getting larger and more complicated than before.

Through statistical analyses on the data obtained from respondents to the surveys, we arrived at several notable results, as shown in Chaps. 2, 3, and 5.

The purpose of the IME study was to clarify the mechanism of how IT creates business value, particularly from the viewpoint of IT management in IT user companies. To do this, we developed a hypothetical structural model that consists of the six factors, namely, "Top management's awareness of and actions relating to IT", "Linkage between management and IT", "IT development capability", "IT investment and deployment", "IT readiness", and "Business value creation from IT". Based on analysis of the data collected from 509 major companies comprising various types of business in Japan, we found that awareness and actions of top management lead to the creation of business value from IT via other intermediate factors, such as the linkage between management and IT, etc. (Fig. 6.2, AGFI = 0.982). Based on statistical methods, we propose a framework called IT Management Effectiveness (IME), by which to measure the overall effectiveness of IT management (Kadono and Tsubaki 2002).

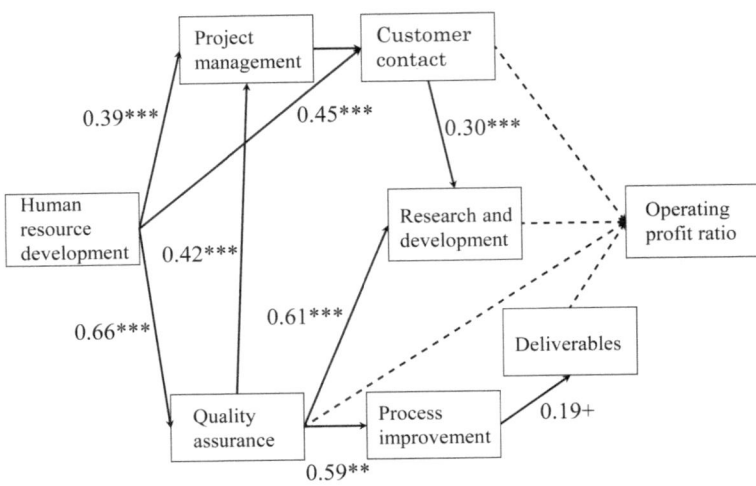

Fig. 6.3 Path analysis results of the SEE survey for 2007. ***$p<0.001$, **$p<0.01$, *$p<0.05$, +$p<0.10$

The purpose of the SEE study was to clarify the mechanism of how software engineering capabilities relate to the business performance of IT vendors in Japan. To do this, we developed a structural model using factors related to software engineering capabilities, business performance and the competitive environment. We then developed the SEE indicator which consists of deliverables, project management, quality assurance, process improvement, research and development, human resource development, and customer contact. By analyzing the data collected in 2006 from 78 major IT vendors in Japan, we found that superior deliverables and business performance were correlated with the effort expended particularly on human resource development, quality assurance, research and development, and process improvement (Kadono 2013).

Additionally, based on the data collected from 100 major IT vendors in the 2007 SEE survey, we constructed a well-fitted path model by a trial and error method, as shown in Fig. 6.3. We reproducibly observed that the level of effort expended on human resource development, quality assurance and project management significantly improved the performance of IT vendors in Japan in customer contact, research and development, process improvement, and deliverables, the same correlation we had found in 2006. By contrast, the paths from customer contact, research and development, quality assurance, and deliverables to operating profit ratio are not significant. Also, we verified that the relationship between software engineering capabilities and business performance varies significantly depending on origin of vendor: manufacturer spin-off, user spin-off or independent (Kadono 2012).

The five surveys on IT management were trial experiments to pursue desirable future-oriented goals for IT management from both viewpoints—the IT user side and the IT vendor side.

If we redefine intellectual activities, whether theoretical or empirical, aimed at *recognition* of phenomena as "recognition science", we can newly define intellectual activities, whether theoretical or empirical, aimed at *creation* and *improvement* of phenomena as "science for society" (Science Council of Japan 2003).

From this perspective, the five surveys fall into the category of science for society, and have the following characteristics.

First, since an aim of the five surveys was to encourage innovation, we surveyed state-of-the-art cases, paying attention to the management of innovation in developing our measurement model. To achieve this aim, we conducted interviews with IT management experts, and conducted literature searches (Barney 2007; Bollen 1989; Carnegie Mellon University 2014; Cusumano 2004; Dodgson et al. 2008; Fujimoto 2003; IEEE 2004; Ministry of Economy, Trade and Industry 2011; Porter 1980). For example, the scope of the survey included the resource-based view, in which we paid attention to factors such as degrees of rarity, and inimitability of management resources (Barney 2007). Also, based on an understanding of service science (Stauss et al. 2008), since project management and customer contact are on the boundary between user and vendor of software, we expanded the SEE questionnaire to include user-side items.

Second, the surveys anticipated innovative consilience among the fields of management, statistics, and simulation, as well as among people in academia, industry, and government.

Third, the surveys were designed to promote continuous learning and, especially, an interaction between overall future goals and individual current realities. This is consistent with the understanding that, once the future-oriented goals of social systems are set, the paths from individual current realities to the overall goals tend to emerge through information circulation between the goals and the current realities. Indeed, we supplied feedback information on rankings and deviation scores to all who responded to the IME surveys, and to some who responded to the SEE surveys; the feedback had a positive impact on the business behavior of individual respondents.

However, the five surveys on IT management focused on either user-side or vendor-side, based on the "goods dominant" logic. Similarly, previous surveys, administered by the Japanese Ministry of Economy, Trade and Industry (METI 2011), the Japan Users Association of Information Systems (JUAS 2011), the Japan Information Technology Services Industry Association (JISA 2011), and other relevant organizations, have focused on either user-side or vendor-side.

For example, JUAS has administered an annual questionnaire survey on IT usage by big business in Japan since 1994. The survey instrument consists of standard questionnaire items every year, addressing IT budgets, return on investment in IT, IT organization, IT staff, and systems development, etc. Beyond these standard items, new questionnaire items are sometimes added to address emerging issues such as information security, and credibility assessment of IT systems. However, the survey focuses only on the user's viewpoint, and it could be regarded as a serious deficiency that it pays no attention to the vendor's viewpoint.

By contrast, since 1999, JISA has published an annual white paper on the information services industry. The white paper focuses only on the vendor's viewpoint, paying attention to IT market growth, technological trends, and skill trends, etc.

However, in an IT project, the achievement of an optimal level of quality, cost, and delivery (QCD) is a goal shared by both IT user companies and IT vendors in common. In the present Chapter, therefore, based on the "service dominant" logic (Vargo and Lusch 2006) of service science (Stauss et al. 2008)and science for society, we have focused on the connection points between user-side and vendor-side, and designed a social research scheme to examine improved sophistication in IT management from both user-side and vendor-side simultaneously.

In this Chapter we use a case study method as a bridge between user-side and vendor-side to elicit a new perspective on improving the sophistication of management; we take up concepts that are equally valid for both user and vendor of software, e.g., QCD achievement, a stationary measurement tool of IT projects on the information circulation platform, a worldwide community of excellence for IT project comparisons, and spill-over effects from the visualization of value-creation mechanisms in the information services towards other industries in the service sector.

6.2 Design of Social Research Scheme for IT Management

Based on the concepts of service science and science for society, we focus on improving the sophistication of services between the demand side, i.e., IT user companies, and the supply side, i.e., IT vendors, simultaneously. In order to do so, we assume that the following three characteristics are crucial: common language, stage of development, and international competitiveness.

First, since deliverables of information services are intangible, we need to identify common language for communication between the IT user company and the IT vendor. Second, since IT services characteristically involve constant innovation and improvement, and constant user problem-solving, the argument about the stage of development is important. Third, since the IT industry is borderless, IT vendors have to cast wide-open eyes on the global market. At the same time, IT vendors should be fully aware of the global competitiveness of the individual industries in which IT user companies are active.

We therefore design a scheme of social research that meets the above three requirements, with a view towards improving the sophistication of services between IT user companies and IT vendors. This scheme aims at the following two objectives from the viewpoint of service science and science for society: (1) to improve management sophistication through the use of IT, and (2) to construct an information circulation platform.

The argument about **IT management sophistication** calls for improvement through three stages as shown in Fig. 6.4: (a) QCD assessment, (b) potential growth factor analysis, and (c) benchmark with world-class cases.

a. The *QCD assessment* means how the IT vendor achieves the levels of quality, cost, and delivery on which the vendor has agreed with the IT user. QCD is one of the most important common languages in IT development between IT user companies and IT vendors. Therefore, the QCD assessment is the starting point

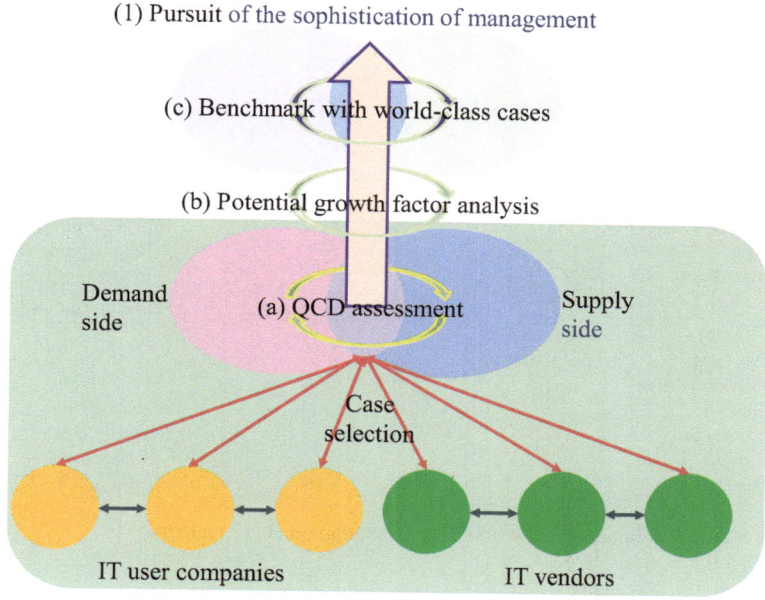

Fig. 6.4 Design of social research scheme on IT management

    from which to discuss improvement in the sophistication of the services between IT user companies and IT vendors.

b. The *potential growth factor analysis* suggests the possibility of improvement in QCD based on the causal relationships empirically confirmed in the IME surveys and the SEE surveys. As shown in the left side of Fig. 6.5, in the IME survey results, top management's awareness of and actions relating to IT, linkage between management and IT, IT investment and deployment, and IT readiness have positive impacts on IT development capability including QCD. At the same time, IT development capability significantly influences business value creation from IT, as shown in Fig. 6.2.

    On the other hand, as shown in the right side of Fig. 6.5, in the SEE survey, human resource development, research and development, project management, customer contact, quality assurance, and process improvement significantly influence deliverables, including QCD. In other words, QCD is the most downstream factor among the core competence factors of IT vendors, as shown in Fig. 6.3. Also, since project management and customer contact are the boundaries between user and vendor of software, we enhanced the question items on these factors, e.g., top management involvement, and quality of user requirement specification, consistent with insights from service science (Stauss et al. 2008).

c. Regarding the *benchmark with world-class cases*, we analyse the gap between the case at hand, as opposed to the most advanced case in the industry, anywhere in the world. We assume that, in the most advanced case worldwide, the use of IT inevitably contributes to a competitive advantage for the user company and is

IT user companies   IT vendors

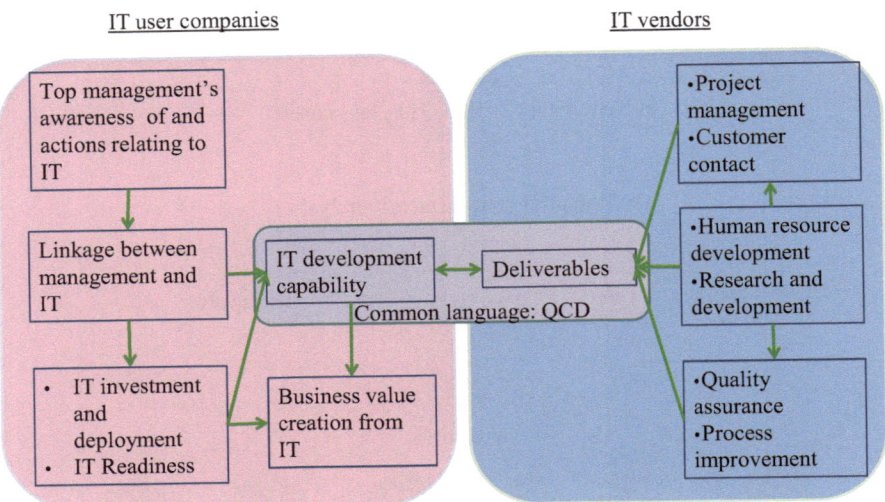

Fig. 6.5 Causal relationships between IT user companies and IT vendors

valid as a benchmark of best practice; and an IT user in any other given case can utilize this benchmark to develop a vision for future progress towards parity with the most advanced case worldwide.

To **construct an information circulation platform**, we accumulate information and understanding on cases that we investigate for objective (1), the process of improving management sophistication through the use of IT, as shown in Fig. 6.4. In other words, information circulation, which occurs within the community of participants in this social research, will result in improved IT management sophistication through the three stages: QCD assessment, potential growth factor analysis, and the benchmark with world-class cases.

6.3 Methods

In the previous surveys on IME and SEE, we investigated through literature searches, statistical methods, and case studies the mechanism of how management and operations of companies influence business performance. In particular, thanks to receiving research support from industry, government, and academia, we conducted interviews with industry experts, administered the large-scale surveys, and performed the statistical analyses.

In the present social research scheme, we adopt a case study approach for the initial round of research, before undertaking a statistical approach.

To achieve objective (1), i.e., to improve management sophistication through the use of IT, first, we choose target projects to be studied in collaboration with industry, government, and academic bodies, such as JUAS, JISA, and METI. As shown in Table 6.2, we adopt approximately ten IT projects, spanning a variety of industries

Table 6.2 List of case studies

| Project case no. | IT user company | | | | IT vendor (counterpart) | | |
	Industry and case	Ranking in the industry	Systems function and adopted technology	Role of IT Division	Business model	Strength	Sub-contractor
1	Electricity	Dominant	Accounting ERP[a]	Plan	System integrator	Management	Yes
2	Construction	Top 5	Purchase mainframe	Develop	Subsidiary	Service	No
3	Steel	No. 2	Logistics, mainframe	Develop	Manufacturer	Technology	Yes
4	Chemical	No. 3	Production client-server	Develop	ERP[a] vendor	Technology	Yes
5	Automobile	Top 3	Sales, web	Develop	Manufacturer	Management	Yes
6	Railroad	Top 3	Purchase client-server	Plan	Manufacturer	Service	No
7	Banking	Top 5	Sales client-server	Plan	System integrator	Management	Yes
8	Insurance	Top 3	Services, cloud	Plan	System integrator	Management	Yes
9	Food	Top 10	Production ERP[a]	Develop	ERP[a] vendor	Service	No
10	Distributor	Top 5	Logistics, cloud	Develop	Subsidiary	Service	No

[a] ERP Enterprise Resource Planning

(financial institutions, manufacturers, distributors, etc.), sizes of companies (number of employees, etc.), systems functions (accounting, production, sales, logistics, services, etc.), adopted technologies (mainframe, client-server, Web, cloud computing, etc.), and roles and positions of IT divisions within IT user companies. At the same time, we examine the IT vendors as the counterparts of the IT user companies from the viewpoint of business model, strengths, and sub-contractor structure.

Second, we use a case study approach to explain factors in the success and/or failure of the IT project from the viewpoint of QCD assessment, potential growth factor analysis, and benchmark with world-class cases. We conduct interviews with both user companies and vendors, and perform quantitative analyses on the IT project. To carry out the QCD assessment, and the potential growth factor analysis, we hold workshops to discuss in depth the potential for improvement towards achieving the targeted QCD goal, and the desirable strategic information systems. Regarding the benchmark with world-class cases, we compare the case at hand with the world's most advanced cases in the U.S., India, and China, in collaboration with an international research network.

To achieve objective (2), i.e., to construct an information circulation platform, we design and develop internet-based systems, endeavouring to achieve the right balance between the freedom of access to information versus the need for cybersecurity and safeguards to privacy, depending on the individual users of the platform.

6.4 Benefits from the New Social Research Scheme

Based on the abovementioned analyses, we expect the following novel and useful results. First, the research should contribute to improving management sophistication based on accumulated data through a case study approach, on both the user-side and the vendor-side. At the same time, we expect common language between the user and the vendor of software, e.g., QCD achievement, to be defined more precisely. Second, the information circulation platform will contribute to establishing a stationary measurement tool for IT projects and an internet-based database under adequate cybersecurity control. Third, in the process of researching the world's most advanced cases, we expect to develop a worldwide community for IT project comparisons. Fourth, the visualization of the value-creation mechanism in information services will have spill-over effects into other service sector industries, even though, in general, visualization of the value-creation mechanism in a service industry appears to be difficult. Therefore, we can expand our vision of science for society to accommodate changes in business environment and sublate the dichotomy between the demand side and the supply side.

Regarding the crucial characteristics to improve the sophistication of services between IT user companies and IT vendors, i.e., common language, stage of development, and international competitiveness (as discussed in the previous section), we can expect improvement in the following ways. The common language, e.g., QCD, will be clarified through continuous discussion between IT user companies and IT vendors. The stage of development in the boundary domain between IT user companies and IT vendors, e.g., project management, and customer contact (as illustrated in Fig. 6.5), will become more sophisticated through potential growth factor analysis. Regarding international competitiveness, the new global benchmark will be developed in the domains of service transformation science, service topic science, and service management science (Stauss et al. 2008)through discussions with world-class communities of practice.

6.5 Conclusions and Future Work

The stakeholders in IT management of enterprise systems include not only the demand side, i.e., IT user companies, but also the supply side, i.e., IT vendors. The present Chapter aims at designing a new social research scheme integrating both the demand side and the supply side, with a view to accelerating innovation in IT management.

To assess the sophistication of the social research, we analyzed the processes and results of the surveys investigating IT management effectiveness on the demand side and SEE on the supply side, which we have conducted five times over 10 years.

Based on "service dominant" logic (Vargo and Lusch 2006), we constructed a new social research scheme for IT management innovation which is dynamic and interactive between IT user companies and IT vendors, compared with the traditional social research scheme which is static and unidirectional based on "goods dominant" logic. The benefits obtainable from this new social research scheme include being able to (1) promote sophistication in management by the use of IT through the three stages: (1) QCD assessment, (2) potential growth factor analysis, and (3) benchmark with world-class cases; and (2) construct an information circulation platform, accumulating information and understanding from the cases observed in that process, i.e., the process of promoting sophistication in management by the use of IT.

Furthermore, through a case in the information service industry, we consider the role of science for society in a future-oriented manner that co-creates value beyond the border, i.e., aufheben, between the supply side and the demand side. This includes the spill-over effects into industries in the service sector other than information services.

For future study, we are planning to implement the research scheme introduced in the present Chapter, in collaboration with industry groups, e.g., JUAS, and JISA.

References

Barney, J. B. (2007). *Gaining and sustaining competitive advantage*. New Jersey: Pearson Prentice Hall.
Bollen, K. (1989). *Structural equation with latent variables*. New York: Wiley-Interscience Publication.

Brynjolfsson, E., & Hitt, L. M. (1998). Beyond the productivity paradox: Computers are the catalyst for bigger changes. *Communications of the ACM, 41*(8), 49–55.

Carnegie Mellon University (CMU) (2014). Software Engineering Institute. http://www.sei.cmu.edu/cmmi/. Accessed 14 Aug 2014.

Cusumano, M. (2004). *The business of software*. New York: Free Press.

Dodgson, M., Gann, D., & Salter, A. (2008). *The management of technological innovation*. Oxford: Oxford University Press.

Fujimoto, T. (2003). *Capability-building competition*. Tokyo: Chuohkouronshinsya.

IEEE, Computer Society. (2004). Guide to the Software Engineering Body of Knowledge (SWEBOK). http://www.computer.org/portal/web/swebok. Accessed 14 Aug 2014.

Japan Information Technology Services Industry Association (JISA). (2011). Fact-finding investigation on the IT usage in Japan. JISA.

Japan Users Association of Information Systems (JUAS). (2011). Fact-finding investigation on the information services industry in Japan. JUAS.

Kadono, Y. (2004). *Evolution of IT management creating business value*. Tokyo: Nikkagiren.

Kadono, Y. (2012). The differences in structural relationships among software engineering capabilities and business performance depending on origin of IT firm in Japan. *International Journal of Innovation and Learning, 14*(3/4), 308–328.

Kadono, Y. (2013). Managing innovation in software engineering in Japan. Proceedings of World Conference on Engineering, Computer Science, UC Berkeley, USA. (Keynote speaker).

Kadono, Y., & Tsubaki H. (2002). IT management effectiveness: An empirical study in Japanese companies. Proceedings of Pacific Asia Conference of Information Systems, Tokyo, Japan.

Ministry of Economy, Trade and Industry, and Information-Technology Promotion Agency, Japan. (METI & IPA) (2007). Fact-finding investigation on software engineering capabilities of enterprise systems in Japan (The responsibility for the investigation lies with Yasuo Kadono). sec.ipa.go.jp/reports/20071204/SE_level_research_2006_2.pdf. Accessed 18 Aug 2014.

Ministry of Economy, Trade and Industry, Japan (METI). (2011). Fact-finding investigation on the software industry in Japan.

Porter, M. (1980). *Competitive strategy*. New York: Free Press.

Science Council of Japan. (2003). Science for society.

Stauss, B., Engelmann, K., Kremer, A., & Luhn, A. (2008). *Services science: Fundamentals, challenges and future developments*. New York: Springer-Verlag.

Vargo, S. L., & Lusch, R. F. (2006). The service-dominant logic: What it is, what it is not, what it might be. In S. L. Vargo & R. F. Lusch (Eds.), *The service-dominant logic of marketing: Dialogue, debate, and directions*. M.E. Sharpe, Inc.

Chapter 7
Agent-Based Modeling of the Software Industry Structure in Japan: Preliminary Consideration of the Influence of Offshoring in China

Abstract In Chap. 7, our goal is a preliminary assessment of the future software industry structure in Japan, giving priority to the effects of offshoring in China, based on surveys on software engineering capabilities of Japanese IT vendors conducted together with the Japanese Ministry of Economy, Trade and Industry (METI). An agent-based simulation model, focusing mainly on customers' price preferences and on the quality of vendors' communication with customers, concludes that Japanese vendors can possibly lose market share if Japanese customers prefer the lower prices offered by offshore vendors. The results suggest that Japanese vendors should improve their communication skills to satisfy their customers' requirements regarding the quality of enterprise software, while also taking into account their customers' price preferences to avoid direct price competition with Chinese vendors. Otherwise, some Japanese vendors within the current man-month-based multilayered software industry culture will not survive in the drastically changing Japanese market.

Keywords Japan · China · Offshoring · Future scenario · Simulation Software industry · Agent-based modeling · Innovation

7.1 Introduction

The information service industry was a 10,427,909 million yen market in Japan, of which 7,502,070 million yen was for software development and programming; orders for software totaled 6,365,857 million yen, accounting for 61.0 % of the entire information service industry, while the software products market was 1,136,213 million yen in 2013 fiscal year (Ministry of Economy, Trade and Industry, Japan (METI) 2014).

As shown in Chap. 1, however, software vendors in Japan are facing drastic changes in their business environment due to technology innovations and new entrants from emerging countries, such as China, India, and others, while the domestic Japanese software industry has been growing only slowly. Also, particular issues in the IT industry in Japan have been pointed out, such as the multilayer subcontractors and the business model depending on custom-made applications for the domestic market. The industry structure, consisting of multilayer subcontractors, implies the

© Springer Japan 2015

Y. Kadono, *Management of Software Engineering Innovation in Japan*,
DOI 10.1007/978-4-431-55612-1_7

possibility of accelerating growth in offshoring of software development to China and other countries (Cusumano 2004; Kadono 2007).

The Japanese information service industry continues to have a considerable presence in the world, although its total sales have grown at a sluggish pace since it passed 10 trillion yen in 2005. However, IT vendors in Japan are facing a wide range of old and new issues in their business environment, such as responses to rapid technological innovations, an orientation of custom-made applications for the domestic market, global competition with new entrants from emerging countries, man-month-based multilayer subcontractors, origin of vendor (e.g., manufacturer spin-offs, user spin-offs, and independents), leadership of senior managers at IT vendors, skill building of software engineers, and IT management in user companies.

Indeed, the offshore software development market has grown strongly: 63.6 billion yen in 2005, 103.5 billion yen in 2007, and an expected 199.5 billion yen in 2010. In 2007, 36.8 % of Japanese software development firms developed software offshore to reduce costs and to circumvent Japan's 80 % deficit in domestic human resources. In 2005, offshore development in China was 53 billion yen, accounting for 83.5 % of the entire offshore development for Japan (Kondo 2009; Ministry of General Affairs, Japan 2007).

Compared to Japan's 10.5 trillion yen market, the information service industry in China is still smaller at 9.3 trillion yen, but has been growing by more than 20 % annually since 2002. Software exports from China were worth 3.6 billion dollars (approximately 396 billion yen) in 2005 and have been growing by over 30 % annually since 2002 (Kondo 2009; Ministry of General Affairs, Japan 2007). Therefore, new entrants from China entering into the Japan market are becoming a threat to domestic Japanese software vendors (Porter 1980).

7.2   Objectives and Method

The focus of this study is to assess the market shares in Japan of Japanese and Chinese software vendors and to assess the necessary conditions to sustain the competitive advantage of Japanese vendors in a situation similar to the current software industry in Japan; these assessments are based on surveys of Software Engineering Excellence (SEE) conducted in 2005, 2006 and 2007 in collaboration with METI. In the surveys, we collected data on software engineering capabilities and the competitive environment from a total of 233 IT vendors in Japan as shown in Chaps. 2 and 3 (Kadono et al. 2006).

The assessments are conducted through an agent-based simulation that is an extension of the Sugarscape model under the assumption that the price preferences of Japanese software customers are changing (Epstein and Axtell 1996; Kadono and Terano 2002; Yamakage 2007).

We assume Japanese and Chinese vendors to be agents and we set parameters such as communication level, service level, cost of switching, and price preference. Also, we assume that a Japanese vendor can outsource projects only to another Japanese vendor, and only under certain conditions.

Then, based on the above conditions, we model the following two scenarios:

- Customers attach equal importance to the communication level and the price level; or
- Customers attach more importance to the price level than the communication level, and this directly influences the quality of the software.

7.3 Simulation Model

7.3.1 Agents and Parameters

We assume the agents are Japanese vendors, Chinese vendors, and customers. We set the following parameters using Artisoc based on the current situation of the Japanese enterprise software service industry (Kozo Keikaku Engineering 2009; Kadono et al. 2006; Kadono 2007; Kadono et al. 2009; Kadono and Imanishi 2011).

- Vendors—Japanese and Chinese

  - *Number of vendors*: Japanese vendors are in the majority in the current Japanese market.
  - *Improvement in communication level*: Chinese vendors have increasingly improved their communication levels to meet the requirements of Japanese customers.
  - *Improvement in price level*: Japanese and Chinese vendors reduce their prices to meet the requirements of Japanese customers.
  - *Switching cost*: Japanese and Chinese vendors need to pay an initial cost for new customers.
  - *Outsourcing scope of Japanese vendors*: a Japanese vendor can outsource a project, though only to another Japanese vendor; a Chinese vendor cannot outsource a project to another vendor.
- Customers

  - *Number of customers*: there is a sufficient number of software customers in the current Japanese market.
  - *Desirable communication level*: Japanese customers take into account the communication level of Japanese vendors.
  - *Preference for low price*: Japanese customers also take the price into account.

7.3.2 Algorithm

In this agent-based simulation, the agents—Japanese vendors, Chinese vendors and Japanese customers—are distributed randomly on a 50x50 matrix, as shown in Fig. 7.1. The mobile direction of each vendor agent is randomly set. Each vendor agent moves one cell per time-step, based on the following algorithm, until either

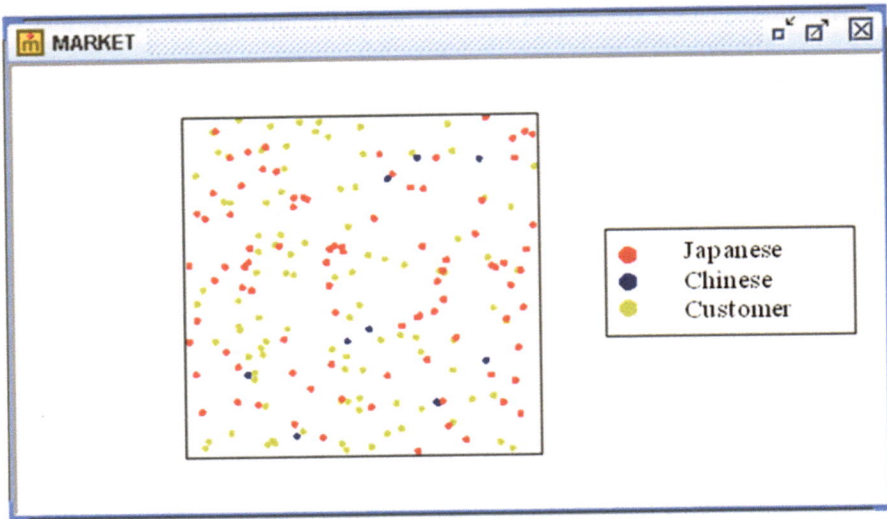

Fig. 7.1 Market with agent-based modeling: Japanese vendors (*red circles*), Chinese vendors (*blue*), and customers (*yellow*), on the market (50×50 matrix)

the Japanese or the Chinese vendors monopolize the market, or until a certain limit in the number time-steps is reached.

Step 1 A vendor moves by one cell randomly.

Step 2 The vendor successfully enters into a contract if encountering a customer whose requirements as to communication level and price are met by the vendor.

Step 3 If the Japanese vendor enters into a contract, it can outsource the project to another Japanese vendor within accessible distance from itself, the Japanese prime contractor.

Step 4 If the vendor cannot get the customer to agree to a contract, the vendor improves its communication level, within the parameter for improvement in the communication level. Also, the vendor reduces its price within the parameter for improvement in the price level.

Step 5 The market share is updated depending on the contracts completed by the Japanese and Chinese vendors, respectively.

7.3.3 Simulation Conditions and Parameters

We assume either of the following two conditions regarding the communication level and the price of software development:

1. Customers attach equal importance to the communication level and the price, i.e., A customer enters into a contract with a vendor if the communication level

Table 7.1 Basic parameters

	Japanese vendors	Chinese vendors
Number of vendors	90	10
Communication level	10	7
Price level	7	10
Switching cost	0.1	0.2
Price reduction (%)	0.02	0.04
Communication level improvement (%)	0.005	0.005
Number of potential customers	100	100
Customer's price preference	0.8	0.8
Outsourcing scope	3	NA

of the vendor $>=$ the communication level the customer requires + the switching cost, and if the price level of the vendor $<=$ the price level the customer requires + the switching cost.

2. Customers attach more importance to the price level than to the communication level, i.e., A customer enters into a contract with a vendor if the price level of the vendor $<=$ the price level the customer requires + (the communication level the customer requires—the communication level of the vendor) * (2—the price preference of the customer) + the switching cost. The price preference of the customer is defined as more than 0.1 and less than 0.9.

In terms of the simulation parameters of the Japanese and Chinese vendors, based on the current industry situation, we assume the number of agents, communication level, price level, switching cost, price reduction and communication level improvement are as shown in Table 7.1. Also, we assume the number of customers is 100 and the price preference is 0.8; and the outsourcing scope of Japanese vendors is three, while the outsourcing scope of Chinese vendors is not applicable (NA).

7.4 Results

First, we investigated the following two cases, within the basic parameters presented in Table 7.1.

Case 1 Simulation subject to condition 1 (customers attach equal importance to the communication level and the price level). The results are shown in Fig. 7.2.

Case 2 Simulation subject to conditions 1 and 2 (customers attach more importance to the price level than the communication level). The results are shown in Fig. 7.3.

In Figs. 7.2 and 7.3, the horizontal axis indicates one-tenth of the number of simulation steps, while the vertical axis indicates the market-share held by the Japanese and the Chinese software vendors.

In Case 1, right up until the end, the Japanese vendors sustain a more competitive position than the Chinese vendors.

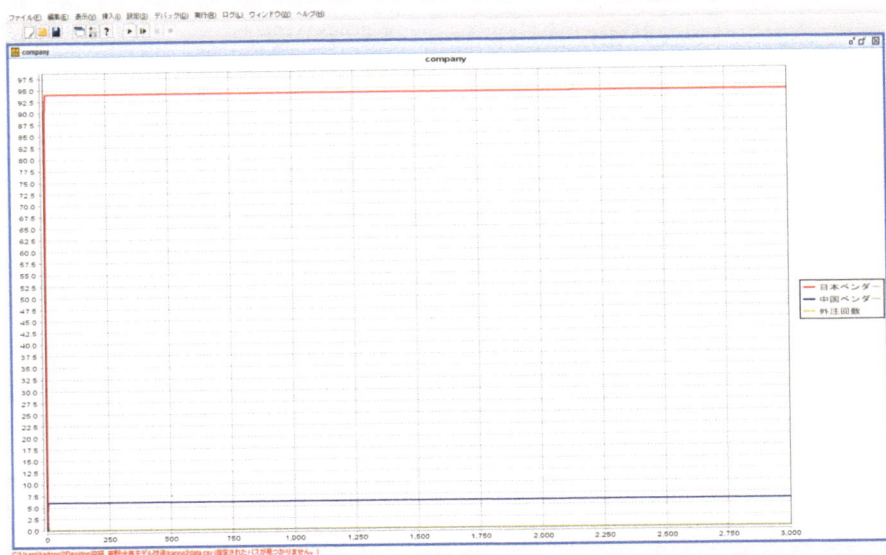

Fig. 7.2 Case 1 results within Table 7.1 parameters. *Vertical axis*: market share of Japanese vendors (*red line*) and Chinese vendors (*blue*) *Horizontal axis*: simulation steps*1/10

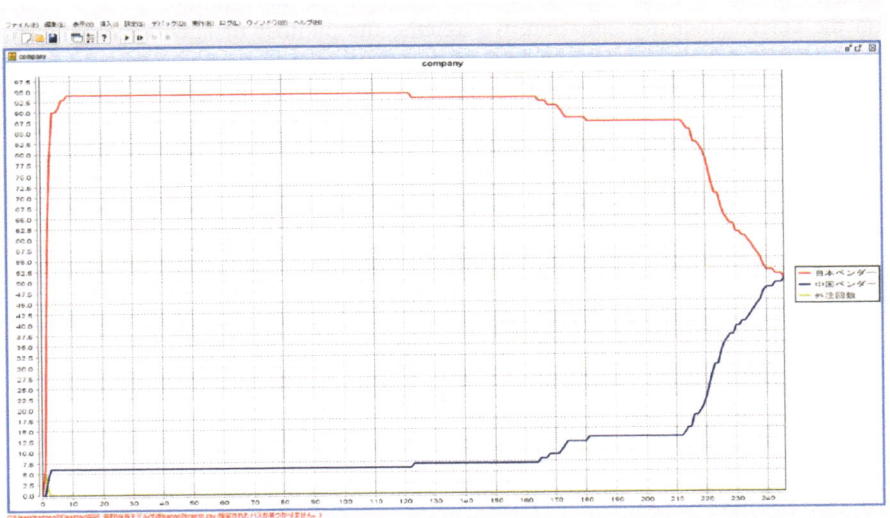

Fig. 7.3 Case 2 results within Table 7.1 parameters

In Case 2, the market-share of the Chinese vendors remains at 7% until the
1650th step, begins to increase from the 1650th step, and surpasses the Japanese
vendors by the 2100th step; in the end, the Chinese vendors dominate the market.

Fig. 7.4 Case 2 results within these parameters: Chinese vendor = 2; Japanese price level = 5

This means that Japanese vendors will probably tend to lose market-share if Japanese customers increasingly attach importance to a lower price; and that Japanese vendors should improve their commitment and skills at communication so as to satisfy their customers' requirements, while minimizing direct price competition with Chinese vendors. Failing this, some Japanese vendors will not survive in the Japanese market.

Second, we performed preliminary analyses for Case 2 with different parameters from those in Table 7.1, such as varying the number of Chinese vendors, the Japanese price level, and the scope for outsourcing from Japanese vendors to other Japanese vendors.

For example, assuming a price level of five, then, even if the number of Chinese vendors is set at two and the number of Japanese vendors at 100, the Chinese vendors end up surpassing the Japanese vendors (Fig. 7.4). On the other hand, if the Japanese vendors improve their price level down to 0.8, the Japanese market rejects one Chinese vendor and the Japanese vendors end up dominating the market. Another set of assumptions is shown: both Japanese and Chinese price levels are 0.8 while the Japanese outsourcing scope is nine. In this case we can observe that, after first losing market-share, Chinese vendors are revitalized by around the 100th step (Kadono and Imanishi 2011; Kadono 2011).

Furthermore, we can observe several phenomena with various combinations of vendor parameters in Table 7.1, such as number of vendors, communication level, improvement in communication level, price level, improvement in price level, switching cost, and outsourcing scope not only for Japanese vendors but also for Chinese vendors. As for the parameters of customers, we can further consider the number of customers, communication level desired by customers, price preference, and other parameters.

7.5   Conclusions and Discussion

In this study we constructed a simplified, agent-based simulation model to make preliminary assessments on the tradeoff between communication skill versus price, contrasting the situations of Japanese versus Chinese software vendors. The results show that Japanese vendors could lose market-share if their Japanese customers increasingly prefer lower prices. Consequently, to survive intense global competition, Japanese vendors will need to increasingly concentrate on and improve their communication skills, so as to deliver more satisfactory software products, while simultaneously improving their price-competitiveness relative to Chinese vendors.

Our focus was on assessing how the Japanese enterprise software service industry will be affected by future offshore development, particularly in relation to Chinese software vendors. However, Japanese software vendors are also facing drastic changes in their domestic business environment due to technology innovations and new competitors from emerging countries, including China, venturing into the low-growth Japanese industry. In order for the Japanese industry to meet these challenges, another important step is to identify and evaluate those software engineering capabilities that are important for achieving medium- and long-term success.

Therefore, we designed surveys on SEE (Barney 2007; Bollen 1989; Carnegie Mellon University 2014; Fujimoto 2003; IEEE,Computer Society 2004; METI 2014) and administered them in 2005, 2006 and 2007, in collaboration with METI (Kadono 2007). By surveying previous papers on the types of Japanese software vendors (Kadono et al. 2009), we found that manufacturer spin-off vendors tend to significantly expand business thanks to well-resourced R&D, while user spin-off vendors seem to depend heavily on demand from their parent companies. As a result, some user spin-off vendors are thought to gain inimitable capabilities. In contrast, many of the independent vendors serve as non-principal contractors that supply personnel without specific strengths as temporary staffing in a multilayer industry structure. However, some independent vendors that do have inimitable assets are thought to be role models for other software vendors in Japan. Based on these results, for future study, we suggest considering the relationship between the types of Japanese software vendor and key factors for the success of offshore software development.

Based on Chaps. 2 and 3, and the previous papers (Kadono et al. 2009), we have found that software vendors in Japan are mainly characterized by their scale and innovation adoption: big software vendors, e.g., system integrators, medium-sized technology-oriented vendors, medium-sized sales-oriented vendors, small subcontractors.

In order to model the current and future structure of the software industry in Japan, we developed another agent-based simulation model that was an extension of the Sugarscape model (Epstein and Axtell 1996; Yamakage 2007; Kadono and Terano 2002). The model consisted of software vendors with varied scale, readiness to innovate, and outsourcing ratios. In the model shown in Fig. 7.5, we assumed that the market would follow the same cycle of technology innovation as for mainframe computers, client servers, Web applications, cloud computing services, and

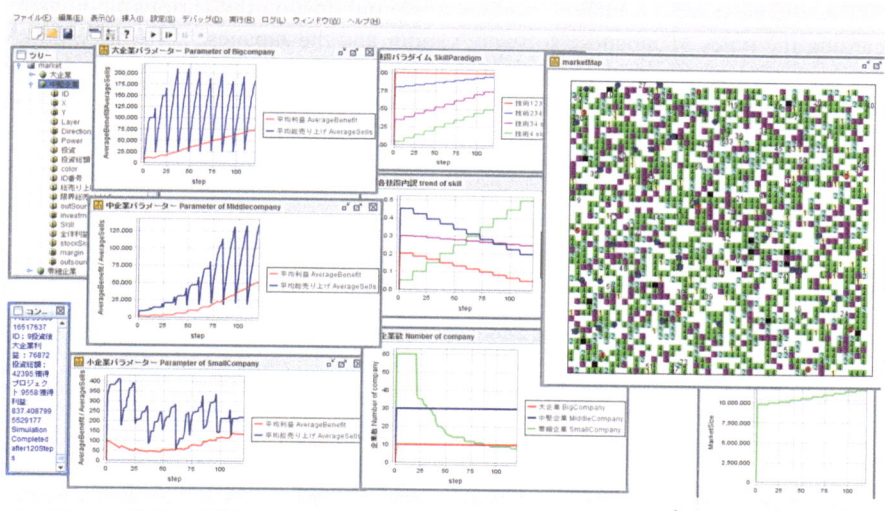

Fig. 7.5 Snapshot of simulation model of software industry structure: duration = 10 years (120 months), matrix = 20×20

so on; and that the larger software vendors would tend to invest more in innovative technology and outsource more jobs to the smaller software vendors in a multilayer industry structure (Kadono et al. 2010).

For the investigation, we set the following three scenarios. In each scenario, we continued to apply the conditions and parameters of availability within the agent-based simulation model.

- *Survival by size and skill*: The big software vendors grow increasingly, thanks to their resourceful staff and skills, exploiting their advantages of scale and scope, whereas the small/medium-sized software vendors do not survive unless they can catch up with rapid technology innovation. As a result, the software industry structure in Japan eventually consists of a smaller number of competitors, each with distinct scale or special skills.
- *Reciprocal relationships*: All current types of market participant survive, thanks to the outsourcing of jobs from big (or medium-sized) software vendors to medium-sized (or small) software vendors in the current multilayer industry structure. In particular, small software vendors do not survive without outsourcing from the big (or medium-sized) vendors.
- *Reverse phenomena*: Some medium-sized technology-oriented vendors outpace big software vendors who tend not to invest as much in innovative technology.

Based on the above scenarios, we suggested that future studies be conducted on the following: interactive behaviors among software vendors, e.g., project-based alliances, and merger and acquisition (M&A); effects of offshore development; and effects of new participants in the Japanese software industry.

Finally, we aspire to integrate into a single publication the various findings regarding the types of Japanese software vendor and the Japanese software industry structure, and so assess the future of the Japanese software industry structure in relation to China, India, the U.S., and the rest of the world.

References

Barney, J. B. (2007). *Gaining and sustaining competitive advantage*. New Jersey: Pearson Prentice Hall.

Bollen, K. (1989). *Structural equation with latent variables*. New York: Wiley-Interscience Publication.

Carnegie Mellon University (2014). Software Engineering Institute. http://www.sei.cmu.edu/cmmi/. Accessed 14 Aug 2014.

Cusumano, M. (2004). *The business of software*. New York: Free Press.

Epstein, J. M., & Axtell, R. (1996). *Growing artificial societies: Social science from the bottom up*. Cambridge, MA: Brookings Institution Press, The MIT Press.

Fujimoto, T. (2003). *Capability-building competition*. Tokyo: Chuohkouronshinsya.

IEEE, Computer Society. (2004). Guide to the software engineering body of knowledge (SWE-BOK). http://www.computer.org/portal/web/swebok. Accessed 14 Aug 2014.

Kadono, Y. (2007). The issues on IT industry in Japan, Nikkei Net. http://it.nikkei.co.jp/business/news/index.aspx?n=MMITac000017122007. Accessed 14 Aug 2014.

Kadono, Y. (2011). Agent-based modeling of the software industry structure in Japan: Preliminary consideration of influence of offshoring in China. Proceedings of TIIM2011.

Kadono, Y., & Imanishi, Y. (2011). A study on the offshore software development of Japanese and Chinese vendors through agent-based simulation. Proceedings of Japan China Conference of Information Systems.

Kadono, Y., & Terano, T. (2002). How information technology creates business value in the past and in the current Electronic Commerce (EC) era. In S.-H. Chen & P. Wang (Eds.), *Computational intelligence in economics and finance* (pp. 449–466). Berlin: Springer-Verlag.

Kadono, Y., Tsubaki, H., & Tsuruho, S. (2006). A study on the reality and economy of software development in Japan. The sixth Asia Pacific Industrial Engineering Management Systems Conference, Bangkok, Thailand (pp. 1425–1433).

Kadono, Y., Tsubaki, H., & Tsuruho, S. (2009). A study on characteristics of software vendors in Japan from environmental threats and resource-based view. Proceedings of Pacific Asia Conference on Information Systems, Indian School of Business, Hyderabad, India.

Kadono, Y., Terano, T., & Ohkuma, Y. (2010). Assessing the current and future structures of software industries in Japan through agent-based simulation. Proceedings of International Conference on Social Science Simulation, Arizona State University.

Kondo, S. (2009). Present status and issues on offshore development in China and future directions. *Machinery Economics Research, 40* (in Japanese).

Kozo Keikaku Engineering. (2009). Artisoc.

Ministry of Economy, Trade, and Industry (METI). (2014). Current survey on selected service industries: Information service industry.

Ministry of General Affairs, Japan. (2007). Study on evolution of offshore development and its influences.

Porter, M. (1980). *Competitive strategy*. New York: Free Press.

Yamakage, S. (2007). *Guidance of designing artificial society* (pp. 148–163). Tokyo: Hayama publishing (in Japanese).

Part III
Epilogue

Chapter 8
A Hybrid Method to Predict Scenarios in the Japanese Software Industry

Abstract In Chap. 8 we investigate the potential to predict future scenarios in the Japanese software industry, making use of a hybrid method: that is, we try to develop a new research framework by integrating data obtained from issue-oriented large-scale fact-finding surveys, statistical analyses based on dynamic modeling, and simulations. On this basis, we suggest guidelines for a global technology strategy for Japan's software industry, with a view to winning a sustainable competitive advantage. Also, it should be possible to develop evidence-based visualizations of industry growth scenarios by integrating intellectual instruments such as management theory, research surveys, statistics, and simulations.

Keywords IT management · Empirical study · Future scenario · Simulation · Software engineering capabilities · Innovation · learning · Social survey · Statistical analysis · Agent-based modeling

8.1 Introduction

IT vendors in Japan are facing drastic changes in their business environment, such as innovations in technology and new competitors from emerging countries, e.g., China and India. Also, many companies in Japan that use enterprise software have not been fully satisfied with the quality, cost, and productivity of software that IT vendors deliver, or the speed of delivery. At the same time, there are particular issues that are special to the IT industry in Japan, such as vendors relying on multilayer subcontractors; and legacy business models that depend on supplying custom-made applications for the domestic market, as shown in Chap. 1. However, this industry is still large. In fact, in 2013 fiscal year, the information service industry was a 10,427,909 million yen market in Japan, of which 7,502,070 million yen was for software development and programming; orders for software totaled 6,365,857 million yen, accounting for 61.0% of the entire information service industry, while the software products market was 1,136,213 million yen (METI 2014).

In order to meet these challenges, in this Chapter we investigate the potential to predict future scenarios in the Japanese software industry, making use of a hybrid method: we integrate large-scale fact-finding surveys; statistical analyses based on dynamic modeling; and simulations. First, we designed a large-scale survey of

Y. Kadono, *Management of Software Engineering Innovation in Japan*,
DOI 10.1007/978-4-431-55612-1_8

the enterprise software industry in Japan, administered it, and developed a tool to measure software engineering capabilities, in collaboration with the Ministry of Economy, Trade and Industry (METI). Second, using dynamic modeling, we empirically verified that human resource development in IT firms leads to improvement in their operational software engineering capabilities; and that improvement in their software engineering capabilities tends to lead to long term improvement in their business performance. Third, we tried to visualize future scenarios in the Japanese software industry through agent-based simulation. Fourth, we developed a new research scheme to integrate issue-oriented large-scale fact-finding surveys, results of statistical analyses, and future scenarios visualized for the Japanese software industry.

8.2   Large-Scale Fact-Finding Surveys on Software Engineering Capabilities in Japan

In order for the IT industry in Japan to meet the challenges mentioned above, an important step is to understand how software engineering capability as a core competence for the industry is significant for achieving medium- and long-term success. Therefore, we designed a research survey on software engineering capabilities and administered it in 2005, 2006, and 2007, in collaboration with METI and the Information-Technology Promotion Agency (IPA), as shown in Chap. 2.

The objectives of the research were to:

- Assess the achievements of the software engineering discipline, as represented by IT vendors in Japan, and
- Better understand the mechanisms of how software engineering capabilities relate to IT vendors' business performance and business environment.

To achieve these objectives, we developed a measurement tool called Software Engineering Excellence (SEE), which can be used to evaluate the overall software engineering capabilities of IT vendors. It consists of seven factors: Deliverables, Project Management, Quality Assurance, Process Improvement, Research and Development, Human Resource Development, and Customer Contact. These seven factors were identified based on interviews with industry experts and literature searches (Barney 2007; Carnegie Mellon University, Software Engineering Institute 2014; Fujimoto 2003; IEEE Computer Society 2013; JISA 2011; Porter 1980; Porter 1990)

We introduced two other indicators as well: Business Performance and Business Environment. Business Performance is a measure of the overall business performance of any given IT vendor, including its profitability, growth, productivity, and management efficiency. Business Environment expresses the company profile and structure of an IT vendor, e.g., origin of vendor, number of software engineers, average age of employees, business model, customer base, and corporate culture.

Table 8.1 Software Engineering Excellence surveys

Fiscal year	2005	2006	2007	Total[a]
Questionnaires sent	230	537	1000	NA
Valid responses	55	78	100	151
Manufacturer spin-off	17	27	27	42
User spin-off	15	15	20	33
Independent	23	36	53	76
Response rate (%)	24	15	10	NA

[a] Total number of unique respondents over the three surveys

In the 2005 survey, there were 55 valid responses, a response rate of 24 %; and in the 2006 survey, there were 78 valid responses, a response rate of 15 %. In the 2007 SEE survey, responses were received from 117 companies, of which 100 were valid responses, a response rate of 10 %. In the 2007 SEE survey, the sample size of each type of vendor, i.e., manufacturer spin-off, user spin-off, and independent, was large enough to perform stratified analysis (Table 8.1).

8.3   Results of Statistical Analyses of Relationship Between Software Engineering Capabilities and Business Performance

After collecting data from vendors in 2005, 2006, and 2007, we calculated the standardized factor loadings for the seven factors—Deliverables, Project Management, Quality Assurance, Process Improvement, Research and Development, Human Resource Development,and Customer Contact—by doing confirmatory factor analysis, based on the responses received to the relevant questions. As shown in Chaps. 2 and 3, we performed statistical analyses to find relationships among software engineering capabilities, business performance, and business environment in short and long term.

Regarding the cross-section analysis, on the basis of the data collected from 78 firms in SEE2006, we succeeded, by a trial and error method, in constructing a well-fitted path model (CFI = 1.0), where all the existing path coefficients are significant at the 5 % level. We did this by using a structural equation model (Bollen 1989). We found that superior Deliverables and Business Performance correlate significantly with effort expended, particularly on Human Resource Development, Quality Assurance, Research and Development, and Process Improvement (Kadono et al. 2008).

To do panel analyses of software engineering capabilities, we integrated 233 valid responses to the SEE surveys, received over 3 years, into a single database, and identified 151 unique IT firms, consisting of 42 manufacturer spin-off vendors, 33 user spin-off vendors, and 76 independent vendors. We then conducted panel analyses of the seven SEE factors, using the 3 years of data, to clarify what influence the

SEE factors have within a year, year-to-year, and mid-term. Based on the results of the panel analyses, our first observation is that most SEE factors in 1 year have significant positive influences on the same factors the next year. Second, within a year, there are three paths to improving the level of Deliverables, i.e., through Project Management, Quality Assurance and Research and Development. Third, some SEE factors have significant positive influence diagonally on different SEE factors in the following year. Fourth, there are some negative paths, implying that efforts put toward a particular factor did not pay off within the duration of our research. Even so, these efforts might be expected to exert longer-term positive effects on other SEE factors (Kadono 2011b). As a result, we confirmed the series correlations throughout the software engineering capabilities, as the previous research showed that firm resorces, including human capital, are relativelly stable (Foss 1997).

To understand the long-term relationship between the software engineering capabilities and business performance of representative IT firms in Japan, we conducted longitudinal analyses of standardized software engineering capability scores, drawing on the three surveys and the 10-year business performance of 151 firms (Meredith and Tisak 1990). Through the panel analyses, we found that IT firms maintaining high levels of deliverables, derived from high levels of human resource development, quality assurance, project management and process improvement, tend to sustain high profitability, while IT firms with high levels of project management and customer contact tend to be highly productive, and continue to improve productivity in the long-term. Concerning business performance, profitable IT firms tend to be stable, and become increasingly more stable, thanks to steady improvements in deliverables and R&D. However, productive IT firms are not necessarily profitable; probably this is because they are handicapped by the multi-layered structure of the industry in Japan (Kadono and Tsubaki 2012).

8.4   New Research Framework to Predict Future Scenarios

In order to predict future scenarios in the Japanese software industry, we try to develop a new research framework as shown in Fig. 8.1. We do this by integrating data obtained from large-scale fact-finding surveys; results obtained from statistical analyses, using dynamic modeling; and visualization of future scenarios obtained through simulations (Kadono 2015).

First, we try to understand the overall structure of Japan's current enterprise software industry, paying attention to scale of company, path dependence, software engineering capabilities, technological base, and customer base, based on fact-finding surveys and statistical analyses, as discussed above.

Second, regarding the structure of Japan's enterprise software industry, we hypothesize that it is unstable, as it is multi-layered, consisting of large-scale system integrators, mid-size software houses, and small temporary manpower companies.

Third, more advanced technology paradigms have arrived from the U.S. and other countries over the years, e.g., mainframe computing, client-server architecture, personal computers, the internet, and cloud computing (Greengard 2013; McKinsey & Company 2013). Meanwhile, Japan's enterprise software industry has fallen behind that in the U.S. and some other countries. We take it to be predictable what advanced technology paradigm will arrive next from abroad, although the timing of the arrival may be less predictable.

Fourth, global competition and collaboration, such as offshore developments in China, India, and other countries, have become more and more prominent.

Next, we try to predict industry scenarios 5–10 years into the future, considering factors such as these four: results of statistical analyses; changes in industry structure; any shift in technology paradigms; and global competition and collaboration. We do this using agent-based simulation (Epstein and Axtell 1996). We need to carefully experiment on how fast any new technology paradigm penetrates into the Japanese market; the speed of changes in the cost structure in emerging countries; and improvements in communication between Japanese IT user companies and offshore vendors. As a preliminary, shown in Chap. 7, we observe a tradeoff: lower costs imply a less satisfactory quality of communication between IT vendors in Japan and China. We investigate this tradeoff using agent-based simulation (Kadono 2011a).

A main aim of this current study is to produce a assessment of the future software industry structure in Japan, looking especially at the effects of offshoring to China, based on surveys of software engineering capabilities of Japanese IT vendors, conducted in collaboration with METI. Using an agent-based simulation model, we focus mainly on price preferences of Japanese customers; and on quality of communication between offshore vendors and Japanese customers. The results suggest that Japanese vendors risk losing market share should Japanese customers prefer the service and lower prices offered by offshore vendors; and that Japanese vendors should seek to improve their communication skills, to satisfy customers' requirements on the quality of enterprise software, while also seeking to accommodate customers' price preferences, and so avoiding direct price competition with the Chinese vendors. Otherwise, some Japanese vendors within the current multi-layered software industry culture will not survive in the drastically changing Japanese market.

8.5 Conclusions and Future Work

This Chapter investigates the potential to predict future scenarios in the Japanese software industry through a hybrid method: that is, we try to develop a new research framework by integrating data obtained from issue-oriented large-scale fact-finding investigations, statistical analyses based on dynamic modeling, and simulation of future scenarios.

This endeavor should be significant both as academic research and in its practical implications, as follows. First, by integrating large-scale surveys, statistical

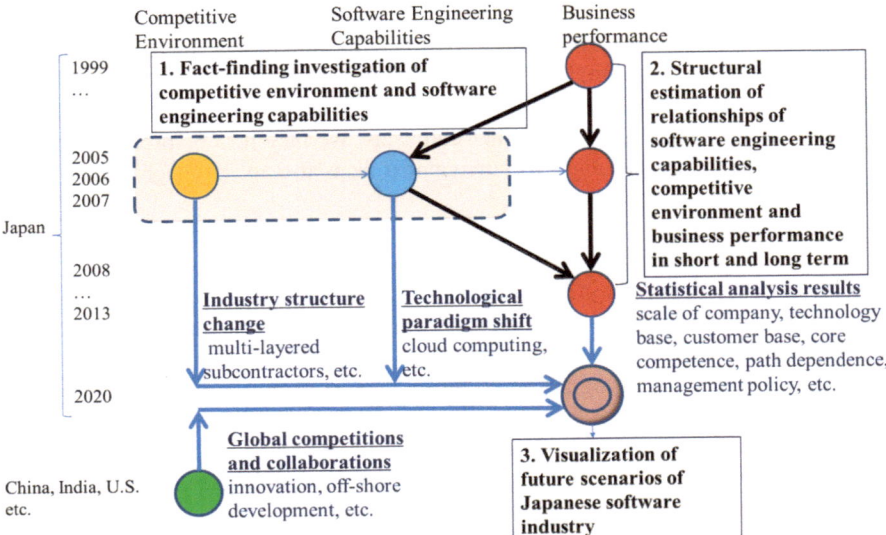

Fig. 8.1 Integration of large-scale fact-finding surveys, statistical analyses, and visualization of future scenarios

analyses, and future prospects, we suggest guidelines for a global technology strategy for Japan's software industry, with a view to obtaining sustainable competitive advantage.

Second, the research throws up a significant challenge: it should be possible to develop evidence-based visualization of industry growth scenarios by integrating intellectual instruments that have hitherto evolved separately, such as fact-finding surveys (as conducted by METI and IPA); management theory, including resource-based views, competitive threats, and diverse competitive advantages of diverse nations; statistical analyses, such as dynamic covariance modeling; and social simulation models.

Third, methods can perhaps be developed to design plans for the management of technology as a national strategy, through visualization of a variety of scenarios, ranging from optimistic to pessimistic. We do not aspire to predict future scenarios precisely, but do aim for a deeper understanding of the complex and multifaceted issues to be managed by policymakers and leading companies in the software industry in Japan, focusing on the management of technology, considering especially the scale of industry participants, technology paradigm shifts, and global competition and collaboration.

Fourth, the method, especially the integration of large-scale surveys, statistical analyses, and future prospects, though developed primarily to illuminate the software industry in Japan, has potential to be expanded and generalized to illuminate any industrial sector in any country.

We would like to extend our research to do the following work in the future:

- Estimate more precisely the population of the software industry in Japan; and
- Do more simulation analyses on the speed of penetration of new technology paradigms into the Japanese market; and the speed of change in cost structure in emerging countries (Fig. 8.1).

References

Barney, J. B. (2007). *Gaining and sustaining competitive advantage*. New Jersey: Pearson Prentice Hall.

Bollen, K. (1989). *Structural equation with latent variables*. New York: Wiley-Interscience Publication.

Carnegie Mellon University (2014). Software Engineering Institute. Capability Maturity Model Integration (CMMI). http://www.sei.cmu.edu/cmmi/. Accessed 14 Aug 2014.

Epstein, J., & Axtell, R. (1996). *Growing artificial societies: Social science from the bottom up*. Washington D.C.: Brookings Institution Press.

Foss, J. N. (1997). *Resource firms and strategy*. Oxford: Oxford University Press.

Fujimoto, T. (2003). *Capability-building competition*. Tokyo: Chuokoron-sha, Inc.

Greengard, S. (2013). Six top tech trends to watch in 2014. http://www.baselinemag.com/innovation/six-top-tech-trends-to-watch-in-2014.html/. Accessed 14 Aug 2014.

IEEE Computer Society. (2013). SWEBOK V3.0. http://www.computer.org/portal/web/swebok/swebokv3. Accessed 14 Aug 2014.

Japan Information Technology Services Industry Association(JISA). (2011). *Fact-finding investigation on the IT usage in Japan*. JISA.

Kadono, Y. (2011a). Agent-based modeling of the software industry structure in Japan: Preliminary consideration of influence of offshoring in China. Proceedings of Technology Innovation and Industrial Management, Oulu, Finland.

Kadono, Y. (2011b). A study on management of software engineering capability in Japan using panel analysis. *International Journal of Service Science, Management, Engineering, Technology, 2*(3), 20–32.

Kadono, Y. (2015). A hybrid method to predict scenarios in the Japanese software industry. *International Journal of Innovation and Learning, 17*(2), 254–261.

Kadono, Y., & Tsubaki, H. (2012). A study on the relationships between software engineering capabilities and business performance of Japanese it firms through longitudinal modeling. Proceedings of the 16th Pacific Asia conference on information systems (Pacis2012), Ho Chi Minh, Vietnam.

Kadono, Y., Tsubaki, H., & Tsuruho, S. (2008). A survey on management of software engineering In Japan. In Sio-long Ao (Ed.), *Current themes in engineering technologies* (pp. 267–277). The American Institute of Physics.

McKinsey & Company, Bughin, J., Chui, M., & Manyika, J. (2013). Ten IT-enabled business trends for the decade ahead. *McKinsey Quarterly*.

Meredith, W., & Tisak, J. (1990). Latent curve analysis. *Psychometrika, 55*, 107–122.

Ministry of Economy, Trade, and Industry (METI). (2014). Current survey on selected service industries: Information service industry. Accessed 14 Aug 2014.

Porter, M. (1980). *Competitive strategy*. New York: Free Press.

Porter, M. (1990). *The competitive advantage of nations*. New York: Free Press.

Appendix: Results on Software Engineering Survey

The Software Engineering Survey (SEE) measurement model has a hierarchical structure with three layers: observed responses to question items, seven detailed factors, and SEE as a primary indicator. SEE as we have defined it consists of the following seven factors. In the appendix, summaries of observed responses to major question items relevant to the following seven SEE factors at SEE2007 survey are shown: Deliverables, Project Management, Quality Assurance, Process Improvement, Research and Development, Human Resource Development, and Customer Contact.

1. Deliverables: achievement ratios on quality, cost, and delivery (QCD), ratio of a money-losing project, understanding of project information

  • Achievement ratios of quality, cost, and delivery (QCD)

   The median QCD achievement ratios are over 70 % for all three types of vendor (Fig. 1).

Fig. 1 QCD achievement (N=92)

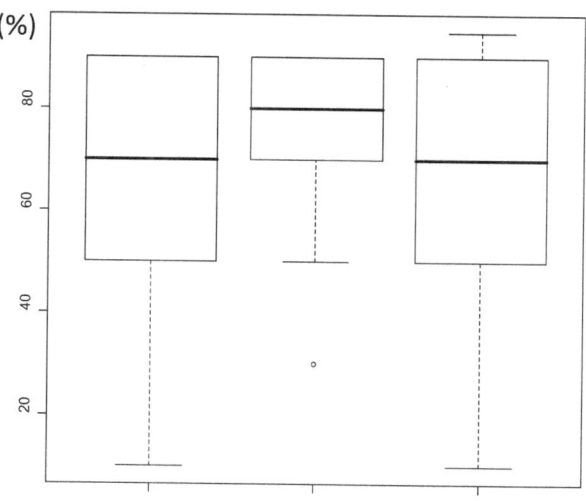

Manufacturer spin-off   User spin-off   Independent

© Springer Japan 2015
Y. Kadono, *Management of Software Engineering Innovation in Japan,*
DOI 10.1007/978-4-431-55612-1

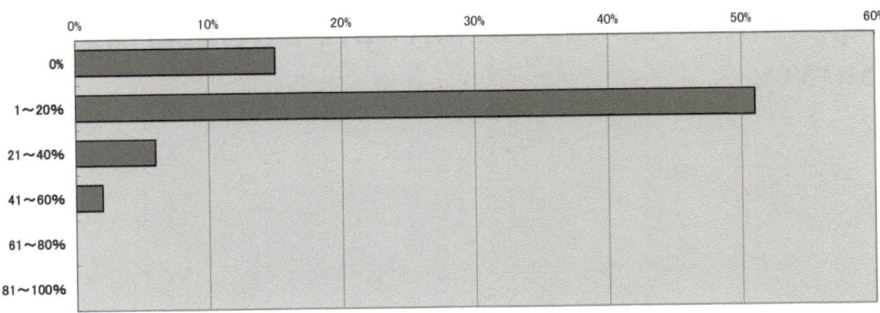

Fig. 2 Ratio of a money-losing project ($N=74$)

Fig. 3 Understanding of project information. Level of understanding: 1.no, 2.little, 3.in-between, 4.almost, 5.fully

- Ratio of a money-losing project

Ratio of IT vendor whose ratio of a money-losing project is less than 20% is over 60% (Fig. 2).

- Understanding of project information

Project information on cost (C) and delivery (D), i.e., dead line, are perfectly understood at 80%, on profitability at almost 70%, and on quality (Q) at almost 60%.On the other hand, project information on customer satisfaction is perfectly understood at less than 30% (Fig. 3).

2. Project Management: project planning capability, project monitoring (scope, frequency)

- Project planning capability

60% of IT vendors make a final decision on a project plan based on clear corporate decision-making standard (Fig. 4).

- Project monitoring: scope

Several project monitoring operations are carried out within the section at around 20–40%, and within the company at around 80% (Fig. 5).

- Project monitoring: frequency

Most project monitoring operations are carried monthly or weekly (Fig. 6).

Fig. 4 Project planning
capability ($N=100$)

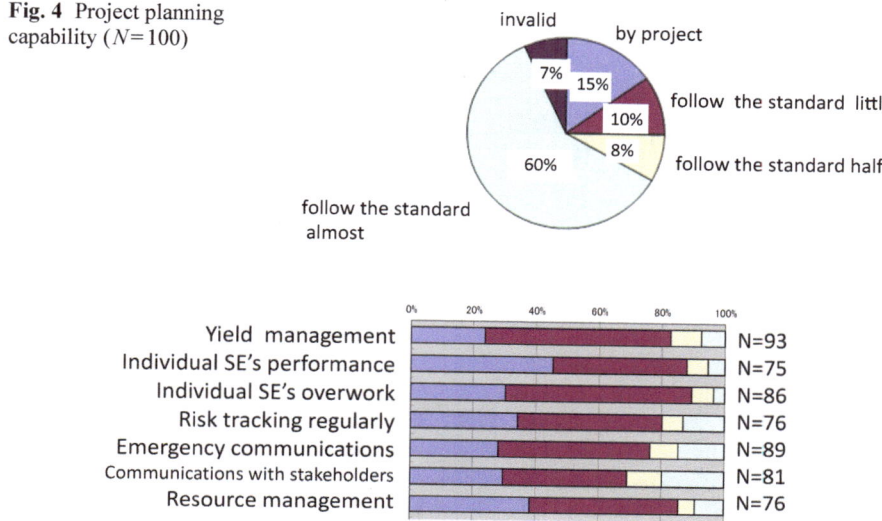

Fig. 5 Project monitoring: scope. 1.department, 2.company, 3.group company, 4.outsoucer

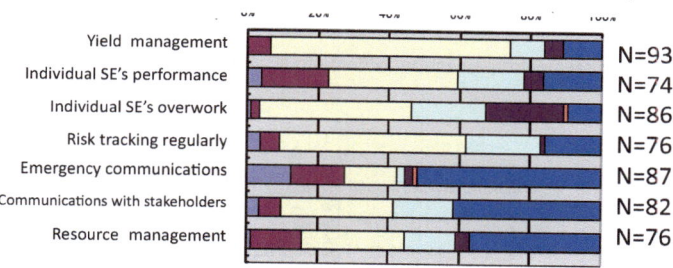

Fig. 6 Project monitoring: frequency. 1.anually, 2.three/six-month period, 3.monthly, 4.weekly, 5.daily, 6.every few hours, 7.anytime

3. Quality Assurance: review process, quality management organization (requirement definition, schematic design, detail design, development, test, operation and manual), management of outsourcees

- Review process

Almost half of IT vendors carry out quality reviews according to standard procedures of corporates through the project management process, i.e., requirement definition, schematic design, detailed design, programming, testing, operation and manual (Fig. 7).

- Quality management organization: schematic design

Project manager is the most important person in charge of quality management at schematic design phase at most of IT vendors. On the other hand, developer itself is sometimes the person in charge of the quality management, instead of line manager, project management office (PMO), and so on (Fig. 8).

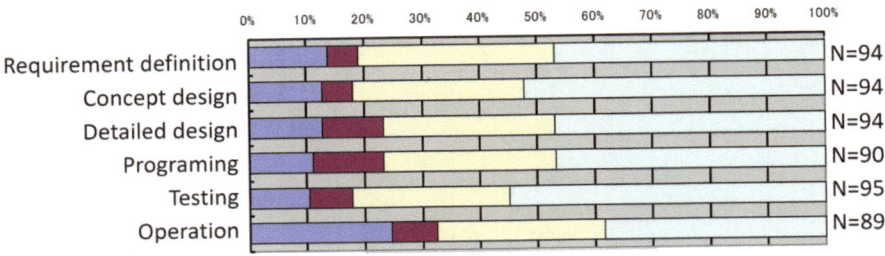

Fig. 7 Review process. 1. no review procedure, 2. little review with procedure, 3. half review with procedure, 4. almost review with procedure

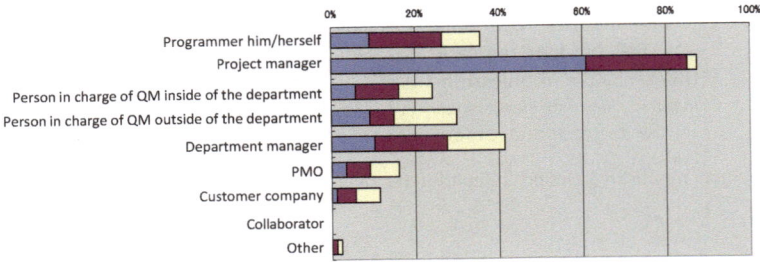

Fig. 8 Quality management organization: schematic design ($N=87$). Rank: 1. first, 2. second, 3. third

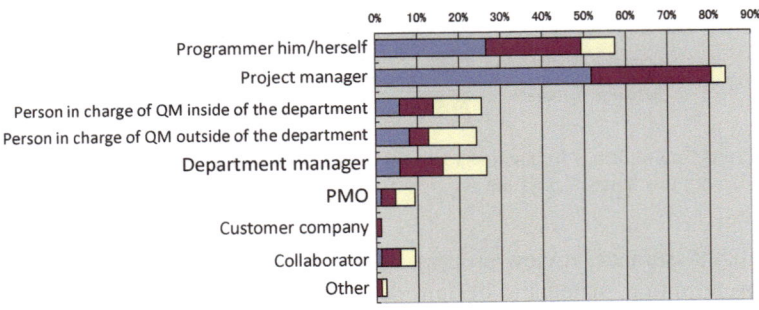

Fig. 9 Quality management organization: development ($N=87$). Rank: 1. first, 2. second, 3. third

- Quality management organization: development

Project manager is the most important person in charge of quality management at development phase at most of IT vendors. Developer itself is the person in charge of the quality management at development phase much more than at schematic design phase (Fig. 9).

- Management of outsourcees

Over 80 % of IT vendors have guidelines of assessment of the outsourcees before contract. However, only 30–40 % of them understand individual skills of the outsources (Fig. 10).

Fig. 10 Management of outsourcees

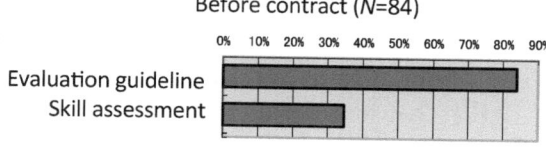

Before contract (*N*=84)

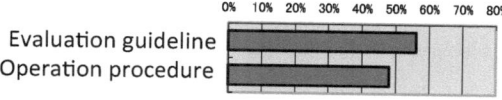

Acceptance inspection of design (*N*=75)

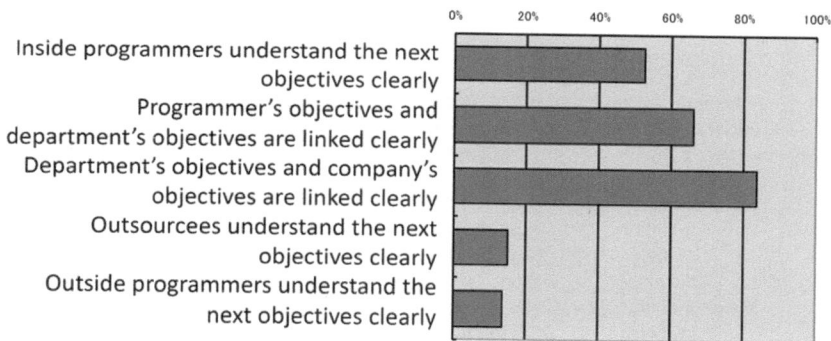

Fig. 11 Objectives management of process improvement (*N*=75)

4. Process Improvement: objectives management, data collection, data utilization, improvement of estimation

- Objectives management of process improvement

At over 80% of IT vendors, objectives of process improvement are shared between development division level and corporate level of the IT vendor (Fig. 11).

- Data collection for process improvement

Some companies have collected data for process improvement on bugs, quality assurance, productivity, quality of life (QOL), technical skills, and cost for more than 20 years (Fig. 12).

- Data utilization for process improvement

Among IT vendors who have collected data for process improvement, some companies effectively utilize data for process improvement on bugs, quality assurance, productivity, quality of life (QOL), technical skills, cost, as well as customer satisfaction (Fig. 13).

- Improvement of estimation

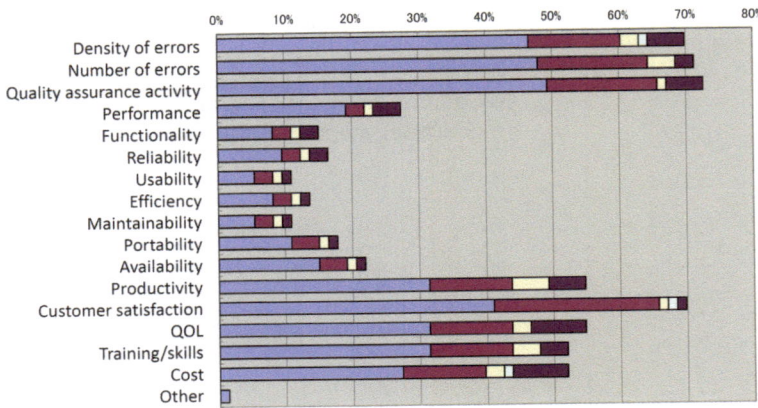

Fig. 12 Accumulated numbers of Years of Data collection for process improvement ($N=73$). Accumulated numbers of years: 1. –5 years, 2. 6–10 years, 3. 11–15 years, 4. 16–20 years, 5. 20– years

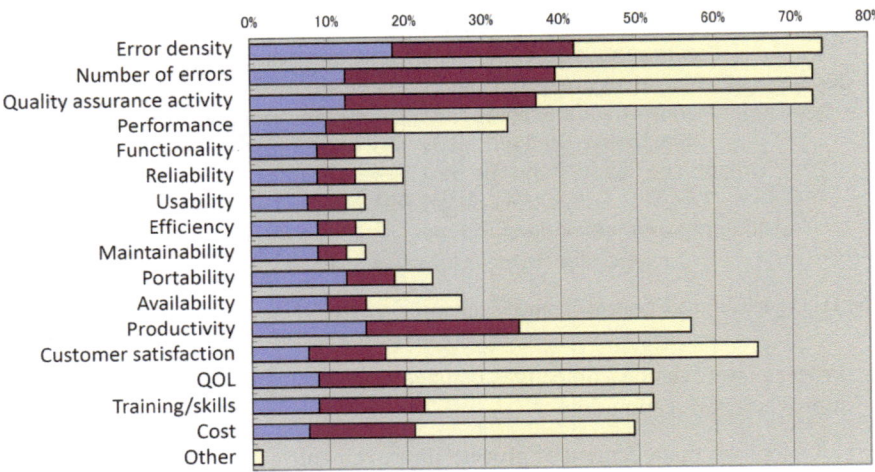

Fig. 13 Data utilization for process improvement ($N=81$). Accumulation and utilization of collected data: 1. accumulated data but not utilized, 2. utilized data but not linked to process improvement, 3. utilized data for process improvement

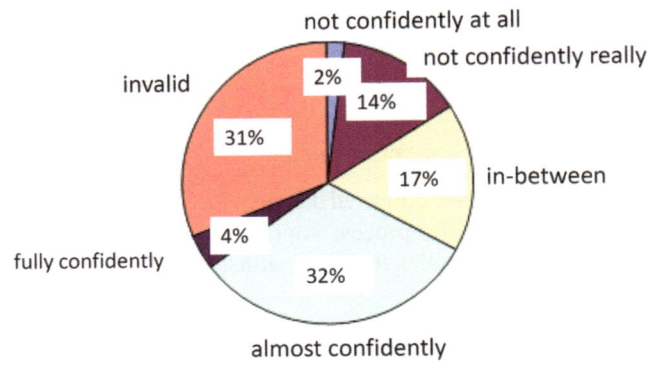

Fig. 14 Data utilization for estimations ($N=100$)

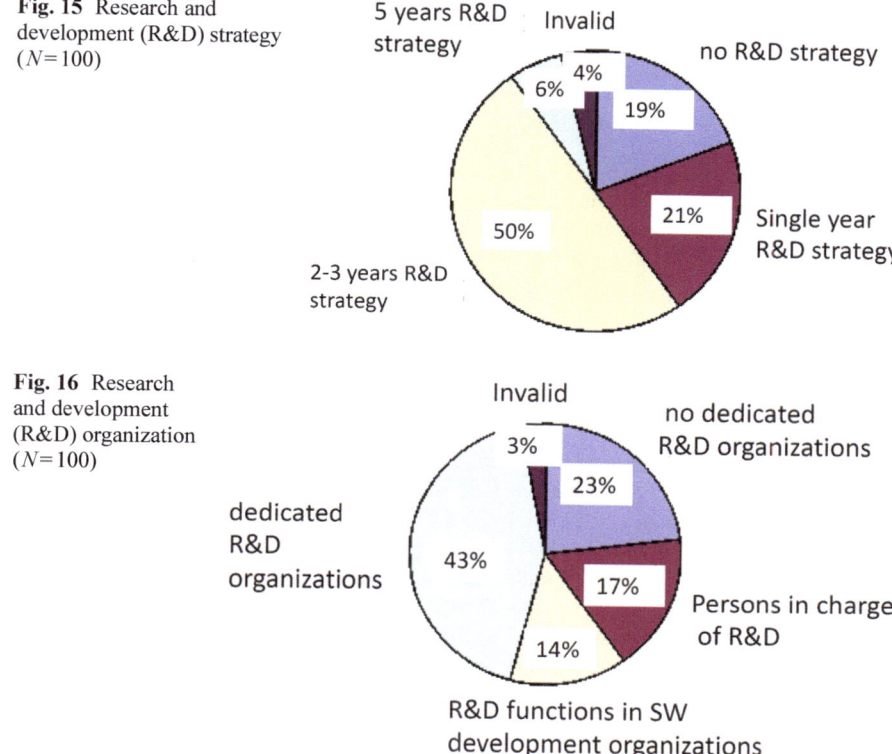

Fig. 15 Research and development (R&D) strategy ($N=100$)

Fig. 16 Research and development (R&D) organization ($N=100$)

Particularly, one third of IT vendors who have collected data for process improvement effectively utilize the accumulated data for estimations (Fig. 14).

5. Research and Development (R&D): strategy, organization, learning organization, readiness for state-of-the-art technology, development methodology, reuse of software resources, effect of R&D

- Research and development (R&D) strategy

Half of IT vendors have R&D strategies at least of a couple of years. On the other hand, 40% of them have either no R&D strategies or single year R&D plans (Fig. 15).

- Research and development (R&D) organization

Almost half of IT vendors have dedicated R&D organizations (Fig. 16).

- Learning organization

Knowledge sharing is active particularly inside of a company, e.g., case study in a company and a team, internal website, towards learning organization (Fig. 17).

- Readiness for state-of-the-art technology

Only 10–20% of IT vendors have positive attitude toward state-of-the-art technologies (Fig. 18).

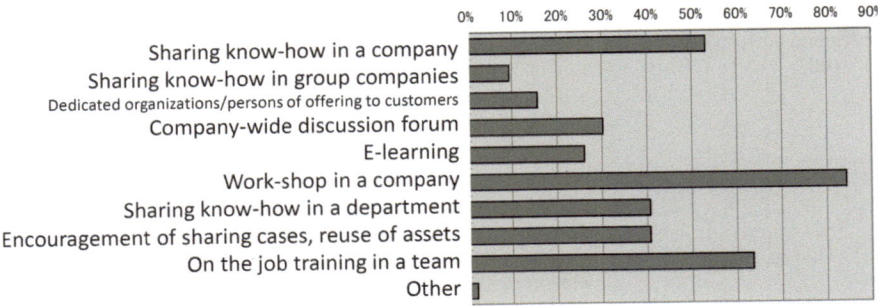

Fig. 17 Learning organization (*N*=100)

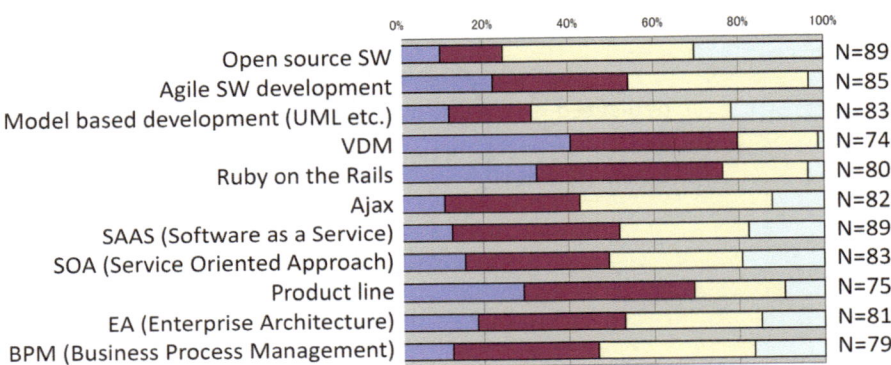

Fig. 18 Readiness for state-of-the-art technology. Readiness: 1. no plan, 2. research, 3. tentative adoption, 4. aggressive adoption

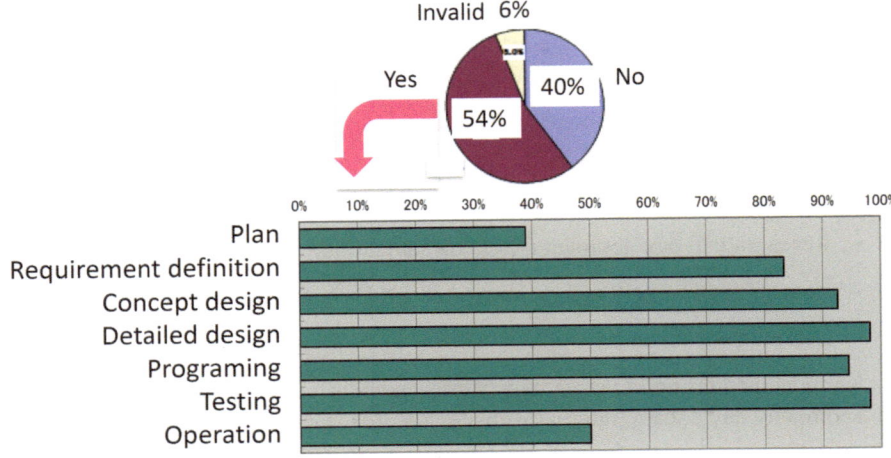

Fig. 19 Development methodology by phase (*N*=100)

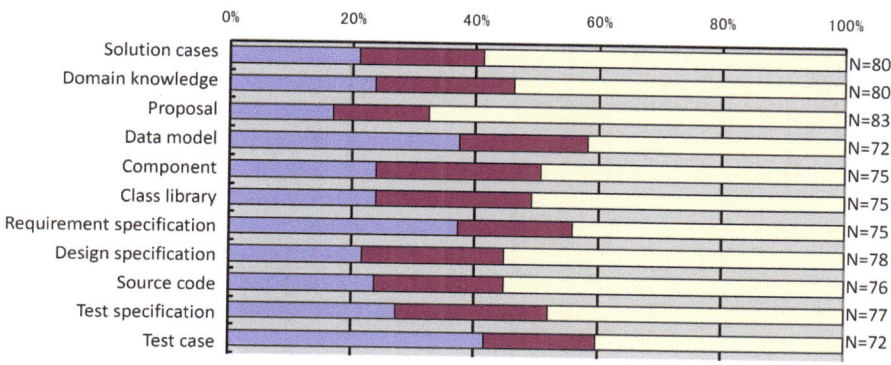

Fig. 20 Reuse of software resources. Stage: 1. have no plan, 2. have a plan, 3. in practice

Fig. 21 Effect of R&D
(*N*=82)

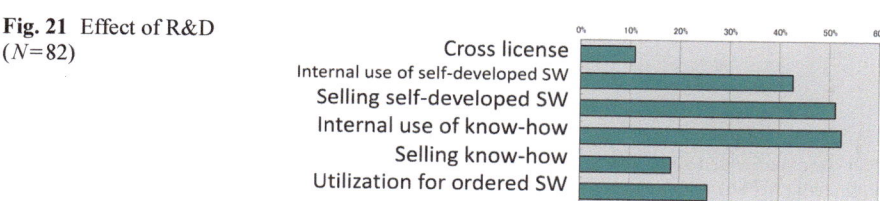

- Development methodology

Development methodology is mainly utilized requirement definition phase through test phases by 40% of IT vendors (Fig. 19).

- Reuse of software resources

Almost half of IT vendors have positive attitude toward the reuse of software resources (Fig. 20).

- Effect of R&D

At almost half of IT vendors, R&D activities, such as in-house product development and knowledge sharing, contribute to business administration and sales increase (Fig. 21).

6. Human Resource Development: training hours for new recruits, training hours for experienced software engineers, skill development program, skills inventory, incentives for skill development, skill development method, programs for high motivation

- Training hours for new recruits

For new recruits, the median is over 400 training hours per year (*N*=85) (Fig. 22).

- Training hours for experienced software engineers

For other experienced software engineers, the median is almost 40 h per year (*N*=86) (Fig. 23).

- Skill development program

Fig. 22 Training hours per
year for new recruits (*N*=85)

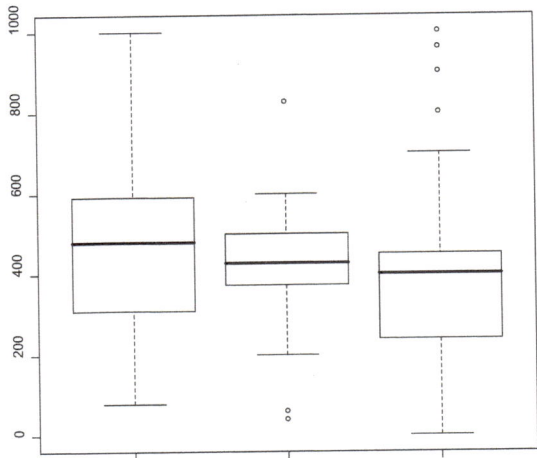

Fig. 23 Training hours per
year for experienced software
engineers (*N*=86)

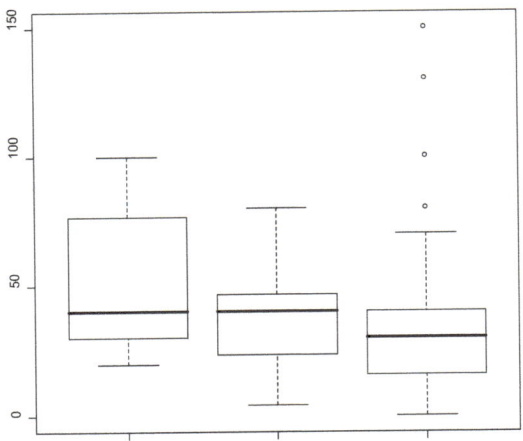

Fig. 24 Skill development
program (*N*=100)

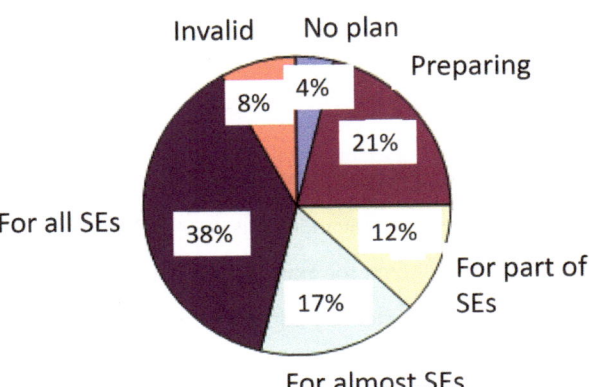

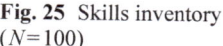

Fig. 25 Skills inventory
(N=100)

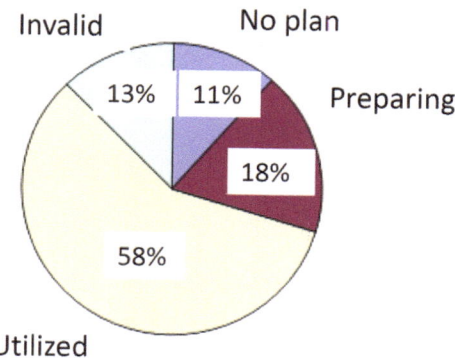

Fig. 26 Incentives for skill
development (N=92)

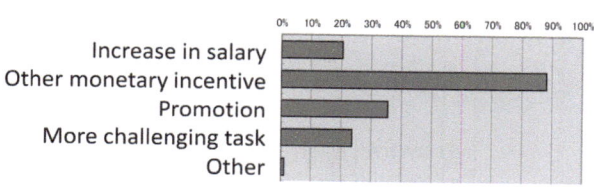

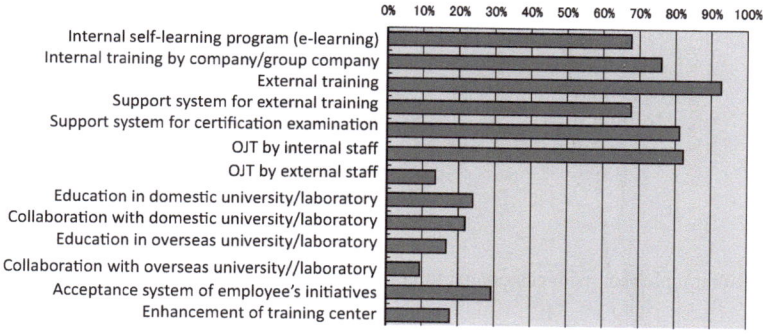

Fig. 27 Skill development method (N=96)

Almost half of IT vendors prepare in-company skill development programs for software engineers (Fig. 24).

- Skills inventory

At almost 60% of IT vendors prepare in-company skills inventory of software engineering (Fig. 25).

- Incentives for skill development

Almost 90% of IT vendors prepare wage incentive plan relating to skill development (Fig. 26).

- Skill development method

Most IT vendors prepare variety of skill development methods, such as external and internal seminars, e-learning systems, and on-the-job training (OJT) (Fig. 27).

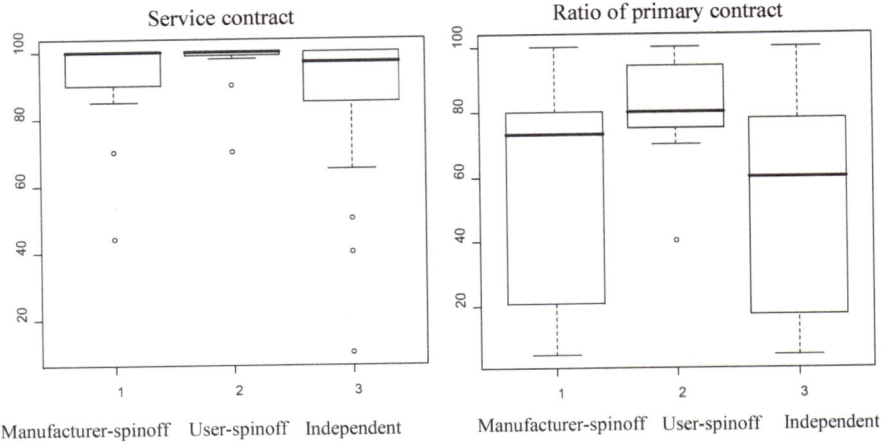

Fig. 28 Ratio of prime contracts (%)

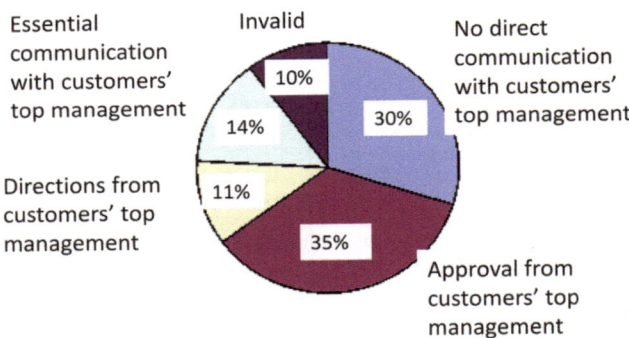

Fig. 29 Communication with customers' top management ($N=100$)

7. Customer Contact: ratio of prime contracts, direct communication with customers' top management, understanding of proposal by vendors' top management, scope of services offered, clarification of user requirements, prevention against unprofitable project

• Ratio of prime contracts

User-spinoff vendors tend to get much more prime contracts than manufacturer-spinoff and independent vendors (Fig. 28).

• Communication with customers' top management

One fourth of IT vendors have direct communication with customers' top management (Fig. 29).

• Understanding of proposal by vendors' top management

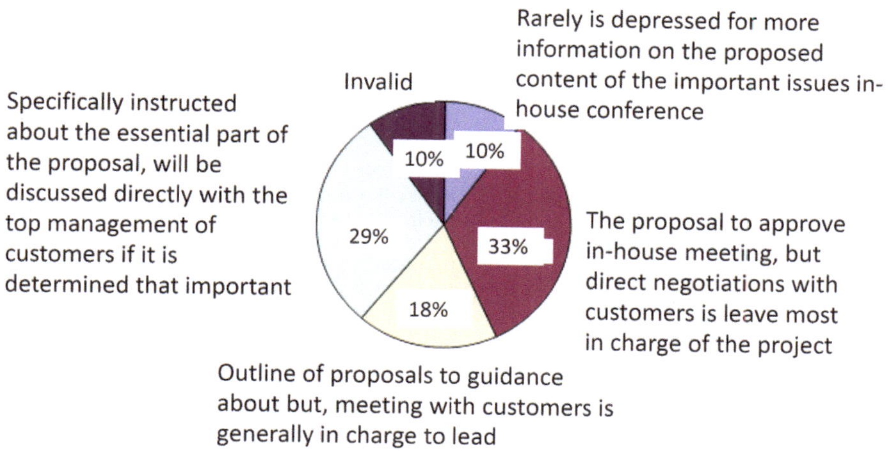

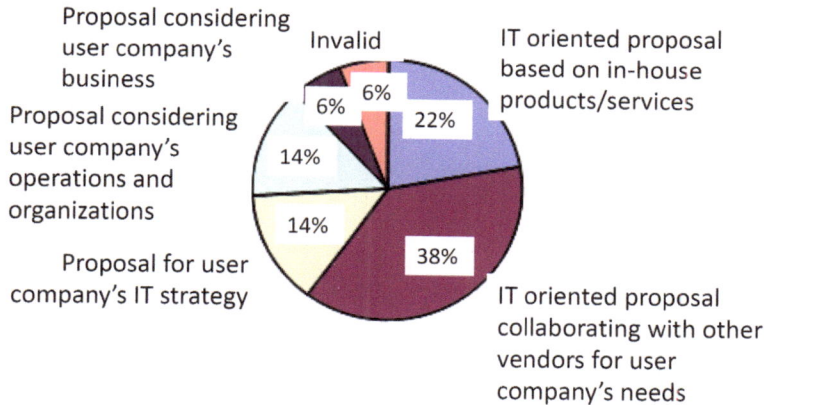

Rarely is depressed for more information on the proposed content of the important issues in-house conference

Invalid

Specifically instructed about the essential part of the proposal, will be discussed directly with the top management of customers if it is determined that important

The proposal to approve in-house meeting, but direct negotiations with customers is leave most in charge of the project

Outline of proposals to guidance about but, meeting with customers is generally in charge to lead

Fig. 30 Understanding of proposal by vendors' top management ($N=100$)

Proposal considering user company's business

Proposal considering user company's operations and organizations

Proposal for user company's IT strategy

Invalid

IT oriented proposal based on in-house products/services

IT oriented proposal collaborating with other vendors for user company's needs

Fig. 31 Scope of proposal ($N=100$)

At almost half of IT vendors, top management understands the contents of proposal for the customer company (Fig. 30).

• Scope of proposal

60 % of IT vendors focus on technology-oriented proposals, while less than 40 % of them consider business related proposals (Fig. 31).

Index